PREFACE.

Who is sufficient for these things? is a question which any one may well ask when sitting down to the preparation of a treatise on popular education. The author of this work would have shrunk from the undertaking, but from deference to the judgment of the honorable body that unanimously invited its preparation. He has also been encouraged not a little by many kind friends, one of whom, distinguished for his labors in the department of public instruction, writing from New England, says, "I rejoice at your good beginnings at the West. You have a noble and inspiring field of action. 'No pent-up Utica contracts your powers.' I beseech you, fail not to fill it with your glorious educational truth, though you should pour out your spirit and your life to do so."

The duties required by law of the Superintendent of Public Instruction in the State of Michigan are comparatively few. The author, however, five years ago, and soon after entering upon the discharge of those duties, undertook *voluntary labors* for the purpose of awakening a deeper interest with all classes of the community in behalf of common schools, and of inspiring confidence in their redeeming power, when improved as they may be, constituting, as they do, *the only reliable instrumentality for the proper training of the rising generation*. These labors, which were hailed as promising great usefulness, and which were prosecuted in every county of the state, were every where received with unexpected favor, and constitute the foundation of the present volume. Many of the subjects then discussed are here greatly amplified.

Among the lectures referred to in the resolution under which this work has been undertaken, was one on the "Michigan School System." But as the Convention for the revision of the Constitution of this state is now in session, it has been deemed advisable to omit, in this connection, the extensive consideration of the details of that system. This may constitute the theme of a small manual which shall hereafter appear.

In the present volume the author has endeavored so to present the subject of popular education, which should have reference to the *whole man*—the body, the mind, and the heart—and so to unfold its nature, advantages, and claims, as to make it every where acceptable. Nay, more, he would have a good common education considered as the inalienable right of every child in the community, and have it placed *first among the necessaries of life*. For the better accomplishment of his object, he has freely drawn from the writings of practical educators, his aim being usefulness rather than originality. This course has been adopted, in some instances, for the sole purpose of enforcing the sentiments inculcated by the authority of the names introduced. Acknowledgments have generally been made in the body of the work. These may have been unintentionally omitted in some instances, and especially in those portions of the work which were written several years ago, and the sources whence information was drawn are now unknown.

An examination of the table of contents, and especially of the index at the end of the volume, will show the range of subjects considered, and their adaptation to the wants and *necessities*, I may say, of the several classes of persons named in the title-page, for whose use it was undertaken. Written, as it has been, for Parents and Teachers, and for Young Persons of both sexes, it is what its title implies—a treatise on Popular Education—and is equally applicable to the wants of families and schools in every portion of our wide-spread country.

With all its imperfections, of which no one can be more sensible than the author, this volume is given to the public, with the hope that it may contribute, in some degree, to advance the work of general education in the United States, but more especially in the State of Michigan.

IRA MAYHEW.

Monroe, Mich., July 4th, 1850.

CONTENTS.

CHAPTER I.
In what does a correct Education consist? — Page 13

CHAPTER II.
The Importance of Physical Education — 28

CHAPTER III.
Physical Education—The Laws of Health — 44

CHAPTER IV.
The Laws of Health—Philosophy of Respiration — 81

CHAPTER V.
The Nature of Intellectual and Moral Education — 111

CHAPTER VI.
The Education of the Five Senses — 146

CHAPTER VII.
The Necessity of Moral and Religious Education — 193

CHAPTER VIII.
The Importance of Popular Education — 224

Education dissipates the Evils of Ignorance — 226

CHAPTER I.

IN WHAT DOES A CORRECT EDUCATION CONSIST?

I call that education which embraces the culture of the whole man, with all his faculties—subjecting his senses, his understanding, and his passions to reason, to conscience, and to the evangelical laws of the Christian revelation.—DE FELLENBERG.

From the beginning of human records to the present time, the inferior animals have changed as little as the herbage upon which they feed, or the trees beneath which they find shelter. In one generation, they attain all the perfection of which their nature is susceptible. That Being without whose notice not even a sparrow falls to the ground, has provided for the supply of their wants, and has adapted each to the element in which it moves. To birds he has given a clothing of feathers; and to quadrupeds, of furs, adapted to their latitudes. Where art is requisite in providing food for future want, or in constructing a needful habitation, as in the case of the bee and the beaver, a peculiar aptitude has been bestowed, which, in all the inferior races of animals, has been found adequate to their necessities. The crocodile that issues from its egg in the warm sand, and never sees its parent, becomes, it has been well said, as perfect and as knowing as any crocodile.

Not so with man! "He comes into the world," says an eloquent writer, "the most helpless and dependent of living beings, long to continue so. If deserted by parents at an early age, so that he can learn only what the experience of one life may teach him—as to a few individuals has happened, who yet have attained maturity in woods and deserts—he grows up in some respect inferior to the nobler brutes. Now, as regards many regions of the earth, history exhibits the early human inhabitants in states of ignorance and barbarism, not far removed from this lowest possible grade, which civilized men may shudder to contemplate. But these countries, occupied formerly by straggling hordes of miserable savages, who could scarcely defend themselves against the wild beasts that shared the woods with them, and the inclemencies of the weather, and the consequences of want and fatigue; and who to each other were often more dangerous than any wild beasts, unceasingly warring among themselves, and destroying each other with every species of savage, and even cannibal cruelty—countries so occupied formerly, are now become the abodes of myriads of peaceful, civilized, and friendly men, where the desert and impenetrable forest are changed into cultivated fields, rich gardens, and magnificent cities.

"It is the strong intellect of man, operating with the faculty of language as a means, which has gradually worked this wonderful change. By language, fathers communicated their gathered experience and reflections to their children, and these to succeeding children, with new accumulation; and when, after many generations, the precious store had grown until memory could contain no more, the arts of writing, and then of printing, arose, making language visible and permanent, and enlarging illimitably the repositories of knowledge. Language thus, at the present moment of the world's existence, may be said to bind the whole human race of uncounted millions into one gigantic rational being, whose memory reaches to the beginnings of written records, and retains imperishably the important events that have occurred; whose judgment, analyzing the treasures of memory, has discovered many of the sublime and unchanging laws of nature, and has built on them all the arts of life, and through them, piercing far into futurity, sees clearly many of the events that are to come; and whose eyes, and ears, and observing mind at this moment, in every corner of the earth, are watching and recording new phenomena, for the purpose of still better comprehending the magnificence and beautiful order of creation, and of more worthily adoring its beneficent Author.

"It might be very interesting to show here, in minute detail, how the arts of civilization have progressed in accordance with the gradual increase of man's knowledge of the universe; but it would lead too far from the main subject." The preceding sketch may remind us of the low condition of man in a state of ignorance and barbarism, and of the high condition to which he may be brought by cultivation. We possess a material and an immaterial part, mutually dependent on each other. On one hand, we may well say to corruption, Thou art my father; and to the worm, Thou art my mother and my sister. On the other hand, the Psalmist says of man, Thou hast made him a little lower than the angels.

In the Scriptures we learn the origin and history of man—the subject of education. He was created in the image of his Maker. It was his delightful employment, in innocency, to dress the beautiful garden in which he dwelt. Presently we learn he transgressed. His subsequent career becomes infelicitous. In the earlier history of the human race, the days of his pilgrimage were protracted several hundred years. In process of time, because of the prevalence of sin, a universal deluge swept away the entire family of man, save *one*—a preacher of righteousness—and those of his household. Subsequently his days were shortened to three score years and ten. Much of this time is consumed in helpless infancy, in sleep, and in securing the necessary means of supporting animal life. This, it would seem, is calamity enough; but not so. Man finds himself beset with temptations on every side, to deepen and perpetuate his degradation, by giving reign to unbridled passion.

But a Light has shined upon his dark pathway, pointing him to a brighter country, and beckoning him thither. Under these adverse circumstances, it becomes the duty of the Educator to unfold the opening energies of his youthful charge; to mold their plastic character, and to assist their efforts in the recovery of that which was lost, and in the attainment of immortality and eternal life.

These are strong views, I am aware; but nothing less would be adequate to the nature and wants of man. In these views I am fully sustained by nearly every writer of any distinction in Europe and America. In a volume of prize essays on the expediency and means of elevating the profession of the educator in society, published in London, under the direction of the central society of education, one of the writers, introducing a quotation from an American author, says, I can not resist the pleasure of quoting a few of Alcott's brief sentences, by way of conclusion to the present division of the argument. The voice that has been sent athwart the Atlantic may find an echo in some British bosoms.

These are its words: "Education includes all those influences and disciplines by which the faculties of man are unfolded and perfected. It is that agency that takes the helpless and pleading infant from the hands of its Creator, and, apprehending its entire nature, tempts it forth, now by austere, and now by kindly influences and disciplines, and thus molds it at last into the image of a perfect man; armed at all points to use the body, nature, and life for its growth and renewal, and to hold dominion over the fluctuating things of the outward. It seeks to realize in the soul the image of the Creator. Its end is a perfect man. Its aim, through every stage of influence, is self-renewal. The body, nature, and life are its instruments and materials. Jesus is its worthiest ideal—Christianity its purest organ. The Gospels are its fullest text-book—genius is its inspiration—holiness its law—temperance its discipline—immortality its reward."

Says Dr. Howe, in a lecture before the American Institute of Instruction, "Education should have for its aim the development and greatest possible perfection of the whole nature of man: his moral, intellectual, and physical nature. My *beau ideal* of human nature would be a being whose intellectual faculties were active and enlightened; whose moral sentiments were dignified and firm; whose physical formation was healthy and beautiful: whoever falls short of this, in one particular—be it in but the least, beauty and vigor of body—falls short of the standard of perfection. To this standard, I believe, man is approaching; and I believe the time will soon be when specimens of it will not be rare."

The following thoughts are drawn from a treatise on the "Mental Illumination and Moral Improvement of Mankind," by that very judicious and celebrated writer, Dr. Dick, of Scotland. The education of human beings, considered in its most extensive sense, comprehends every thing which is requisite to the cultivation and improvement of the faculties bestowed upon them by the Creator. It ought to embrace every thing that has a tendency to strengthen and invigorate the animal system; to enlighten and expand the understanding; to regulate the feelings and dispositions of the heart; and, in general, to direct the moral powers in such a manner as to render those who are the subjects of instruction happy in themselves, useful members of society, and qualified for entering upon the scenes and employments of a future and more glorious existence.

It is a very common but absurd notion, and one that has been too long acted upon, that the education of youth terminates, or should terminate, about the age of thirteen or fourteen years. Hence, in an article on this subject in one of our encyclopedias, education is defined to be "that series of means by which the human understanding is gradually enlightened, between infancy and the period when we consider ourselves as qualified to take a part in active life, and, *ceasing to direct our views to the acquisition of new knowledge or the formation of new habits,* are content to act upon the principles we have already acquired."

This definition, though accordant with general opinion and practice, is certainly a very limited and defective view of the subject. In the ordinary mode of our scholastic instruction, education, so far from being *finished* at the age above stated, can scarcely be said to have *commenced*. The *key* of knowledge has indeed been put into the hands of the young; but they have never been taught to unlock the gates to the temple of science, to enter within its portals, to contemplate its treasures, and to feast their minds on the entertainments there provided. Several moral maxims have been impressed on their memories; but they have seldom been taught to appreciate them in all their bearings, or to reduce them to practice in the various and minute ramifications of their conduct. Besides, although every rational means were employed for training the youthful mind till the age above named, no valid reason can be assigned why regular instruction should cease at this early period.

Man is a progressive being; his faculties are capable of an indefinite expansion; the objects to which these faculties may be directed are boundless and infinitely diversified; he is moving onward to an eternal world, and, in the present state, can never expect to grasp the universal system of created objects, or to rise to the highest point of moral excellence. His tuition, therefore, can not be supposed to terminate at any period of his terrestrial existence; and the course of his life ought to be considered as nothing more than the course of his education. When he closes his eyes in death, and bids a last adieu to every thing here below, he passes into a more permanent and expansive state of existence, where his education will likewise be progressive, and where intelligences of a higher order may be his instructors; and the education he received in this transitory scene, *if it was properly conducted,* will found the ground-work of all his future progressions in knowledge and virtue throughout the succeeding periods of eternity.

There are two very glaring defects which appear in most of our treatises on education. In the first place, the moral tuition of youthful minds, and the grand principles of religion which ought to direct their views and conduct, are either entirely overlooked, or treated of in so vague and general a manner, as to induce a belief that they are considered matters of very inferior moment; and, in the business of teaching, and the superintendence of the young, the moral precepts of Christianity are seldom made to bear with particularity upon every malignant affection that manifests itself, and every minor delinquency that appears in their conduct, or to direct the benevolent affections how to operate in every given circumstance, and in all their intercourses and associations. In the next place, the idea that man is a being destined to an immortal existence, is almost, if not altogether overlooked. Volumes have been written on the best modes of training men for the profession of a soldier, of a naval officer, of a merchant, of a physician, of a lawyer, of a clergyman, and of a statesman; but I know of no treatise on this subject which, in connection with other subordinate aims, has for its grand object to develop that train of instruction which is most appropriate for man considered as a candidate for immortality. This is the more unaccountable, since, in the works alluded to, the eternal destiny of human beings is not called in question, and is sometimes referred to as a general position which can not be denied; yet the means of instruction requisite to guide them in safety to their final destination, and to prepare them for the employments of their everlasting abode, are either overlooked, or referred to in general terms, as if they were unworthy of particular consideration. To admit the doctrine of the immortality of the human soul, and yet to leave out the consideration of it, in a system of mental instruction, is both impious and preposterous, and inconsistent with the principle on which we generally act in other cases, which requires that affairs of the greatest moment should occupy our chief attention. If man is only a transitory inhabitant of this lower world; if he is journeying to another and more important scene of action and enjoyment; if his abode in this higher scene is to be permanent and eternal; and if the course of instruction through which he now passes has an important bearing on his happiness in that state, and his preparation for its enjoyments—if all this be true, then surely every system of education must be glaringly defective which either overlooks or throws into the shade the immortal destination of human beings.

If these sentiments be admitted as just, the education of the young becomes a subject of the highest importance. There can not be an object more interesting to Science, to Religion, and to general Christian society, than the forming of those arrangements, and the establishing of those institutions, which are calculated to train the minds of all to knowledge and moral rectitude, and to guide their steps in the path which leads to a blessed immortality. In this process there is no period in human life that aught to be overlooked. We must commence the work of instruction when the first dawning of reason begins to appear, and continue the process through all the succeeding periods of mortal existence, till the spirit takes its flight to the world unknown.

While we would bring clearly into view the nature of that education which is needful for man, considered as a candidate for immortality, we would by no means overlook those subordinate aims which have reference to his present condition, and the relations he sustains in this life. The two are so intimately connected, and sustain such a reciprocal relation to each other, that each is best secured by that system of training and in the use of those appliances by which the other is most successfully promoted. In training the rising generation for the proper discharge of their duty to themselves and to one another—as children, and subsequently as parents; as members of society and citizens of free and independent states—we at the same time best promote their interests as candidates for immortality. It is equally true that any system of education which omits to provide for man's highest and enduring wants as an immortal being, in a proportionate degree falls short of providing for his dearest interests and best good in this life.

The system of education which we should promote comprehends whatever may have any good influence in developing the mind, by giving direction to thought, or bias the motives of action. To lead infancy in the path of duty, to give direction to an immortal spirit, and to teach it to aspire by well-doing to the rewards of virtue, is the first step of instruction. To youth, education imparts that knowledge whose ways are usefulness and honor, and by due restraint and subordination, makes individual to intwine with public good in a just observance of laws, comprehending the path of duty. To manhood, it "leads him to reflect on the ties that unite him with friends, with kindred, and with the great family of mankind, and makes his bosom glow with social tenderness; it confirms the emotions of sympathy into habitual benevolence, imparts to him the elating delight of rejoicing with those who rejoice, and, if his means are not always adequate to the suggestions of his charity, soothes him at last with the melancholy pleasure of weeping with those who weep." To age, it gives consolation, by remembrance of the past, and anticipation of the future. Wisdom is drawn from experience, to give constancy to virtue; and amid all the vicissitudes of life, it enables him to repose unshaken confidence in that goodness which, by the arrangement of the universe, constantly incites him to perpetual progress in excellence and felicity. Education is the growth and improvement of the mind. Its great object is immediate and prospective happiness. That, then, is the best education which secures to the individual and to the world the greatest amount of permanent happiness, and that the best system which most effectually accomplishes this grand design. How far this is accomplished by the present systems of education is not easily determined, but that it fails in many important considerations can not admit of a doubt.

It is feared that, by a great majority, a wrong estimate is made of education. Is it not generally considered as a *means* which must be employed to accomplish *some other purpose*, and consequently made subservient and secondary to the employments of life? Is it not considered as being contained in books, and a certain routine of studies, which, when gone through with, is believed to be accomplished, and consequently laid by, to be used as interest may suggest or convenience demand? Education comprehends all the improvements of the mind from the cradle to the grave. Every man is what education has made him, whether he has drunk deep at the Pierian spring, or sipped at the humblest fountain. The philosopher, whose comprehensive mind can scan the universe, and read and interpret the phenomena of nature; whose heaven-aspiring spirit can soar beyond the boundaries of time, indulge in the anticipation of immortality, and discern in the past, the present, and the future the all-pervading spirit of benevolence, is equally the child of education with him whose soul proud science never taught to feel its wants, and know how little may be known.

As we have already said, man possesses a material and an immaterial part, mutually dependent on each other. These are so intimately connected, and sustain such a reciprocal relation to each other, that neither can be neglected without detriment to both. The body continually modifies the state of the mind, and the mind ever varies the condition of the body. Mental and physical training should, then, go together. That system of instruction which relates exclusively to either, is a partial system, and its fate must be that of a house divided against itself. Education has reference to the *whole man*. It seeks to make him a complete creature after his kind, giving to both mind and body all the power, all the beauty, and all the perfection of which they are capable.

Our systems of education have hitherto fallen far short of this high and only true standard. Education, in too many instances, has been confined, almost entirely, to either the physical, intellectual, or moral energies of men. With the greater part, it has been limited to the *physical powers*. No effort has been made to develop any but their bodily strength, animal passions, and instinctive feelings. Accordingly, the great mass of mankind are raised but little above inferior animals. They labor hard, and boast of their strength; gratify their passions, and glory in their shame; eat and drink, sleep and wake, supposing to-morrow will be like the present. They are scarcely aware of their rational, intellectual powers, much less of their ever-expanding and never-dying spirits; consequently they feel but imperfectly their responsibility, and are governed principally by the fear of human authority. They have been taught to fear or reverence nothing higher. Their education is confined to animal feeling—physical energies. They have no conception of any thing beyond. The whole intellectual world, and all hereafter, is narrowed down to the animal feeling of the present time. How erroneous! How badly educated! And what are we to anticipate when only the physical energies of men generally are thus developed? Why, surely, what we are beginning to witness—namely, physical power, trampling on all authority.

The education of others is confined principally to *intellect*. Not that their physical powers are not necessarily more or less developed, but that their attention is directed almost exclusively to intellectual attainments. From the earliest infancy their minds are taxed, though their bodies are neglected, and their souls forgotten. Nor is it unfrequent that their physical strength gives way under the constant pressure of intellectual studies. And thus they are subjected to all the evils of physical inability—the sufferings of living death, in consequence of an erroneous education. Besides, they are destitute of all those kinder feelings and sympathetic emotions which alone result from the cultivation of the moral susceptibilities, and become insensible to the more delicate affections of the soul, and elevating hopes of the truly virtuous. They have nothing on which to rest for enjoyment but intellectual attainments. And even these are small compared with what they might have been under a different course of education. Yet with what delight are the first developments of intellect discovered by the natural guardian of the infant mind! and with what anxious solicitude are they watched through advancing youth and manhood by those employed in their education. In either stage the development of intellect alone seems worthy of an effort. And yet, when carried to the utmost, what may we expect of one destitute of virtue, and without strength of body? Little to benefit himself or others. Like Columbus, Franklin, or La Place, he may employ his intellect in useful discoveries; or, like Hume, Voltaire, and Paine, to curse the world. In either case he may lead astray, and should never be trusted implicitly. As the bark on the ocean without compass or chart, that rides out the storm or sinks to the bottom, he may guide us in safety, or ruin us forever!

The education of others, again, is confined mostly to their *moral energies*. Those of the body are almost forgotten, only as nature forces their development upon the reluctant soul within. And those of intellect are deemed unworthy of a thought, except as necessary in the rudest stages of society; while the moral susceptibilities are cultivated to the utmost. They are brought into action in every situation. They are employed in private, in the social circle, and around the public altar. Nor are those employing them ever satisfied. They become fanatics—religious enthusiasts. They have zeal without knowledge, and seem resolved on bringing all to their standard. They enlist in the work all the sympathies of the soul—its tenderest sensibilities and most compassionate feelings. Without intellect to guide, and physical strength to sustain them, they sink under moral excitement, and become deranged: a result that might be anticipated from such an education; and one that is often developed, in some of its milder features, among the reformers of the day. Nor may you reason with them. Reckless of consequences and regardless of authority, they are not to be convinced or persuaded. They are right, and *know* they are right, for the plain reason that they know nothing else, and will not be diverted from their course. What degradation! Who would not shrink from such an education? the development of the moral energies merely? It never qualified men for the highest attainment—the utmost dignity of which they are susceptible.

Diversified as are the developments of human character, and dissimilar as they may appear to the careless observer, there are peculiar characteristics of men that render them similar to one another, and unlike every other being. In their natures, original susceptibilities, and ultimate destinies, they are alike. They are material, intellectual, and spiritual; animal, rational, and immortal. On these uniform traits of character education should be based. It should develop and strengthen the animal functions; classify and improve the rational faculties; and purify and elevate the spiritual affections in harmonious proportion and perfect symmetry.

The animal functions of the human system are to be developed and strengthened by education. Hitherto they have been assigned to the province of nature, and deemed foreign to the objects of education. But a more unphilosophical and dangerous theory has seldom been embraced, as the melancholy results abundantly testify. We shall therefore devote a chapter to physical education, which seems to lie at the foundation of the great work of human improvement; for, as we have seen, in the present state the mind can manifest itself only through the body; after which we shall proceed to the consideration of the other grand divisions of the great work of education.

CHAPTER II.

THE IMPORTANCE OF PHYSICAL EDUCATION.

The influence of the physical frame upon the intellect, morals, and happiness of a human being, is now universally admitted. The extent of this influence will be thought greater in proportion to the accuracy with which the subject is examined. Bodily pain forms a large proportion of the amount of human misery. It is, therefore, of the highest importance that a child should grow up sound and healthy in body, with the utmost degree of muscular strength that education can communicate.—LALOR.

The importance of the department of the great work of education which we now approach has not hitherto been duly appreciated by parents and teachers generally. I shall therefore devote more space to this subject than is usual in works on education, but not more, I trust, than its relative importance demands. Physical, intellectual, and moral education are so intimately connected, that, in order duly to appreciate the importance of either, we must not view it separate and alone merely, but in connection with both of the others. And especially is this true of physical education. However much value, then, we may attach to it on its own account, considering man as a corporeal being, we shall have occasion greatly to magnify its importance when we come to direct our attention to his intellectual culture, and still more when we view it in connection with his moral training. Then, and not till then, shall we be enabled, in some degree, properly to appreciate the importance of physical education.

It has been objected, says Dr. Combe,[1] that to teach any one how to take care of his own health, is sure to do harm, by making him constantly think of this and the other precaution, to the utter sacrifice of every noble and generous feeling, and to the certain production of peevishness and discontent. The result, however, he adds, is exactly the reverse; and it would be a singular anomaly in the constitution of the moral world were it otherwise. He who is instructed in, and is familiar with grammar and orthography, writes and spells so easily and accurately as scarcely to be conscious of attending to the rules by which he is guided; while he, on the contrary, who is not instructed in either, and knows not how to arrange his sentences, toils at the task, and sighs at every line. The same principle holds in regard to health. He who is acquainted with the general constitution of the human body, and with the laws which regulate its action, sees at once his true position when exposed to the causes of disease, decides what ought to be done, and thereafter feels himself at liberty to devote his undivided attention to the calls of higher duties. But it is far otherwise with the person who is destitute of this information. Uncertain of the nature and extent of the danger, he knows not to which hand to turn, and either lives in the fear of mortal disease, or, in his ignorance, resorts to irrational and hurtful precautions, to the certain neglect of those which he ought to use. It is ignorance, therefore, and not knowledge, which renders an individual full of fancies and apprehensions, and robs him of his usefulness. It would be a stigma on the Creator's wisdom if true knowledge weakened the understanding, and led to injurious results. Those who have had the most extensive opportunities of forming an opinion on this subject from extensive experience, bear unequivocal testimony to the advantages which knowledge confers in saving health and life, time and anxiety.

If, indeed, ignorance were itself a preventive of the danger, or could provide a remedy when it approached, then it might well be said that "ignorance is bliss;" but as it gives only the kind of security which shutting the eyes affords against the dangers of a precipice, and consequently leaves its victim doubly exposed, it is high time to renounce its protection, and to seek those of a more powerful and beneficent ally. Every medical man can testify that, natural character and other circumstances being alike, those whose knowledge is the most limited are the fullest of whims and fancies; the most credulous respecting the efficacy of every senseless and preposterous remedy; the most impatient of restraint, and the most discontented at suffering.

If any of my readers be still doubtful of the propriety or safety of communicating physiological knowledge to the public at large, continues the author from whom we last quoted, and think that ignorance is in all circumstances to be preferred, I would beg leave to ask him whether it was knowledge or ignorance which induced the poorer classes in every country of Asia and Europe to attempt to protect themselves from cholera by committing ravages on the medical attendants of the sick, under the plea of their having poisoned the public fountains? And whether it was ignorance or knowledge which prompted the more rational part of the community to seek safety in increased attention to proper food, warmth, cleanliness, and clothing? In both cases, the desire of safety and sense of danger were the same, but the modes resorted to by each were as different in kind as in result, the efficacy of the one having formed a glaring contrast to the failure of the other.

Dr. Southwood Smith, the able author of a volume entitled "The Philosophy of Health," says, The obvious and peculiar advantages of this kind of knowledge are, that it would enable its possessor to take a more rational care of his health; to perceive why certain circumstances are beneficial or injurious; to understand, in some degree, the nature of disease, and the operation as well of the agents which produce it as of those which counteract it; to observe the first beginnings of deranged function in his own person; to give to his physician a more intelligible account of his train of morbid sensations, as they arise; and, above all, to co-operate with him in removing the morbid state on which they depend, instead of defeating, as is now, through ignorance, constantly the case, the best concerted plans for the renovation of health. It would likewise lay the foundation for the attainment of a more just, accurate, and practical knowledge of our *intellectual* and *moral nature*. There is a *physiology* of the *mind* as well as of the *body*, and both are so intimately united that neither can be well understood without the study of the other. The physiology of man comprehends both. Were even what is already known of this science and what might be easily communicated made a part of general education, how many evils would be avoided! how much light would be let in upon the understanding! and how many aids would be afforded to the acquisition of a sound body and a vigorous mind! prerequisites more important than are commonly supposed to the attainment of wisdom and the practice of virtue.

Human physiology, says Dr. Combe, in his admirable treatise on that subject, from which I have already quoted, is as important in its practical consequences as it is attractive to rational curiosity. In its widest sense, it comprehends an exposition of the functions of the various organs of which the human frame is composed; of the mechanism by which they are carried on; of their relations to each other, or the means of improving their development and action; of the purposes to which they ought severally to be directed, and of the manner in which exercise ought to be conducted, so as to secure for the organ the best health, and for the function the highest efficacy. A true system of physiology comes thus to be the proper basis, not only of a sound *physical*, but of a sound *moral* and *intellectual* education, and of a rational hygiene; or, in other words, it is the basis of every thing having for its object the physical and mental health and improvement of man; for, so long as life lasts, the mental and moral powers with which he is endowed manifest themselves through the medium of organization, and no plan which he can devise for their cultivation, that is not in harmony with the laws which regulate that organization, can possibly be successful.

Let it not be said that knowledge of this description is superfluous to the unprofessional reader; for society groans under the load of suffering inflicted by causes susceptible of removal, but left in operation in consequence of our unacquaintance with our own structure, and of the relation of different parts of the system to each other and to external objects. Every medical man must have felt and lamented the ignorance so generally prevalent in regard to the simplest functions of the animal system, and the consequent absence of the judicious co-operation of friends in the care and cure of the sick. From ignorance of the commonest facts in physiology, or from want of ability to appreciate their importance, men of much good sense in every other respect not only subject themselves unwittingly to the active causes of disease, but give their sanction to laws and practices destructive equally to life and to morality, and which, if they saw them in their true light, they would shrink from countenancing in the slightest degree.

Were the intelligent classes of society better acquainted with the functions of the human body and the laws by which they are regulated, continues this judicious writer, the sources of much suffering would be dried up, and the happiness of the community at large would be essentially promoted.

Medical men would no longer be consulted so exclusively for the cure of disease, but would be called upon to advise regarding the best means of strengthening the constitution, from an early period, against any accidental or hereditary susceptibility which might be ascertained to exist. More attention would be paid to the *preservation* of health than is at present practicable, and the medical man would then be able to advise with increased effect, because he would be proportionally well understood, and his counsel, in so far, at least, as it was based on accurate observation and a right application of principles, would be perceived to be, not a mere human opinion, but, in reality, an *exposition of the will and intentions of a beneficent Creator*, and would therefore be felt as carrying with it an *authority* to which, as the mere dictum of a fallible fellow-creature, it could never be considered as entitled.

It is true that, as yet, medicine has been turned to little account in the way of directly promoting the physical and mental welfare of man. But the day is, perhaps, not far distant, when, in consequence of the improvements both in professional and general education now in progress, a degree of interest will be attached to this application of its doctrines far surpassing what those who have not reflected on the subject will be able to imagine as justly belonging to it, but by no means exceeding that which it truly deserves.

Every person should be acquainted with the organization, structure, and functions of his own body—the house in which he lives: he should know the conditions of health, and the causes of the numerous diseases that flesh is heir to, in order to avoid them, prolong his life, and multiply his means of usefulness. If these things are not otherwise learned, they should be taught —the elements of them at least—in our primary schools. This instruction would come, perhaps, most appropriately from the members of the medical profession. But either society generally, or physicians themselves, or both, have mistaken the true sphere of a physician's usefulness, and what ought to constitute the grand object of his profession, namely, the *prevention of disease*, and the *general improvement of the health*, and not the CURING of diseases merely. The physician, like the clergyman in his parish, should receive a salary; and he should be occupied, chiefly, in teaching the laws of health to his employers; in imparting to them instruction in relation to the means of avoiding the diseases to which they are more particularly exposed, and in laying before them such information as shall be needful, in order to the highest improvement of their physical organization, and the transmission to posterity of unimpaired constitutions. This he may do by public lectures, at suitable seasons of the year; and by visiting from house to house, and imparting such information as may be particularly needed. The physician should not allow any of his employers blindly to disregard the laws of health, or, knowing them, to violate them unreproved. *He* should be accounted the *best physician*, other things being equal, whose employers have the *least sickness*, and uniformly enjoy the *best health*. When the relation existing between the members of the medical profession and the well-being of society generally comes to be better understood, and physicians are employed in accordance with the principles just stated, their greatest usefulness to the communities they serve will be found to consist in teaching well men and women how to retain and improve their health, and rear a healthy offspring, and not in partially curing diseased persons who are constantly violating the laws of health. These views will doubtless be new to many of my readers, and seem to them very strange! But let me inquire of such what they would think of the clergyman who should neglect to instruct his parishioners in the ennobling doctrines of morality and religion, and should suffer them to go on in sin unrebuked, until they become a burden to themselves? who should wait until his counsels were solicited before he sounds the note of alarm, and points the guilty sinner to "the Lamb of God which taketh away the sin of the world?" and who should confine his labors almost entirely to *condemned criminals*? Such conduct on the part of clergymen would doubtless be regarded by these very persons as passing strange! The course commonly pursued in the employment of physicians is equally unphilosophical, and floods society with a legion of evils—physical and intellectual, social and moral—three fourths of which might be avoided, by the proper exercise of the medical profession, in *one generation*; and ultimately, nineteen twentieths, if not ninety-nine one hundredths of them. As I have already said, this instruction would come, perhaps, most appropriately from the members of the medical profession. But if these things are not taught elsewhere, I repeat it, they should be taught—the elements of them at least—in our primary schools.

I can not better enforce the importance of physical education than by quoting from a lecture "on the education of the blind," by one of the most distinguished practical educators[2] in this country. "That the proportion of the blind to the whole population might be diminished by wise social regulations, and by the dissemination of knowledge of the organic laws of man, there is not a doubt; but whether the time has come, or ever will come, is another question. At any rate, to so enlightened a body[3] as I have the honor of addressing, suggestions of methods by which the extent of blindness may be limited will neither be misapplied, nor liable to offend a mawkish sensibility. That the blindness of a large proportion of society is a social evil will not be denied, nor will the right which society has to diminish that proportion be questioned. But how? in a very simple way; by preventing the transmission of an hereditary blindness to another generation; by preventing the marriage of those who are congenitally blind, or who have lost their sight by reason of hereditary weakness of the visual organs, which disqualifies them to resist the slightest inflammation or injury in childhood.

"I am aware that many people would condemn this proposition as cruel, because it might add to the sadness of the sufferers; and that the whole seven thousand five hundred blind in this country would rise up and scout it, as barbarous and unnatural; for I have experienced the effects of contradiction to the wills of individual blind persons in this respect. But my rule is, the good of the community before that of the individual; the good of the race before that of the community. To give you an instance: the city of Boston, with a population of eighty thousand, is represented in the Institution for the Blind by two blind children only; and I know of but four in the whole population; while Andover, with but five thousand, is fully and ably represented by seven;[4] and it has three more growing up.

"Now how is this? Why, the blind of Andover are mostly from a common stock; three of them are born of one mother, who has had four blind children. Another of the pupils is cousin, in the first degree, to these three; and two other pupils are cousins in a remote degree. Then, from other places, there are two brothers, who have a third at home. There is one blind girl, who has two blind sisters at home. Then there are two pairs of sisters.

"In the immediate vicinity of Boston, I know of a family in which blindness is hereditary; the last generation there were five. Of these five one is married, and has four children, not one of whom can see well enough to read; and if the others marry, they may increase the number to twelve or twenty.

"Now apply this state of things to the whole country, and have you any difficulty in conceiving how it happens that there are seven thousand five hundred blind in the United States? And can you doubt whether or not this great proportion of blind to the whole community might not be considerably diminished, if men and women understood the organic laws of their nature? understood that, very often, blindness is the punishment following an infringement of the natural laws of God; and if they could be made to act upon the holy Christian principles, that we should deny ourselves any individual gratification, any selfish desire, that may result in evil to the whole community?

"I would that every individual whom I have the honor to address would assist in the education of the blind, so far as to give them just and Christian views of this subject. I would that all should work for society; not for society to-day alone, but for the society of future ages; not in any one narrow, partial way, but upon a broad scale, and in every way in which they can be useful. If a person congenitally blind, or strongly predisposed to become so, or one who marries a person so born or so disposed, has blind offspring in consequence of it, I ask, is he not as responsible, in a moral point of view, for the infirmity of his children as though he had put out their eyes with his own hands?

"You may suppose, perhaps, that the infirmity of blindness would incapacitate sufferers from winning the affections of seeing persons; and that, with respect to two blind persons, the sense of incapacity to support a family would prevent them from uniting themselves. In the first place, I answer, that seeing people do no better than the blind. Even a blind man may perceive that many marriages are mere matters of course, resulting from juxtaposition of parties; and rarely matters where the purer affections and higher moral sentiments are consulted. And, in the second place, that incapacity of supporting a family will not weigh a feather in the balance with desire, unless the intellectual and moral nature is enlightened and cultivated. Do we not see, every day, cases of misery entailed upon whole families, because one of the parties had overlooked or disregarded *moral infirmity,* which ought to have been a greater objection than any *physical defect*—than even blindness or deafness?

"But no process of reasoning is required, for there stand the facts. The blind not only seek for partners in life, but are sometimes sought by seeing persons; and numerous instances have occurred within my knowledge. It is true, that despair of success in any other quarter, or an equally unworthy motive, may induce some to seek for partners among the blind, or the blind to unite with the blind; but still, there is the evil.

"My observation induces me to think that the blind, far more than seeing persons, are fond of social relations, and desirous of family endearments. A moment's thought would induce one to conclude that this would naturally be the case; a moment's observation convinces one that it is so. Now I have found among them some of the most pious, intelligent, and disinterested beings I ever knew; but hardly more than one who was prepared to forego the enjoyments of domestic relations. And how can we expect them to be so, more than seeing people? The fact is, but very few persons in the community give any attention to the laws of their organic nature, and the tendency to hereditary transmission of infirmities. Very few consider that they owe more to society than to their individual selves; that if we are to love our neighbor *as ourself,* we must, of course, love *all* our neighbors, collectively, more than the single unit which each one calls I.

"I would that considerations of this kind had more weight with the community generally. I would that the subject were more attended to, and that the violation of the laws of our organic nature were less frequent in our country. There is one great and crying evil in our system of education; it is, that but part of man's nature is educated, and that our colleges and schools doom young men for years to an uninterrupted and severe exercise of the intellectual faculties, to the comparative neglect of their moral, and still more of their physical nature. Nay, not only do they *neglect* their physical nature—they ABUSE it; they sin against themselves and against God; and though they sin in ignorance, they do not escape the penalties of His violated laws. Hence you see them pale, and wan, and feeble; hence you find them acknowledging, when too late, the effects of severe application. But do they acknowledge it humbly and repentingly, as with a consciousness of sin? No, they often do it with a secret exultation, with a lurking feeling that you will say or think, 'Poor fellow, his mind is too much for his body!' Nonsense! his mind is too weak; his knowledge too limited; he is an imperfect man; he knows not his own nature. But if he has no conscientiousness, no scruple about impairing his own health and sowing the seeds of disease, he has less about entailing them upon others. And a consumptive young man or woman—the son or daughter of consumptive parents—hesitates not to spread the evil in society, and entail puny faces, weakness, pain, and early death upon several individuals, and punish their children for their own sins.

"Is this picture too high-colored? Alas! no. And if I showed you satisfactorily that sin against the organic laws caused so great a proportion of blindness, how much more readily will you grant that the same sin gives to so many of our population the narrow chest, the hectic flush, the hollow cough, which makes the *victim doomed*, by his *parent*, to consumption and early death! Do you not see, every Sabbath, at church, the young man or woman, upon whose fair and delicate structure the peculiar impress of the EARLY DOOMED is stamped? and as a slight but hollow cough comes upon your ear, does it not recall the death-knell which rang in the same sad note before to the father or mother? Who of you has not followed some young friend to his long resting-place, and found that the grass had not grown rank upon the grave of his brother? that the row of white marbles, beneath which slept his parents and sisters, were yet glistering in freshness, and that the letters which told their names and their early death seemed clear as if cut but yesterday?

"They tell us that physical education is attended to in this country; and yet, where is the teacher, where is the clergyman even, who dares to step forth in these cases, and say to those who are *doomed*, you must not and shall not marry? and where are the young men and women who would listen to them if they did? It is not that they are wanting in conscientiousness; they may be conscientious and disinterested; but they do not know that they are doing wrong, because they are not acquainted with the organic laws of their nature. All that is done in schools or colleges toward physical education is the mere strengthening of the muscular system by muscular exercise; but this is not half enough. These remarks may be deemed irrelevant to my subject, but they can not be lost to an audience whose highest interest is the education of man; and if I am mistaken in supposing that little attention has been paid to the subject, its importance will guaranty its repetition."

Before dismissing this subject, I will introduce two additional quotations from American authors, whose opinions are received by the medical profession in this country not only, but throughout Europe. In both instances, I copy from works published in Great Britain, into which the opinions of these American writers have been quoted. In regard to hereditary transmission, Dr. Caldwell observes: "Every constitutional quality, whether good or bad, may descend, by inheritance, from parent to child. And a long-continued habit of drunkenness becomes as essentially constitutional as a predisposition to gout or pulmonary consumption. This increases, in a manifold degree, the responsibility of parents in relation to temperance. By habits of intemperance, they not only degrade and ruin *themselves*, but transmit the elements of like degradation and ruin to their posterity. This is no visionary conjecture, the fruit of a favorite and long-cherished theory. It is a settled belief resulting from observation—an inference derived from innumerable facts. In hundreds and thousands of instances, parents, having had children born to them while their habits were temperate, have become afterward intemperate, and had other children subsequently born. In such cases, it is a matter of notoriety that the younger children have become addicted to the practice of intoxication much more frequently than the older, in the proportion of five to one. Let me not be told that this is owing to the younger children being neglected, and having corrupt and seducing examples constantly before them. The same neglects and profligate examples have been extended to all, yet all have not been equally injured by them. The children of the earlier births have escaped, while those of the subsequent ones have suffered. The reason is plain. The latter children had a deeper animal taint than the former."—*Transylvania Journal*.

Physiologists in general coincide in the belief that a vigorous and healthy physical and mental constitution in the parents communicates existence in the most perfect state to their offspring, while impaired constitutions, from whatever cause, are transmitted to posterity. In this sense, all who are competent to judge are agreed that the Giver of life is a jealous God, visiting the iniquity of the fathers upon the children unto the third and fourth generation of them that hate him or violate his laws. Strictly speaking, it is not *disease* which is transmitted, but organs of such imperfect structure that they are unable to perform their functions properly, and so weak as to be easily put into a morbid state or abnormal condition by causes which unimpaired organs are able to resist.

My last quotation on this point is from a lecture delivered by Dr. Warren before the American Institute of Instruction, copied into the "Schoolmaster," a work published in London under the superintendence of the Society for the Diffusion of Useful Knowledge:

"Let me conclude by entreating your attention to a revision of the existing plans of education in what relates to the preservation of health. Too much of the time of the better educated part of young persons is, in my humble opinion, devoted to literary pursuits and sedentary occupations, and too little to the acquisition of the corporeal powers indispensable to make the former practically useful. If the present system does not undergo some change, I much apprehend we shall see a degenerate and sinking race, such as came to exist among the higher classes in France before the Revolution, and such as now deforms a large part of the noblest families in Spain;[5] but if the spirit of improvement, so happily awakened, continues—as I trust it will—to animate those concerned in the formation of the young members of society, we shall soon be able, I doubt not, to exhibit an active, beautiful, and wise generation, of which the age may be proud."

CHAPTER III.

PHYSICAL EDUCATION. THE LAWS OF HEALTH.

If man is ever to be elevated to the highest and happiest condition which his nature will permit, it must be, in no small degree, by the improvement—I might say, the redemption—of his physical powers. But knowledge on any subject must precede improvement.—ALCOTT.

Physical and moral health are as nearly related as the body and the soul.—HUFELAND's *Art of Prolonging Life*.

If the reader is persuaded that the views presented in the last chapter on the importance of physical education are truthful—and they are concurred in by physiologists generally—he will naturally desire to become acquainted with the *laws of health*, that, by yielding obedience to them, he may improve his physical condition, and most successfully promote his intellectual and moral well-being. I might, then, here refer to some of the many excellent treatises on this subject; but I shall probably better accomplish the object for which this work has been undertaken by presenting, within as narrow limits as practicable, a summary of these laws.

In every department of nature, *waste* is invariably the result of *action*. In mechanics, we seek to reduce the waste consequent upon action to the lowest possible degree; but to prevent it entirely is beyond the power of man. Every breath of wind that passes over the surface of the earth, modifies the bodies with which it comes in contact. The great toe of the bronze statue of Saint Peter at Rome has been reduced, it is said, to less than half its original size by the successive kisses of the faithful.

In *dead* or *inanimate* matter, the destructive influence of action is constantly forced upon our attention by every thing passing around us, and so much human ingenuity is exercised to counteract its effects that no reflecting person will dispute the universality of its operation. But when we observe shrubs and trees waving in the wind, and animals undergoing violent exertion, year after year, and continuing to increase in size, we may be inclined, on a superficial view, to regard *living* bodies as constituting an exception to this rule. On more careful examination, however, it will appear that waste goes on in living bodies not only without intermission, but with a rapidity immeasurably beyond that which occurs in inanimate objects.

In the vegetable world, for instance, every leaf of a tree is incessantly pouring out some of its fluids, and every flower forming its own fruit and seed, speedily to be separated from, and lost to its parent stem; thus causing in a few months an extent of waste many hundred times greater than what occurs in the same lapse of time after the tree is cut down, and all its living operations are at a close.

The same thing holds true in the animal kingdom: so long as life continues, a copious exhalation from the skin, the lungs, the bowels, and the kidneys goes on without a moment's intermission, and not a movement can be performed which does not in some degree increase the circulation, and add to the general waste. In this way, during violent exertion, several ounces of the fluids of the body are sometimes thrown out by perspiration in a very few minutes; whereas, after life is extinguished, all the excretions cease, and waste is limited to that which results from ordinary chemical decomposition.[6]

So far, then, the law that waste is attendant on action applies to both dead and living bodies; but beyond this point a remarkable difference between them presents itself. In the physical or inanimate world, what is once lost or worn away *is lost forever*; but *living* bodies, whether vegetable or animal, possess the distinguishing characteristic of being able to *repair their own waste* and add to their own substance. The possession of such a power is essential to their existence. But there is a wide difference between them in other respects. In surveying the respective modes of existence of vegetables and of animals, we perceive the fixity of position of the one, and the free locomotive power of the other. The vegetable grows, flourishes, and dies, fixed to the same spot of earth from which it sprang. However much external circumstances change around it, it must remain and submit to their influence. At all hours and at all seasons, it is at home, and in direct communication with the soil from which its nourishment is extracted. But it is otherwise with animals: these not only enjoy the privilege of locomotion, but are compelled to use it, and often to go a distance in search of food and shelter. The necessity for a constant change of place being imposed on them, a different arrangement became indispensable for their nutrition. The method which the Creator has provided is not less admirable than simple. To enable animals to move about, and at the same time to maintain a connection with their food, they are provided with a stomach. In this receptacle they can store up a supply of materials from which sustenance may be gradually elaborated during a period of time proportioned to their necessities and mode of life. Animals thus *carry with them* nourishment adequate to their wants; and the small nutritive vessels imbibe their food from the internal surface of the stomach and bowels, where it is stored up, just as the roots or nutritive vessels of vegetables do from the soil in which they grow. The possession of a stomach or receptacle for food is accordingly a distinguishing characteristic of the animal system.

The sole objects of nutrition being to repair waste and to admit of growth, the Creator has so arranged that within certain limits it is always most vigorous when growth or waste proceeds with the greatest rapidity. Even in vegetables this provision is distinctly observable. It is also strikingly apparent in animals. Whenever growth is proceeding rapidly, or the animal is undergoing much exertion and expenditure of material, an increased quantity of food is invariably required. On the other hand, where no new substance is forming, and where, from bodily inactivity, little loss is sustained, a comparatively small supply will suffice. In endowing animals with the sense of *appetite,* including the sensation of hunger and thirst, the Creator has effectually provided against any inconvenience which might otherwise exist, and given to them a guide in relation to both the quality and quantity of food needful for them, and the times of partaking of it, with that beneficence which distinguishes all his works. He has not only provided an effectual safeguard in the sensations of hunger and thirst, but he has attached to their regulated indulgence a degree of pleasure which never fails to insure attention to their demands, and which, in highly-civilized communities, is apt to lead to excessive gratification. Their end is manifestly to proclaim that nourishment is required for the support of the system. When the body is very actively exercised, and a good deal of waste is effected by perspiration and exhalation from the lungs, the appetite becomes keener, and more urgent for immediate gratification; and if it is indulged, we eat with a relish unknown on other occasions, and afterward experience a sensation of internal comfort pervading the frame, as if every individual part of the body were imbued with a feeling of contentment and satisfaction; the very opposite of the restless discomfort and depression which come upon us, and extend over the whole system, when appetite is disappointed. There is, in short, an obvious and active sympathy between the condition and bearing of the stomach, and those of every part of the animal frame; in virtue of which, hunger is felt very keenly when the general system stands in urgent need of repair, and very moderately when no waste has been suffered.

We have seen that *waste* is every where attendant upon *action*, and that the object of nutrition is to repair waste and admit of growth. We come now to consider the *Process of Digestion*.

All articles used for food necessarily undergo several changes before they are fitted to constitute a part of the body. In the process of digestion, four different changes should be noticed. More might be specified.

1. MASTICATION.—The first step in the preparation of food for imparting nourishment to the system consists in proper mastication, or chewing. Food should be thoroughly masticated before it is taken into the stomach. This is necessary in order to break it up and reduce it to a sufficient degree of fineness for the efficient action of the gastric juice. Besides, the action of chewing and the presence of nutrient food constitute a healthful stimulus to the salivary glands, situated in the mouth. By this means, also, the food not only becomes well masticated, but has blended with it a proper amount of saliva, upon both of which conditions the healthy action of the stomach depends. We have here another illustration of the beneficence of the Creator, who has kindly so arranged that the very act of mastication gratifies taste, the mouth being the seat of this sensation. But if we disregard these benevolent laws, and introduce unmasticated food into the stomach, the gastric juice can act only upon its surface, and changes of a

purely chemical nature frequently commence in food thus swallowed before digestion can take place. Hence frequently arise—and especially in children and persons of delicate constitution—pains, nausea, and acidity, consequent on the continued presence of undigested aliment in the stomach.

2. CHYMIFICATION.—As soon as food has been thoroughly masticated and impregnated with saliva, it is ready for transmission to the stomach. This interesting part of the process of digestion, called deglutition or swallowing, is most easily and pleasantly performed, when the alimentary morsel has been well masticated and properly softened, not by drink, which should never be taken at this time, but by saliva. When the food reaches the stomach, it is converted into a soft, pulpy mass, called *chyme*; and the process by which this change is effected is called *chymification*. This is the second principal step in digestion, and is effected immediately by the action of the *gastric juice*. This powerful solvent is secreted by the gastric glands, which are excited to action by the presence of food in the stomach. In health, the gastric secretion always bears a direct relation to the quantity of aliment required by the system. If too much food is taken into the stomach, indigestion is sure to follow, for the sufficient reason that the gastric juice is unable to dissolve it. This is true even when food has been well masticated; but it becomes strikingly apparent when a full meal has been hastily swallowed, both mastication and insalivation having been imperfectly performed.

The time usually occupied in the process of chymification, when food has been properly masticated, varies from *three to four hours*. Digestion is sometimes effected in less time, as in the case of rice, and pigs' feet soused; but it more commonly requires a longer period, as in the case of salt pork and beef, and many other articles of food, both animal and vegetable.

By the alternate contraction and relaxation of the muscular coat of the stomach, which is excited to action by the presence of food, a kind of churning motion is communicated to its contents that greatly promotes digestion; for by this means every portion of food in turn is brought in contact with the gastric juice as it is discharged from the internal surface of the stomach. This motion continues until the contents of the stomach are converted into chyme, and conveyed into the first intestine, where they undergo another important change.

3. CHYLIFICATION.—As fast as chyme is formed, it is expelled by the contractile power of the stomach into the *duodenum*, or first intestine. It there meets with the *bile* from the liver, and with the pancreatic juice. By the action of these agents, the chyme is converted into two distinct portions: a milky white fluid, called *chyle*, and a thick yellow residue. This process is called *chylification*, or *chyle-making*. The chyle is then taken up by the absorbent vessels, which are extensively ramified over the inner membrane or lining of the bowels. From the white color of the contents of these vessels, they have been named *lacteals* or *milk-bearers*, from *lac*, which signifies milk. These lacteals ultimately converge into one trunk, called the *thoracic duct*, which terminates in the great vein under the clavicle or collar bone, hence called the *subclavian* vein, just before that vein reaches the right side of the heart. Here the chyle is poured into the general current of the venous blood, and, mingling with it, is exposed to the action of the air in the lungs during respiration. By this process, both the chyle and the venous blood are converted into red, arterial, or nutritive blood, which is afterward distributed by the heart through the arteries, to supply nourishment and support to every part of the body. The change which takes place in the lungs is called *sanguification*, or *blood-making*. The chyle is not prepared to impart nourishment to the system until this change takes place. *Respiration*, then, is, in reality, *the completion of digestion*. This interesting and vital part of the process of digestion will be considered more fully in the following chapter.

Before passing from this part of the subject, a few remarks of a more general nature seem called for. The *nerves of the stomach* have a direct relation to *undigested* but *digestible* substances. When any body that can not be digested is introduced into the stomach, distinct uneasiness is speedily excited, and an effort is soon made to expel it, either upward by the mouth or downward by the bowels. It is in this way, says Dr. Combe, that bile in the stomach excites nausea, and that tartar emetic produces vomiting. The *nerves of the bowels*, on the other hand, are constituted in relation to *digested* food; and, consequently, when any thing escapes into them from the stomach in an *undigested* state, it becomes a source of irritative excitement. This accounts for the cholic pains and bowel-complaints which so commonly attend the passage through the intestinal canal of such indigestible substances as fat, husks of fruits, berries, and cherry-stones.

The process of digestion, which commences in the stomach, is completed in the intestines. Physiologists have hence sometimes called the former part of the process, or chymification, by the more simple term *stomach digestion*; and the latter, or chylification, has been termed *intestinal digestion*. The bowels have distinct coats corresponding with those of the stomach. By the alternate contraction and relaxation of the muscular coat, their contents are propelled in a downward direction, somewhat as motion is propagated from one end of a worm to the other. It has hence been called vermicular, or *wormlike motion*. Some medicines have the power of *inverting* the order of the muscular contractions. Emetics operate in this manner to produce vomiting. Other medicines, again, excite the *natural* action to a higher degree, and induce a cathartic action of the bowels. When medicines become necessary to obviate that kind of costiveness which arises from imperfect intestinal contraction, physicians usually administer rhubarb, aloes, and similar laxatives, combined with tonics. But when the muscular coat of the bowels is kept in a healthy condition by a natural mode of life, and is aided by the action of the abdominal muscles, it rarely becomes necessary to administer laxative medicines.

The inner or mucous coat of the stomach and bowels is generally regarded by physiologists as a continuation of the skin. They greatly resemble each other in structure, and they are well known to sympathize with each other. Eruptions of the skin are very generally the result of disorders of the digestive organs. On the other hand, bowel complaints are frequently produced by a chill on the surface. The mucous coat and the skin are both charged with the double function of *excretion* and *absorption*. By the exercise of the *former* function, much of the waste matter of the system, requiring to be removed, is thrown into the intestines, and, mingling with the indigestible portion of the food, forms the common excrement; while by the exercise of the *latter* function the nutritive portion of their contents is taken up, and, as we have seen, passes into the general circulation, and contributes either to promote growth or to repair waste.

4. EVACUATION.—This is the fourth and last principal step in the process of digestion. After the chyle is separated from the chyme and passes into the circulation, the indigestible and refuse portion of the food, which is incapable of nourishing the system, passes off through the intestinal canal. In its course its bulk is considerably increased by the excretion of waste

matter which has served its purposes in the system, and which, mingling with the innutritious and refuse part of the food, is thrown out of the body in the form of excrement. If the contents of the bowels are too long retained, uneasiness is produced. Hurtful matter, also, which should pass off by evacuation, is reabsorbed, passes again into the general circulation, and is ultimately thrown out of the system either by the lungs or through the pores of the skin.

This part of the process of digestion is *very important*, for it is impossible to enjoy good health while this function is imperfectly performed. To secure full and natural action in the intestinal canal, several principal conditions are necessary. These are, first, well-digested chyme and chyle; second, a due quantity and quality of secretions from the mucous or lining membrane of the bowels; third, a free and full contractile power of the muscular coat, and the unrestrained action of the abdominal and respiratory muscles; and, finally, a due nervous sensibility to receive impressions and communicate the necessary stimulus. The contractile power of the muscular coat, and the free passage of the intestinal contents from the stomach downward, are greatly aided by the constant but gentle agitation which the whole digestive apparatus receives during the act of breathing, and from exercise of every description. By free and deep inhalations of air into the lungs, the diaphragm is depressed and the bowels are pushed down. But when the air is thrown out from the lungs, the diaphragm rises into the chest, and the bowels follow, being pressed upward by the contractile power of the abdominal muscles. During exercise, breathing is deeper and more free, which gives additional pressure to the bowels from above. The abdominal muscular contraction is also, in turn, more vigorous and extensive, and thus the motion is returned from below. Persons that take little or no exercise, or who allow the chest and bowels to be confined by tight clothing, lose this natural stimulus, and frequently become subjects of immense suffering from habits of costiveness. These should be removed if possible, and they generally can be by a proper course of discipline. This should have reference to both diet and exercise. Such articles of food should be used as tend to keep open the bowels. This should be combined with the free exercise of the lungs and the abdominal muscles. In addition to these, there should be a determination to secure a natural evacuation of the bowels at least once a day. This is regarded by physiologists generally as essential to health. Efforts should be continued until the habit is established. Some definite period should be fixed upon for this purpose. Soon after breakfast is, on many accounts, generally preferable.

TIME FOR MEALS.—Before passing from the subject of digestion, I will submit a few thoughts in relation to the times for eating. It has already been observed that *three or four hours* are generally necessary for the digestion of a simple meal. Usually, perhaps, a greater length of time is required. It is also an established doctrine, based upon the results of careful examination and experiment, that *the stomach requires an interval of rest*, after the process of digestion is finished, to enable it to recover its tone before it can again enter upon the vigorous performance of its function. As a general rule, then, *five or six hours should elapse between meals*. If the mode of life is indolent, a greater time is required; if active, less time will suffice. Where the usages of society will allow the principal meal to be taken near the middle of the day, the following time for meals is approved by physiologists generally: breakfast at 7 o'clock, dinner at half past 12, and tea at 6. Luncheons and late suppers should be avoided; for the former will always be found to interfere with the healthful performance of the function of digestion, and the latter will induce restlessness, unpleasant dreams, and pain in the head. "A late supper," says the author of the Philosophy of Health, "generally occasions deranged and disturbed sleep; there is an effort on the part of the nerves to be quiet, while the burdened stomach makes an effort to call them into action, and between these two contending efforts there is disturbance—a sort of gastric riot—during the whole night. This disturbance has sometimes terminated in a fit of apoplexy and in death."

THE SKIN.—This membranous covering, which is spread over the surface of the body to shield the parts beneath, serves also as an excreting and secreting organ. By the great supply of blood which it receives, it is admirably fitted for this purpose. The whole animal system, as we have seen, is in a state of transition, decay and renovation constantly succeeding each other. While the stomach and alimentary canal take in new materials, the skin forms one of the principal outlets by which particles that are useless to the system are thrown out of the body. Every one knows that the skin perspires, and that checked perspiration is a powerful cause of disease and death; but few have any just notion of the extent and influence of this exhalation. When the body is overheated by exercise, a copious sweat breaks out, which, by evaporation, carries off the excess of heat, and produces an agreeable feeling of coolness and refreshment. The sagacity of Franklin led him to the first discovery of the use of perspiration in reducing the heat of the body, and to point out the analogy subsisting between this process and that of the evaporation of water from a rough porous surface, so constantly resorted to in the East and West Indies, and in other warm countries, as an efficacious means of reducing the temperature of the air in rooms, and of wine and other drinks, much below that of the surrounding atmosphere. This is the higher and more obvious degree of the function of exhalation. But in the ordinary state of the system, the skin is constantly giving out a large quantity of waste materials by what is called *insensible perspiration*; a process which is of great importance to the preservation of health, and which is called *insensible*, because the exhalation, being in the form of vapor, and carried off by the surrounding air, is invisible to the eye. But its presence may often be made manifest, even to the sight, by the near approach of a dry cool mirror, on the surface of which it will soon be condensed so as to become visible. It is this which causes so copious deposits upon the windows of a crowded school-room in cold weather. A portion of these exhalations, however, proceed from the lungs.

There is an experiment that may be easily tried, which affords conclusive evidence that the amount of insensible perspiration is much greater than it is ordinarily supposed to be. Take a dry glass jar, with a neck three or four inches in diameter, and thrust the hand and a part of the fore-arm into it, closing the space in the neck about the arm with a handkerchief. After the lapse of a few minutes, it will be seen, by drawing the fingers across the inside of the jar, that the insensible perspiration even from the hand is very considerable. Many attempts have been made to estimate accurately the amount of exhaled matter carried off through the skin; but many difficulties stand in the way of obtaining precise results. There is a great difference in different constitutions, and even in the same person at different times, in consequence of which we must be satisfied with an approximation to the truth.

Although the precise amount of perspiration can not be ascertained, it is generally agreed that the cutaneous exhalation is greater than the united excretions of both bowels and kidneys. Great attention has been given to this subject. Sanctorius, a celebrated medical writer, weighed himself, his food, and his excretions, daily, for thirty days. He inferred from his experiments that *five pounds* of every eight, of both food and drink, taken into the system, pass out through the skin. All physiologists agree that from twenty to forty ounces pass off through the skin of an adult in usual health every twenty-four hours. Take the lowest estimate, and we find the skin charged with the removal of *twenty ounces* of waste matter from the system *every day*. We can thus see ample reason why checked perspiration proves so detrimental to health; for every twenty-four hours during which such a state continues, we must either have this amount of useless and hurtful matter accumulating in the system, or some of the other organs of excretion must be greatly overtasked, which obviously can not happen without disturbing their regularity and well-being. It is generally known that continued exposure in a cold day produces either a bowel complaint or inflammation of some internal organ. Instead of expressing surprise at this, if people generally understood the structure and uses of their own bodies, they would rather wonder why one or the other of these effects is not *always* attendant upon so great a violation of the laws of health, *which are the laws of God*.

The lungs also excrete a large proportion of waste matter from the system. So far, then, their office is similar to that of the kidneys, the liver, and the bowels. In consequence of this alliance with the skin, these parts are more intimately connected with each other, in both healthy and diseased action, than with other organs. Whenever an organ is unusually delicate, it will be more easily affected by any cause of disease than those which are sound. Thus, in one instance, checked perspiration may produce a bowel complaint, and in another, inflammation of the lungs, and so on. Hence the fitness, in prescribing remedies, of adapting them not only to the *disease* itself, but of taking into the account the *cause* of the disease. A bowel complaint, for example, may arise either from overeating or from a check to perspiration. The thing to be cured is the same in both cases, but the *means of cure* ought obviously to be different. In one instance, an emetic or laxative, to carry off the offending cause, would be the most rational and efficacious remedy; in the other, a diaphoretic should be administered, to open the skin and restore it to a healthy action. Facts like these expose the ignorance and impudence of the quack, who undertakes to cure every form of disease by one remedy.

It has already been remarked that the skin is charged with the double function of *excretion* and *absorption*. We have a striking illustration of the exercise of the latter function in the vaccination of children and others, to protect them from small-pox. A small quantity of cow-pox matter is inserted under the external layer of the skin, where it is acted upon, and in a short time taken into the system by the absorbent vessels. In like manner, when the perspiration is brought to the surface of the skin, and confined there, either by injudicious clothing or by want of cleanliness, there is much reason to believe that its residual parts are again absorbed. It is established by observation that concentrated animal effluvia form a very energetic poison. We can, then, see why the absorption of the residual parts of perspiration produces fever, inflammation, and even death itself, according to its quantity and degree of concentration. This leads me to notice the importance of

BATHING.—The exhalation from the skin being so constant and extensive, and the bad effects of it when confined being so great, it becomes very important that we provide for its removal. This can be most easily and effectually accomplished by frequently bathing the whole body. This is a luxury within the reach of all, but one which is unappreciated by those who have not enjoyed it. An aged gentleman said to me recently, that in early life he "used to go a swimming frequently and enjoyed it much; but," he added, "I have not bathed or washed myself all over *for the last thirty years*!" This, it is believed, is an extreme case. But it is to be feared there are not wanting instances in which persons do not bathe the entire person once a month, or once a year even! When the residual parts of the perspiration are not removed by washing or bathing, they at last obstruct the pores and irritate the skin. It is apparently for this reason that, in the Eastern and warmer countries, where perspiration is very copious, ablution and bathing have assumed the rank and importance of *religious observances*. Those who are in the habit of using the flesh-brush daily are at first surprised at the quantity of white dry scurf which it brings off; and those who take a warm bath for half an hour at long intervals can not have failed to notice the great amount of impurities which it removes, and the grateful feeling of comfort which its use imparts. It is remarked by an eminent physician, that the warm, tepid, cold, or shower bath, as a means of preserving health, ought to be in as common use as a change of apparel, for it is equally a measure of necessary cleanliness. Many, no doubt, neglect this, and enjoy health notwithstanding; but many more suffer from its omission; and even the former would be greatly benefited by employing it. Cleanliness, then, is as essential to health as to decency. Still more, it promotes not only physical health, but contributes largely to strengthen and invigorate the intellectual faculties, and to elevate and purify the affections. It comes, then, to be ranked among the *cardinal virtues*.

To secure the benefits of bathing or ablution, a great amount of apparatus is not necessary. A shower-bath, or plunge-bath, may not be best for all. Every one can procure a wash-bowl and one or two quarts of water, which are all that is necessary. To prevent the reduction of heat in the system by evaporation, and especially in cold weather, it will usually be found best to bathe the body *by sections*. It is generally agreed that the morning is the best time for bathing. Immediately on rising, then, the clothing being removed, let the head, face, and neck be washed as usual, and thoroughly dried by the use of a towel. Proceed to wash the chest and abdomen, which may be dried as before, after which a coarse towel or a flesh-brush should be vigorously applied, until the skin is perfectly dry, and there is a pleasant glow upon the surface. The back and limbs, in turn, should be washed, dried, and excited to a healthy and pleasant glow by friction. This last is of the utmost importance. If not easily secured, salt or vinegar may be added to the water, both of which are excellent stimulants to the skin.[7] When these are used, and care is taken to excite in the surface, by subsequent friction with a coarse towel, flesh-brush, or hair glove, the healthful glow of reaction, it will be found to contribute largely to both physical and mental comfort. The beneficial results will be more apparent if, while bathing and rubbing the chest and abdomen, pains are taken to throw back the shoulders, expand the lungs, and enlarge the chest.

By an act of the Legislature of the commonwealth of Massachusetts, passed in April last, it is required that "physiology and hygiene shall hereafter be taught in the schools of that commonwealth, in all cases in which the school committee shall deem it expedient."

When physiology is not made a study in school, the teacher should not fail to give familiar and instructive lectures on the subject. I know of instances where, by this simple means, the habits of a whole school, composed of several hundred youth of both sexes, have been radically changed; and the practice of daily ablution has ceased to be the luxury of the few, having become the necessity not only of teachers and scholars, but of the families in which they reside. There is the most satisfactory evidence that cleanliness is conducive to health.[8] How important it is, then, that *habits of cleanliness* be formed at an early age.

Dr. Weiss, a distinguished German physician, in his remarks on this subject, says, the best time, undoubtedly, for these ablutions, is the morning. They are to be performed immediately after rising from the bed, when the temperature of the body is raised by the heat of the bed. The sudden change favors in a great measure the reaction which ensues, and excites the skin, rendered more sensitive by the perspiration during the night, to renewed activity. Cold ablutions, he adds, are fitted for all constitutions; they are best adapted for purifying and strengthening the body; for women, weak subjects, children, and old age. The room in which the ablution is performed may be slightly heated for debilitated patients in winter, to prevent colds in consequence of too low a temperature of the apartment; this exception is, however, only admissible for very weakly persons. Generally speaking, ablutions may be performed in a cold room, especially where persons get through the operation quickly, and can immediately afterward take exercise in the open air.

It is the opinion of Dr. Combe that bathing is a safe and valuable preservative of health, in ordinary circumstances, and an active remedy in disease. Instead of being dangerous by causing liability to cold, it is, he says, when well managed, so much the reverse, that he has used it much and successfully for the express purpose of diminishing such liability, both in himself and in others in whom the chest is delicate. In his own instance, in particular, he is conscious of having derived much advantage from its regular employment, especially in the colder months of the year, during which he has found himself most effectually strengthened against the impression of cold by repeating the bath at shorter intervals than usual. I shall conclude my remarks on bathing by presenting a paragraph from this transatlantic author.

If the bath can not be had at all places, soap and water may be obtained every where, and leave no apology for neglecting the skin. If the constitution be delicate, water and vinegar, or water and salt, used daily, form an excellent and safe means of cleansing and gently stimulating the skin. To the invalid they are highly beneficial, when the nature of the indisposition does not render them improper. A rough and rather coarse towel is a very useful auxiliary in such ablutions. Few of those who have steadiness to keep up the action of the skin by the above means, and to avoid strong and exciting causes, will ever suffer from colds, sore throats, or similar complaints; while, as a means of restoring health, they are often incalculably serviceable. If one tenth of the persevering attention and labor bestowed to so much purpose in rubbing down and currying the skins of horses were bestowed by the human race in keeping themselves in good condition, and a little attention were paid to diet and clothing, colds, nervous diseases, and stomach complaints would cease to form so large an item in the catalogue of human miseries. Man studies the nature of other animals, and adapts his conduct to their constitution; himself alone he continues ignorant of and neglects. He considers himself a being of superior order, and not subject to the laws of organization which regulate the functions of the lower animals; but this conclusion is the result of ignorance and pride, and not a just inference from the premises on which it is ostensibly founded.

CLOTHING.—The skin is very materially affected in the healthy performance of its functions by the nature and condition of the clothing. It is a very commonly received opinion that one principal object in clothing is to impart heat to the body. This, however, is an erroneous idea; the utmost that it can do is to *prevent the escape of heat.* All articles of clothing are not alike in this respect. Some conduct the heat from the body readily, and are hence much used in warm weather; as linen, for example. Others, again, have very little tendency to convey heat from the body, and are hence sought in cold weather. Of this nature are furs, and cloths manufactured from wool. I do not intend in this connection to speak of the merits of different kinds of clothing, but to remark simply upon the necessity of changing clothes often, or at least of ventilating them frequently. This remark applies particularly to all articles of clothing worn next to the skin, and to beds. Clothes worn next to the skin during the day should be removed on going to bed, and a fresh sleeping-gown should be put on. The former should be hung up in a situation that will allow the accumulated perspiration of the day to pass off by evaporation. By this means they will become sufficiently freshened and ventilated, by morning, to be worn another day, when the night-clothes, in turn, should be ventilated. Beds also should be thrown open and exposed to fresh air with open doors, or at least windows, several hours before being made. In our best-regulated boarding schools, and literary and benevolent institutions of all kinds, particular attention is now paid to this subject. In some instances, lodging rooms are furnished with frames for the express purpose of facilitating the ventilation of the bed-clothes. Immediately on rising in the morning, the clothes are removed from the beds, and exposed upon these frames to a current of fresh air for several hours, the windows being opened for that purpose. Notwithstanding care be taken to promote personal cleanliness by daily ablutions, if the ventilation of beds and clothing be neglected, and perspiration be suffered to accumulate in them, it may be reabsorbed, and, passing again into the circulation, produce all the mischief of which I have before spoken.

THE TEETH.—I have already spoken of the relation the teeth sustain to digestion. Their use in the proper mastication of food is essential to the healthy and vigorous performance of this important function. The proper use of a good set of teeth contributes largely to both the physical comfort, and the intellectual and moral well-being of their possessor; but when neglected, they very commonly decay and become useless; nay, more, they are not unfrequently a source of great and almost constant discomfort for years. In order to preserve the teeth, they must be *kept clean*. After every meal, they should be cleaned with a brush and water. A tooth-pick will sometimes be found necessary in the removal of particles of food that are inaccessible to the brush. Metallic tooth-picks injure the enamel, and should not be used. Those made of ivory, or the common goose-quill, are unobjectionable. The brush should be used, not only after each meal, but the last thing at night and the first thing in the morning. This will prevent the accumulation of *tartar*, which so commonly incrusts neglected teeth. If suffered to remain, it gradually accumulates, presses upon the gums, and destroys their health. By this means the roots of the teeth become bare, and thus deprived of their natural stimulus, they prematurely decay. Food or drink either very hot or very cold is exceedingly injurious to the teeth. Sour drops, acidulated drinks, and all articles of food that "set the teeth on edge," are injurious, and should be carefully avoided. Should it become necessary to take sour drops as a medicine, they should be given through a quill, and every precaution should be taken to prevent their coming in contact with the teeth. Even then the mouth should be well rinsed immediately after they are swallowed.

Disordered digestion is a great source of injury to the teeth both in childhood and in mature age. When digestion is vigorous, there is less deposition of tartar, and the teeth are naturally of a purer white. Especially is this true when the general health is good, and the diet plain, and contains a full proportion of vegetable matter. This accounts for the fact that many rustics and savages possess teeth that would be envied in town. Tobacco is sometimes used as a *preservative* of the teeth. It is, indeed, occasionally prescribed as a *curative* by ignorant physicians, and those who are willing to pander to the diseased appetites of their patients. But there is the best medical testimony that the use of this *filthy weed "debilitates the vessels of the gums, turns the teeth yellow, and renders the appearance of the mouth disagreeable."* Dr. Rush informs us that he knew a man in Philadelphia who *lost all his teeth* by smoking. In speaking of the *moral effects* of this practice, he adds, "Smoking and chewing tobacco, by rendering water and other simple liquors insipid to the taste, dispose very much to the stronger stimulus of ardent spirits; hence the practice of smoking cigars throughout our country has been followed by the use of brandy and water as a common drink." A dentist of extensive and successful practice in the Middle and Western States, after listening to the reading of this article, said to me, he had a patient, a young lady, two of whose front teeth had decayed through, laterally, in consequence of smoking. On removing the caries, he found it impossible to fill her teeth, because the openings continued through them. He thinks, as do many others, that the heat of the smoke is a principal cause of the injury.

Among the conditions upon which the healthy action of the voluntary organs depends is a due degree of *appropriate exercise*. This is a *general law*, and holds with reference to the *teeth* as well as to any other organ or set of organs. The proper mastication of healthful and nutritious food constitutes the appropriate exercise of the teeth, and is a condition upon which *their health*, and the healthy exercise of the function of *digestion*, alike depend. If from any cause the teeth of one jaw are removed, the corresponding teeth of the other jaw, being thus deprived of that exercise which is essential to their health, are pressed out of the jaw, appear to grow long, become loose in their sockets, and sometimes fall out. Hence the propriety and advantage of inserting *artificial teeth* where the natural ones fail; an event which rarely happens when they are properly taken care of. I need hardly add that nuts, and other hard substances that break the enamel, are injurious to the teeth, and should be avoided.

THE BONES.—The bones constitute the frame-work of the system. They consist of two substances, being formed of both *animal* and *earthy* matter. To the former belongs every thing connected with their *life* and *growth*, while the latter gives to them *solidity* and *strength*. The proportions of the animal and earthy elements of which the bones are composed vary at different ages. In childhood and early youth, when but *little strength* is needed, and *great growth* of bone is required, the animal part preponderates. As growth advances the animal part *decreases*, and the earthy part *increases*. In middle life, when growth is finished and the strength is greatest, and when nutrition is required only to repair waste, the proportions are changed, and the solid or earthy part exceeds the vital or animal; and in extreme old age, the earthy part so predominates as to cause the bones to become very brittle.

The bones, like other parts of the system, require exercise. If properly used, they increase in size and strength. But while a due degree of exercise is beneficial, it ought to be remarked that severe and continued labor should not be required of children and youth; for its tendency is to increase the deposition of earthy matter to a hurtful extent. It is by this means that many children are made dwarfs for life, their bones being consolidated by an undue amount of exercise and excessive labor before they have attained their full growth. Multitudes of children in our country, from this and kindred causes, fail of attaining the size of their ancestors. These remarks may be turned to a practical account in the family and in the school. At birth, many of the bones are scarcely more than cartilage; yet children are frequently urged to stand and walk long before the bones become sufficiently strong to sustain the pressure; and, as a consequence, their legs become crooked, and they are perhaps other ways deformed for life. Children ought always, when seated, to be able to rest their feet upon the floor. When they occupy a seat that is too high, and especially when they are unable to reach their feet to the floor, the thigh bones very frequently become curved. If, in addition to high seats, the back is not supported, children become round shouldered, their chests contract, their constitutions become permanently enfeebled, and they become peculiarly susceptible to pulmonary disease. The back to the seat should afford a pleasant and agreeable support to the small of the back, but it ought not to reach to the shoulder blades.

Parents and teachers should never forget that children are as susceptible to physical training as to intellectual or moral culture. And here, especially, they should be "trained *up* in the way they should go." Physical uprightness is next to moral. If children are allowed to contract bad physical habits, they are liable not only to grow crooked, but to become deformed in various ways. But so great is the power of education, that by it even the physically crooked may be made straight; the chest may be enlarged, the general health may be improved, and much may be done in many ways to fortify those who have inherited feeble constitutions against the attacks of disease. The benefits resulting from maintaining an upright form, and a free and open chest, have already been considered, and I shall have occasion to refer to them again. The chest of most adults, although *incased with bone*, may be increased several inches by drawing the arms back in the use of *nature's own shoulder-braces*, and at the same time taking deep inhalations of air, and filling the lungs to their utmost capacity. Hundreds of individuals in different parts of the country have borne testimony to the efficacy of this treatment in the improvement of their health. The good results of such discipline in childhood are still more manifest.

A stooping posture is frequently induced by sitting at tables and desks that are too low. It has been erroneously maintained by some that the top of the desk should be on the same plane with the elbow when the arm hangs by the side. When the desk is higher, it has been said the tendency is to elevate one shoulder, to depress the other, and to produce a permanent curvature of the spinal column. Although this may have been frequently the result of sitting at a high desk, yet it is not a *necessary result*. To prevent the projection of one shoulder, and the consequent spinal curvature, *both of the arms must be kept on the same level*. For this purpose, there should be room to support them equally; and care should be taken to see that this support is regularly sought. If this be not done, the right arm will be apt to rise above the left, from its more constant use and elevation. A physician, highly celebrated for the success that has attended his treatment for lung affections, after dwelling upon the injury to the health that frequently results from sitting at too low desks, remarks, that "every parent should go to the school-rooms, and know for a certainty that the desks at which his children write or study are fully up to the arm-pits, and in no case allow them to sit stooping, or leaning the shoulders forward on the chest. If fatigued by this posture, they should be called to stand, or go out of doors and run about." The height of table I find most conducive to comfort for my own use is midway between the two; that is, half way from the elbow (as the arm hangs by the side) to the arm-pit. It is necessary, however, to rest both arms equally upon the table. The secret of posture consists in avoiding all bad positions, and in not continuing any one position too long. The ordinary carriage of the body is an object worthy of the attention of every parent and instructor. The more favorable impression which a man of erect and commanding attitude is sure to make, should not be overlooked. But there is a greater good than this; for he who *walks erect*, enjoys better health, possesses increased powers of usefulness, realizes more that *he is a man*, and has more to call forth gratitude to a beneficent Creator, than he who adopts an *oblique* posture. It was just remarked that "physical uprightness is next to moral." Physical *obliquity*, it may be added, is akin to *moral*. If they are not German-cousins, there can be little doubt but that, considered in all its bearings, the tendency of the former is to induce the latter.

Important as an erect posture and a well-developed chest are to gentlemen, they are in some respects even more so to the fairer sex; for, in addition to the advantages already considered, which both enjoy in common, these impart to them a peculiar charm, that to men of sense is far greater than pretty faces, which Nature has not given to all. "For a great number of years, it has been the custom in France to give young females, of the earliest age, the habit of holding back the shoulders, and thus expanding the chest. From the observations of anatomists lately made, it appears that the clavicle or collar bone is actually longer in females of the French nation than in those of the English. As the two nations are of the same race, as there is no remarkable difference in their bones, and this is peculiar to the sex, it must be attributed, as I believe, to the habit above mentioned, which, by the extension of the arms, has gradually produced an elongation of this bone. Thus we see that habit may be employed to alter and improve the solid bones. The French have succeeded in the development of a part in a way that adds to health and beauty, and increases a characteristic that distinguishes the human being from the brute."[9]

THE MUSCLES.—The muscles consist of compact bundles of fleshy fibers, which are found in animals on removing the skin. They constitute the red fleshy part of meat, and give form and symmetry to the body. In the limbs they surround and protect the bones, while in the trunk they spread out and constitute a defensive wall for the protection of the vital parts beneath. The muscles have been divided into *three parts*, of which the middle and fleshy portion, called the *belly*, is most conspicuous. The other two parts are the opposite ends, and are commonly called the *origin* and *insertion* of the muscle. The *origin* is usually fastened to one bone, and the *insertion* is attached to another. By the contraction of the *belly* of the muscle, the *insertion*, which is *movable*, is drawn toward the *origin*, which is *fixed*, and brings with it the bone to which it is attached. This any one can see illustrated in bending the arm. The muscle which performs this function lies between the elbow and the shoulder. It is attached to the shoulder by its *origin*, and to one of the bones of the fore-arm, just below the elbow, by its *insertion*. By grasping the arm midway between the shoulder and the elbow with the opposite hand, and then bending the arm, the enlargement of the belly of the muscle by the contraction will be at once perceived. Then, by moving the hand down on the inside of the arm toward the elbow, the lessening muscle may be readily traced until it terminates in a *tendon*, of much less size than the muscle, but of great strength, which is inserted into the bone just below the elbow. As the fore-arm is drawn up, and especially if there be a weight in the hand, the *tendon* may be felt just within the elbow-joint, running toward the point of insertion. Extend the arm at the elbow, and the muscle on the outside of the arm will swell and become firm, while the inside muscle, and its tendon at the elbow, will be relaxed. This example well illustrates the principle on which all the joints of the system are moved. Those who are acquainted with mechanics will readily perceive that the action just described is an example of the "*third* kind of lever," where the power is applied between the weight and the fulcrum. The elbow is the fulcrum, the hand contains the weight, and the tendon, inserted into the bone just below the elbow, is the power. This kind of lever requires the power to be greater than the weight, and acts under what is called a *mechanical disadvantage*. What is lost in power, however, is compensated in increased velocity.

There are upward of four hundred muscles in the human body. Some of these are *voluntary* in their motions, as those I have described, while others are *involuntary*, as the action of the heart and the respiratory muscles. Had the action of these depended upon the will, as does the action of the muscles of locomotion, the circulation of the blood and the process of breathing would cease, and life would become extinct whenever sleep or any other cause should overcome the attention. Here, then, we have another beautiful illustration of the wisdom and beneficence of the Creator in so ordering that those muscles which are essential to the continuation of life shall perform their functions without the control or attention of the individual.

The study of the muscular system involves an exposition of the principles by which exercise should be regulated, and can scarcely fail to excite the attention of the general reader, and especially of those who, as parents or teachers, are interested in the education of the young.

The muscles enable us to move the frame-work of the system. Their chief purpose obviously is to enable us to carry into effect the various resolutions and designs which have been formed by the mind. But, while fulfilling this grand object, their active exercise is, at the same time, highly conducive to the well-being of many other important functions. By muscular contraction, the blood is gently assisted in its course through the smaller vessels to the more distant parts of the body; and by it the important processes of digestion, respiration, secretion, absorption, and nutrition are promoted; and by it the health of the whole body is immediately and greatly influenced. The mind itself is exhilarated or depressed by the proper or improper use of muscular exercise. It thus becomes a point of no slight importance to establish general principles by which that exercise may be regulated.

In every part of the animal economy, the muscles are proportioned in size and structure to the efforts required of them. Whenever a muscle is called into frequent use, its fibers increase in thickness within certain limits, and become capable of acting with greater force and readiness. On the other hand, when a muscle is little used, its volume and power decrease in a corresponding degree.

In order to secure the most beneficial results from exercise, reference should be had to the time at which it is taken. Those who are in perfect health may engage in it at almost any hour except immediately after a meal; but those who are not robust ought to confine their hours of exercise within narrower limits. To a person in full vigor, a good walk, or other brisk exercise before breakfast may be highly beneficial and exhilarating, while to an invalid or delicate person it will be likely to prove detrimental. In order to prove beneficial, exercise must be resorted to only when the system is sufficiently vigorous to be able to meet it. This is usually the case after a lapse of from two to four hours after a moderate meal. The forenoon, then, will generally be found the best time for exercise for persons whose habits are sedentary. If exercise be delayed till the system feels exhaustion from want of food, its tendency will be to dissipate the strength that remains and impair digestion; while, if taken at the proper time, it will invigorate the system and promote digestion. The reasons are obvious; for exercise of every kind causes increased action and waste in the organ, and if there be not materials and vigor enough in the system to keep up that action and supply the waste, nothing but increased debility can reasonably be expected.

Active exercise immediately *before* meals is injurious. The reasons are apparent, for muscular exercise directs a flow of blood and nervous energy to the surface and extremities; and it is an established law in physiology, that energetic action can not be kept up in two distant parts of the system at the same time. Hence, whenever a meal is taken immediately after vigorous exercise, the stomach is taken at disadvantage, and, from want of the necessary action in its vessels and nerves, is unable to carry on digestion with success. This is very obviously the case where the exercise has been severe or protracted.

Active exercise ought to be equally avoided immediately *after* a heavy meal, for then the functions of the digestive organs are in the highest state of activity. If the muscular system be called into vigorous action under such circumstances, it will cause a withdrawal of the vital stimuli of the blood and nervous influence from the stomach to the extremities, which can not fail greatly to retard the digestive process. In accordance with this well-established fact, there is a natural and marked aversion to active pursuits after a full meal. A mere stroll, which requires no exertion and does not fatigue, will not be injurious before or after eating; but exercise beyond this limit is at such times hurtful. All, therefore, who would preserve and improve their health, will find it to their advantage to observe faithfully this important law, otherwise they will deprive themselves of most of the benefits that are usually attendant upon judicious exercise. All, then, who are forced to much exertion immediately after eating, should satisfy themselves with partaking of a very moderate meal. These remarks apply to both physical and mental exercise; for if the intellect be intently occupied in profound and absorbing thought, the nervous energy will be concentrated in the brain, and any demands made on it by the stomach or muscles will be very imperfectly attended to. So, also, if the stomach be actively engaged in digesting a full meal, and some subject of thought be presented to the mind, considerable difficulty will be felt in pursuing it, and most probably both thought and digestion will be disturbed.

Another law of the muscular system requires that relaxation and contraction should alternate; or, in other words, that rest should follow exercise. In accordance with this law, it is easier to walk than to stand; and in standing, it is easier to change from one foot to the other than to stand still. To require a child to extend his arm and hold a book in his hand, or even to keep the arm extended but a short time, is a violation of this law which should never be permitted. Akin to this is the very injudicious practice, which is sometimes resorted to in schools, of requiring a boy to stoop over, and, placing his finger upon a nail in the floor, "hold it in." Teachers who are disposed to inflict punishments like these ought first to try the experiment themselves. Such protracted tension of the muscles enfeebles their action, and ultimately destroys their power of contraction.

These remarks sufficiently explain why small children, after sitting a while in school, become restless. Proper regard for this organic law requires that the smaller children in school be allowed a recess as often, at least, as once an hour; and that all be allowed and encouraged frequently to change their position. I fully concur in the opinion expressed by Dr. Caldwell, who says, "It would be infinitely wiser and better to employ suitable persons to superintend the exercises and amusements of children under seven years of age, in the fields, orchards, and meadows, and point out to them the richer beauties of nature, than to have them immured in crowded school-rooms, in a state of inaction, poring over torn books and primers, conning words of whose meaning they are ignorant, and breathing foul air."

A change of position calls into action a different set of muscles, and relieves those that are exhausted. The object of exercise is to employ all the muscles of the body, and especially to strengthen those that are weak. It ought hence to be frequently varied, and always adapted to the peculiarities of individuals. Different kinds of exercise will therefore be found to suit different constitutions. Sedentary persons best enjoy, and will be most profited by, that kind of exercise which brings into action the greatest number of muscles.

To give exercise its greatest value, it should be taken at the same hour every day. This is well-nigh as important as the rule that requires meals to be taken regularly. If exercise be taken irregularly, one day in the morning, another day at noon, and another day at night, if at all, it is possible that good may result from it, but its beneficial effects would be greatly increased if the same amount of exercise were taken every day at the same hours. Give the system an opportunity of establishing *good habits* in this respect, and it will derive great advantage from them; but it is difficult for it to derive any benefit from a *habit of irregularity*, if such may be called a habit. Students, teachers, and all persons who lead sedentary lives, should have their regular times for exercise as well as for meals, and if they find it necessary to do without one, they will generally find it advantageous to dispense with the other also.

Walking, it has been said, agrees with every body. But as it brings into play chiefly the lower limbs and muscles of the loins, and affords little scope for the play of the arms and muscles of the chest, it is of itself insufficient to constitute adequate exercise. To render it most beneficial, the shoulders should be drawn back, and the chest should be enlarged by taking deep inspirations of pure air. The muscles of the chest, and of every part of the body, should be free to move and unconfined by tight clothing. Fencing, shuttlecock, and such other useful sports as combine with them free movements of the upper part of the body, are doubly advantageous, for they not only exercise the muscles of the whole body, but possess the additional advantage of animating the mind and increasing the nervous stimulus, by which exercise is rendered easy, pleasant, and invigorating. For the purpose of developing the chest, physiologists generally concur in recommending *fencing* as a good exercise for boys. Shuttlecock is a very beneficial exercise for females, calling into play, as it does, the muscles of the chest, trunk, and arms. It ought to be practiced in the open air. When played with both hands, as it may be after a little practice, it is very useful in preventing curvature, and in giving vigor to the spine. It is an excellent plan to play with a battledore in each hand, and to strike with them alternately. The graces is another play well adapted for expanding the chest, and giving strength to the muscles of the back, and has the advantage of being practicable in the open air. It is very important that the muscles of the back be strengthened by due exercise, for their proper use contributes to both health and beauty.

When managed with due regard to the natural powers of the individual, and so as to avoid effort and fatigue, *reading aloud* becomes a very useful and invigorating exercise. In forming and undulating the voice, not only the chest, but also the diaphragm and abdominal muscles are in constant action, and communicate to the stomach and bowels a healthy and agreeable stimulus. Where the voice is raised and the elocution is rapid, the muscular effort becomes fatiguing; but when care is taken not to carry reading aloud so far at one time as to excite a sensation of soreness or fatigue in the chest, and the exercise is duly repeated, it is extremely useful in developing and giving tone to the organs of respiration and to the general system.

"Vocal music is also very useful, by its direct effect on the constitution. It was the opinion of Dr. Rush, that young ladies especially, who, by the custom of society, are debarred from many kinds of salubrious exercise, should cultivate singing, not only as an accomplishment, but as a means of preserving health. He particularly insists that it should never be neglected in the education of females; and states that, besides its salutary operation in enabling them to soothe the cares of domestic life, and quiet sorrow by the united assistance of the sound and sentiment of a properly chosen song, it has a still more direct and important effect. 'I here introduce a fact,' he remarks, 'which has been suggested to me by my profession, and that is, that the exercise of the organs of the breast by singing contributes very much to defend them from those diseases to which the climate and other causes expose them. The Germans are seldom afflicted with consumption, nor have I ever known but one instance of spitting blood among them. This,

I believe, is in part occasioned by the strength which their lungs acquire by exercising them frequently in vocal music, for this constitutes an essential branch of their education. The music-master of our academy has furnished me with an observation still more in favor of this opinion. He informed me that he had known several instances of persons who were strongly disposed to consumption, who were restored to health by the exercise of their lungs in singing.'"[10]

Bathing or ablution, when conducted as recommended on pages 60 and 61, is not only a means of cleanliness and of exciting a healthy action in the skin, but it constitutes, at the same time, a most *admirable exercise*. If a lodging-room has been properly ventilated by leaving open windows, or otherwise, so that the air is pure and healthful in the morning, ten or fifteen minutes spent in bathing and friction, with a proper exercise of the muscles of the back and abdomen, will contribute more to invigorate the system and promote the general health than twice the amount of exercise taken at any other time or in any other way.

From the foregoing remarks, it appears that the most perfect of all exercises are those which combine the free play of all the muscles of the body, mental interest and excitement, and the unrestrained use of the voice.

CHAPTER IV.

THE LAWS OF HEALTH. PHILOSOPHY OF RESPIRATION.

We instinctively shun approach to the dirty, the squalid, and the diseased, and use no garment that may have been worn by another. We open sewers for matters that offend the sight or the smell, and contaminate the air. We carefully remove impurities from what we eat and drink, filter turbid water, and fastidiously avoid drinking from a cup that may have been pressed to the lips of a friend. On the other hand, we resort to places of assembly, and draw into our mouths air loaded with effluvia from the lungs, skin, and clothing of every individual in the promiscuous crowd—exhalations offensive, to a certain extent, from the most healthy individuals; but when arising from a living mass of skin and lungs in all stages of evaporation, disease, and putridity, they are in the highest degree deleterious and loathsome.—BIRNAN.

Respiration is usually defined as the process by which air is taken into the lungs and expelled from them. It explains the changes that take place in these organs, in the conversion of *chyle* and *venous*, or worn-out blood, into *arterial* or nutrient blood. In order to be clearly understood, I must premise a few observations on the circulation of the blood.[11] The blood circulating through the body is of two different kinds; the one *red* or *arterial*, and the other *dark* or *venous* blood. The former alone is capable of affording nourishment and supporting life. It is distributed from the *left* side of the heart all over the body by means of a great *artery*, which subdivides in its course, and ultimately terminates in myriads of very minute ramifications closely interwoven with, and in reality constituting a part of, the texture of every living part. On reaching this extreme point of its course, the blood passes into equally minute ramifications of the *veins*, which in their turn gradually coalesce, and form larger and larger trunks, till they at last terminate in two large veins, by which the whole current of the venous blood is brought back in a direction contrary to that of the blood in the arteries, and poured into the *right* side of the heart. On examining the quality of the blood in the arteries and veins, it is found to have undergone a great change in its passage from the one to the other. The florid hue which distinguished it in the arteries has disappeared, and given place to the dark color characteristic of venous blood. Its properties, too, have changed, and it is now no longer capable of sustaining life.

Two conditions are essential to the reconversion of venous into arterial blood, and to the restoration of its vital properties. The first is an adequate provision of *new materials* from the *food* to supply the place of those which have been expended in nutrition, and the second is the free exposure of the *venous blood* to the *atmospheric air*. The first condition is fulfilled by the chyle, or nutrient portion of the food, being regularly poured into the venous blood just before it reaches the right side of the heart, and the second by the important process of *respiration*, which takes place in the air-cells of the lungs. The venous blood, having arrived at the right side of the heart, is propelled by the contraction of that organ into a large artery, leading directly, by separate branches, to the two lungs, and hence called the *pulmonary* artery. In the innumerable branches of this artery expanding themselves throughout the substance of the lungs, the dark blood is subjected to the contact of the air inhaled in breathing, and a change in the composition both of the blood and of the inhaled air takes place, in consequence of which the former is found to have reassumed its florid or arterial hue, and to have regained its power of supporting life. The blood then enters minute venous ramifications, which gradually coalesce into larger branches, and at last terminate in four large trunks in the left side of the heart, whence the blood, in its arterial form, is again distributed over the body, to pursue the same course and undergo the same change as before.

It will be perceived that there are two distinct circulations, each of which is carried on by its own system of vessels. The one is from the *left* side of the *heart* to *every part of the body*, and back to the *right* side of the *heart*. The other is from the *right* side of the *heart* to the *lungs*, and back to the *left* side of the *heart*. The former has for its object nutrition and the maintenance of life; and the latter, the restoration of the deteriorated blood, and the *animalization* or *assimilation* of the *chyle* from which the *blood* is formed. This process has already been referred to as the *completion of digestion*; for *chyle* is not fitted to nourish the system until, by its exposure to the atmospheric air in the lungs, it is converted into *arterial blood.*

As the food can not become a part of the living animal, or the venous blood regain its lost properties until they have undergone the requisite changes in the air-cells of the lungs, the function of respiration by which these are effected is one of pre-eminent importance in the animal economy, and well deserves the most careful examination. The term respiration is frequently restricted to the mere inhalation and expiration of air from the lungs, but more generally it is employed to designate the whole series of phenomena which occur in these organs. The term *sanguification* is occasionally used to denote that part of the process in which the blood, by exposure to the action of the air, passes from the venous to the arterial state. As the chyle does not become assimilated to the blood until it has passed through the lungs, this term, which signifies *blood-making*, is not unaptly used.

The *quantity* and *quality* of the blood have a most direct and material influence upon the condition of every part of the body. If the *quantity* sent to the arm, for example, be diminished by tying the artery through which it is conveyed, the arm, being then imperfectly nourished, wastes away, and does not regain its plumpness till the full supply of blood be restored. In like manner, when the *quality* of that fluid is impaired by deficiency of food, bad digestion, impure air, or imperfect sanguification in the lungs, the body and all its functions become more or less disordered. Thus, in consumption, death takes place chiefly in consequence of respiration not being sufficiently perfect to admit of the formation of proper blood in the lungs. A knowledge of the structure and functions of the lungs, and of the conditions favorable to *their* healthy action, is therefore very important, for on their welfare depends that of every organ of the body.

The exposure of the blood to the action of the air seems to be indispensable to every variety of animated creatures. In man and the more perfect of the lower animals, it is carried on in the lungs, the structure of which is admirably adapted for the purpose. In many animals, however, the requisite action is effected without the intervention of lungs. In fishes, for example, that live in water and do not breathe, the blood circulates through the gills, and in them is exposed to the air which the water contains. So necessary is the atmospheric air to the vitality of the blood in all animals, that the want of it inevitably proves fatal. A fish can no more live in water deprived of air, than a man could in an atmosphere devoid of oxygen, which is the element that unites with the blood in the lungs in sanguification.

In man the lungs are those large, light, spongy bodies which, along with the heart, completely fill up the cavity of the chest. They vary much in size in different persons; and as the chest is formed for their protection, it is either large and capacious, or the reverse, according to the size of the lungs.

The substance of the lungs consists of bronchial tubes, air-cells, blood-vessels, nerves, and cellular membrane. The bronchial tubes are merely continuations and subdivisions of the windpipe, and serve to convey the external air to the air-cells of the lungs. The air-cells constitute the chief part of the lungs, and are the termination of the smaller branches of the bronchial tubes. When fully distended, they are so numerous as in appearance to constitute almost the whole lung. They are of various sizes, from the twentieth to the hundredth of an inch in diameter, and are lined with an exceedingly fine, thin membrane, on which the minute capillary branches of the pulmonary arteries and veins are copiously ramified. It is while circulating in the small vessels of this membrane, and there exposed to the air, that the blood undergoes the change from the venous to the arterial state. So numerous are these air-cells, that the aggregate extent of their lining membrane in man has been computed to exceed twenty thousand square inches, or about ten times the surface of the human body. Some writers place the estimate considerably higher.

A copious *exhalation* of moisture takes place in breathing, which presents a striking analogy to the exhalation from the surface of the skin already described. In the former as in the latter instance, the exhalation is carried on by the innumerable minute capillary vessels in which the small arterial branches terminate in the air-cells. Pulmonary exhalation is, in fact, one of the chief outlets of waste matter from the system; and the air we breathe is thus vitiated, not only by the subtraction of its oxygen and the addition of carbonic acid gas, but also by animal effluvia, with which it is loaded when returned from the lungs. In some individuals this last source of impurity is so great as to render their vicinity offensive, and even insupportable. It is this which gives the disagreeable, sickening smell to crowded rooms. The air which is expired from the lungs is rendered offensive by various other causes. When spirituous liquors are taken into the stomach, for example, they are absorbed by the veins and mixed with the venous blood, in which they are carried to the lungs to be expelled from the body. In some instances, when persons have drank copiously of spirits, their breath has been so saturated with them as actually to *take fire* and *burn*. An instance of this kind has recently been communicated to me by several reliable witnesses, in which the flame was extinguished by closing the mouth and nose, thus excluding the pure air that supported the combustion, until the unfortunate experimenter could remove the candle by which his breath had taken fire. This illustration will explain how the odor of different substances is frequently perceptible in the breath long after the mouth is free from them.

The lungs not only exhale waste matter, but *absorption* takes place from their lining membrane. In both of these respects there is a striking analogy between the functions performed by the lungs and the skin. When a person breathes an atmosphere loaded with the fumes of spirits, tobacco, turpentine, or of any other volatile substance, a portion of the fumes is taken up by the absorbing vessels of the lungs, and carried into the system, and there produces precisely the same effects as if introduced into the stomach. Dogs, for example, have been killed by being made to inhale the fumes of prussic acid for a few minutes. The lungs thus become a ready inlet to contagion, miasmata, and other poisonous influences diffused through the air we breathe.

From this general explanation of the structure and uses of the lungs, it is obvious that several conditions which it is our interest to know and observe are essential to the healthy performance of the important function of respiration. The first among these is a healthy original formation of the lungs. No fact in medicine is better established, says Dr. Combe, than that which proves the hereditary transmission, from parents to children, of a constitutional liability to pulmonary disease, and especially to consumption; yet, continues he, no condition is less attended to in forming matrimonial engagements.

Another requisite to the well-being of the lungs, and to the free and salutary exercise of respiration, is a due supply of rich and healthy blood. When, from defective food or impaired digestion, the blood is impoverished in quality, and rendered unfit for adequate nutrition, the lungs speedily suffer, and that often to a fatal extent. The free and easy expansion of the chest is also indispensable to the full play and dilation of the lungs. Whatever interferes with or impedes it, either in dress or in position, is obviously prejudicial to health. On the other hand, whatever favors the free expansion of the chest equally promotes the healthy action of the respiratory organs. Stays and corsets, and tight vests and waistbands, operate most injuriously, compressing as they do the thoracic cavity, and interfering with the healthy dilation of the lungs.

The admirable harmony established by the Creator between the various constituent parts of the animal frame, renders it impossible to pay regard to the conditions required for the health of any one, or to infringe the conditions required therefor, without all the rest participating in the benefit or injury. Thus, while cheerful exercise in the open air and in the society of equals is directly and eminently conducive to the well-being of the muscular system, the advantage does not stop there, the beneficent Creator having kindly so ordered it that the same exercise shall be scarcely less advantageous to the important function of respiration. Active exercise calls the lungs into play, favors their expansion, promotes the circulation of the blood through their substance, and leads to their complete and healthy development. The same end is greatly facilitated by that free and vigorous exercise of the voice, which so uniformly accompanies and enlivens the sports of the young, and which doubles the benefits derived from them considered as exercise. The excitement of the social and moral feelings which children experience while engaged in play is another powerful tonic, the influence of which on the general health ought not to be overlooked; for the nervous influence is as indispensable to the right performance of respiration as it is to the action of the muscles or to the digestion of food.

The regular supply of pure fresh air is another essential condition of healthy respiration, without which the requisite changes in the constitution of the blood, as it passes through the lungs, can not be effected. To enable the reader to appreciate this condition, it is necessary to consider the nature of the changes alluded to.

It is ascertained by analysis that the air we breathe is composed chiefly of the two gases *nitrogen* and *oxygen,* united in the ratio of four to one by volume, with exceedingly small and variable quantities of carbonic acid and aqueous vapor. No other mixture of these, or of any other gases, will sustain healthy respiration. To be more specific—atmospheric air consists of about seventy-eight per cent. of nitrogen, twenty-one per cent. of oxygen, and not quite one per cent. of carbonic acid. Such is its constitution when taken into the lungs in the act of breathing. When it is expelled from them, however, its composition is found to be greatly altered. The quantity of nitrogen remains nearly the same, but eight or eight and a half per cent. of the oxygen or vital air have disappeared, and been replaced by an equal amount of carbonic acid. In addition to these changes, the expired air is loaded with moisture. Simultaneously with these occurrences, the blood collected from the veins, which enters the lungs of a dark color and unfit for the support of life, assumes a florid hue and acquires the power of supporting life.

Physiologists are not fully agreed in explaining the processes by which these changes are effected in the lungs. All, however, agree that the change of the blood in the lungs is essentially dependent on the supply of oxygen contained in the air we breathe, and that air is fit or unfit for respiration in exact proportion as its quantity of oxygen approaches to, or differs from, that contained in pure air. If we attempt to breathe nitrogen, hydrogen, or any other gas that does not contain oxygen, the result will be speedy suffocation. If, on the other hand, we breathe air containing too great a proportion of oxygen, the vital powers will speedily suffer from excess of stimulus.

The chief chemical properties of the atmosphere are owing to the presence of *oxygen.* Nitrogen, which constitutes about four fifths of its volume, has been supposed to act as a mere diluent to the oxygen. *Increase* the proportion of oxygen in the atmosphere, and, as already stated, the vital powers will speedily suffer from excess of stimulus, the circulation and respiration become *too rapid,* and the system generally becomes highly excited. *Diminish* the proportion of oxygen, and the circulation and respiration become *too slow,* weakness and lassitude ensue, and a sense of heaviness and uneasiness pervades the entire system. As has been observed, air *loses* during each respiration a portion of its oxygen, and gains an equal quantity of *carbonic acid,* which is an *active poison.* When mixed with atmospheric air in the ratio of one to four, it extinguishes animal life. It is this gas that is produced by burning charcoal in a confined portion of common air. Its effect upon the system is well known to every reader of our newspapers. It causes dimness of sight, weakness, dullness, a difficulty of breathing, and ultimately *apoplexy* and *death*.[12]

Respiration produces the same effect upon air that the burning of charcoal does. It converts its oxygen, which is the aliment of animal life, into carbonic acid, which, be it remembered, is an active poison. Says Dr. Turner, in his celebrated work on chemistry, "An animal can not live in air which is unable to support combustion." Says the same author again, "An animal can not live in air which contains sufficient carbonic acid for extinguishing a candle." It will presently be seen why these quotations are made.

It is stated in several medical works that the quantity of air that enters the lungs at each inspiration of an adult varies from thirty-two to forty cubic inches. To establish more definitely some data upon which a calculation might safely be based, I some years ago conducted an experiment whereby I ascertained the medium quantity of air that entered the lungs of myself and four young men was thirty-six cubic inches, and that respiration is repeated once in three seconds, or twenty times a minute. I also ascertained that *respired air will not support combustion*. This truth, taken in connection with the quotations just made, establishes another and a *more important* truth, viz., that AIR ONCE RESPIRED WILL NOT FURTHER SUSTAIN ANIMAL LIFE. That part of the experiment by which it was ascertained that respired air will not support combustion is very simple, and I here give it with the hope that it may be tried at least in every *school-house*, if not in every family of our wide-spread country. It was conducted as follows:

I introduced a lighted taper into an inverted receiver (glass jar) which contained seven quarts of atmospheric air, and placed the mouth of the receiver into a vessel of water. The taper burned with its wonted brilliancy about a minute, and, growing dim gradually, became extinct at the expiration of three minutes. I then filled the receiver with water, and inverting it, placed its mouth beneath the surface of the same fluid in another vessel. I next removed the water from the receiver by *breathing into it*. This was done by filling the lungs with air, which, after being retained a short time in the chest, was exhaled through a siphon (a bent lead tube) into the receiver. I then introduced the lighted taper into the receiver of respired air, by which it was *immediately extinguished*. Several persons present then received a quantity of respired air into their lungs, whereupon the premonitory symptoms of apoplexy, as already given, ensued. The experiment was conducted with great care, and several times repeated in the presence of respectable members of the medical profession, a professor of chemistry, and several literary gentlemen, to their entire satisfaction.

Before proceeding further, I will make a practical application of the principles already established. Within the last ten years I have visited half of the states of the Union for the purpose of becoming acquainted with the actual condition of our common schools. I have therefore noticed especially the condition of school-houses. Although there is a great variety in their dimensions, yet there are comparatively few school-houses less than sixteen by eighteen feet on the ground, and fewer still larger than twenty-four by thirty feet, exclusive of our principal cities and villages. From a large number of actual measurements, not only in New York and Michigan, but east of the Hudson River and west of the great lakes, I conclude that, exclusive of entry and closets, when they are furnished with these appendages, school-houses are not usually larger than twenty by twenty-four feet on the ground, and seven feet in height. They are, indeed, more frequently smaller than larger. School-houses of these dimensions have a capacity of 3360 cubic feet, and are usually occupied by at least forty-five scholars in the winter season. Not unfrequently sixty or seventy, and occasionally more than a hundred scholars occupy a room of this size.

A simple arithmetical computation will abundantly satisfy any person who is acquainted with the composition of the atmosphere, the influence of respiration upon its fitness to sustain animal life, and the quantity of air that enters the lungs at each inspiration, that a school-room of the preceding dimensions contains quite too little air to sustain the healthy respiration of even *forty-five* scholars three hours—the usual length of each session; and frequently the school-house is imperfectly ventilated between the sessions at noon, and sometimes for several days together.

Mark the following particulars: 1. The quantity of air breathed by forty-five persons in three hours, according to the data just given, is 3375 cubic feet.

2. *Air once respired will not sustain animal life.* 3. The school-room was estimated to possess a capacity of 3360 cubic feet—*fifteen feet less than is necessary to sustain healthy respiration.* 4. Were forty-five persons whose lungs possess the estimated capacity placed in an air-tight room of the preceding dimensions, and could they breathe pure air till it was all once respired, and then enter upon its second respiration, *they would all die with the apoplexy before the expiration of a three hours' session.*

From the nature of the case, these conditions can not conveniently be fulfilled. But numerous instances of fearful approximation exist. We have no air-tight houses. But in our latitude, comfort requires that rooms which are to be occupied by children in the winter season, be made very close. The dimensions of rooms are, moreover, frequently narrowed, that the *warm breath* may lessen the amount of fuel necessary to preserve a comfortable temperature. It is true, on the other hand, that the quantity of air which children breathe is somewhat less than I have estimated. But the derangement resulting from breathing impure air, in their case, is greater than in the case of adults whose constitutions are matured, and who are hence less susceptible of injury. It is also true in many schools that the number occupying a room of the dimensions supposed is considerably greater than I have estimated. Moreover, in many instances, a great proportion of the larger scholars will respire the estimated quantity of air.

Again, all the air in a room is not respired *once* before a portion of it is breathed the second, or even the *third* and *fourth* time. The atmosphere is not suddenly changed from purity to impurity—from a healthful to an infectious state. Were it so, the change, being more perceptible, would be seen and *felt* too, and a *remedy* would be sought and applied. But because the change is gradual, it is not the less fearful in its consequences. In a room occupied by *forty-five persons,* THE FIRST MINUTE, *thirty-two thousand four hundred cubic inches of air impart their entire vitality to sustain animal life, and, mingling with the atmosphere of the room, proportionately deteriorate the whole mass.* Thus are abundantly sown in early life the fruitful seeds of disease and premature death.

This detail shows conclusively sufficient cause for that uneasy, listless state of feeling which is so prevalent in crowded school-rooms. It explains why children that are amiable at home are mischievous in school, and why those that are troublesome at home are frequently well-nigh uncontrollable in school. It discloses the true cause why so many teachers who are justly considered both pleasant and amiable in the ordinary domestic and social relations, are obnoxious in the school-room, being there habitually sour and fretful. The ever-active children are disqualified for study, and engage in mischief as their only alternative. On the other hand, the irritable teacher, who can hardly look with complaisance upon good behavior, is disposed to magnify the most trifling departure from the rules of propriety. The scholars are continually becoming more ungovernable, and the teacher more unfit to govern them. Week after week they become less and less attached to him, and he, in turn, becomes less interested in them.

This detail explains, also, why so many children are unable to attend school at all, or become unwell so soon after commencing to attend, when their health is sufficient to engage in other pursuits. The number of scholars answering this description is greater than most persons are aware of. In one district that I visited a few years ago in the State of New York, it was acknowledged by competent judges to be emphatically true in the case of not less than *twenty-five scholars*. Indeed, in that same district, the health of more than *one hundred* scholars was materially injured every year in consequence of occupying an old and partially-decayed house, of too narrow dimensions, with very limited facilities for ventilation. The evil, even after the cause was made known, was suffered to exist for years, although the district was worth more than three hundred thousand dollars. And what *was* true[13] of this school, is now, with a few variations, true in the case of scores, if not hundreds of schools with which I am acquainted, from far-famed New England to the Valley of the Mississippi.

This detail likewise explains why the business of teaching has acquired, and *justly too*, the reputation of being unhealthy. There is, however, no reason why the health of either teacher or pupils should sooner fail in a well-regulated school, taught in a house properly constructed, and suitably warmed and ventilated, than in almost any other business. If this statement were not true, an unanswerable argument might be framed against the very *existence* of schools; and it might clearly be shown that it is *policy*, nay, DUTY, to close at once and forever the four thousand school-houses of Michigan, and the hundred thousand of the nation, and leave the rising generation to perish for lack of knowledge. But our condition in this respect is not hopeless. The evil in question may be effectually remedied by enlarging the house, or, which is easier, cheaper, and more effectual, by frequent and thorough ventilation. It would be well, however, to unite the two methods.

In the winter of 1841-2, I visited a school in which the magnitude of the evil under consideration was clearly developed. Five of the citizens of the district attended me in my visit to the school. We arrived at the school-house about the middle of the afternoon. It was a close, new house, eighteen by twenty-four feet on the ground—two feet less in one of its dimensions than the house concerning which the preceding calculation is made. There were present forty-three scholars, the teacher, five patrons, and myself, making fifty in all. Immediately after entering the school-house, one of the trustees remarked to me, "I believe our school-house is too tight to be healthy." I made no reply, but secretly resolved that I would sacrifice my comfort for the remainder of the afternoon, and hazard my health, and my life even, to test the accuracy of the opinions I had entertained on this important subject. I marked the uneasiness and dullness of all present, and especially of the patrons, who had been accustomed to breathe a purer atmosphere. School continued an hour and a half, at the close of which I was invited to make some remarks. I arose to do so, but was unable to proceed till I opened the outer door, and snuffed a few times the purer air without. When I had partially recovered my wonted vigor, I observed with delight the renovating influence of the current of air that entered the door, mingling with and gradually displacing the fluid poison that filled the room, and was about to do the work of death. It seemed as though I was standing at the mouth of a huge sepulcher, in which the dead were being restored to life. After a short pause, I proceeded with a few remarks, chiefly, however, on the subject of respiration and ventilation. The trustees, who had just tested their accuracy and bearing upon their comfort and health, resolved immediately to provide for ventilation according to the suggestions in the article on school-houses in the last chapter of this work.

Before leaving the house on that occasion, I was informed an evening meeting had been attended there the preceding week, which they were obliged to dismiss before the ordinary exercises were concluded, because, as they said, "We all got sick, and the candles went almost out." Little did they realize, probably, that the light of life became just as nearly extinct as did the candles. Had they remained there a little longer, both would have gone out together, and there would have been reacted the memorable tragedy of the *Black Hole* in Calcutta, into which were thrust a garrison of one hundred and forty-six persons, one hundred and twenty-three of whom perished miserably in a few hours, being suffocated by the confined air.

What has been said in the preceding pages on the philosophy of respiration was first given to the public nearly ten years ago, in a report of the author's in the State of New York. He has since seen the same sentiments inculcated by many of our most eminent practical educators, some of whom had written upon the subject at an earlier date. Allen and Pepy showed by experiment that air which has been once breathed contains eight and a half per cent. of carbonic acid, and that no continuance of the respiration of the same air could make it take up more than ten per cent. Air, then, when once respired, has taken up more than *four fifths* of the amount of this noxious gas that it can be made to by any number of breathings.

Dr. Clark, in his work on Consumption, remarks as follows: "Were I to select two circumstances which influence the health, especially during the growth of the body, more than others, and concerning which the public, ignorant at present, ought to be well informed, they would be the proper adaptation of food to difference of age and constitution, and the constant supply of pure air for respiration." Dr. William A. Alcott, who has given especial attention to this subject, after quoting the preceding remark of Dr. Clark, adds: "We believe this is the opinion of all medical men who have studied the constitution of man, and its relation to outward objects."

A distinguished surgeon[14] of Leeds, England, goes somewhat further in praising pure air than most of his contemporaries. "Be it remembered," says he, "that man subsists more upon air than upon his food and drink." There is some novelty in this remark, I admit: but is it not truthful? Men have been known to live *three weeks* without eating. But exclude the atmospheric air from the lungs for the space of *three minutes*, and death generally ensues. We thus see that life will continue with abstinence from food three thousand times as long as it is safe to protract an atmospheric fast.

Let us take another view of the subject. Men usually eat *three times* in twenty-four hours. This is all that is necessary to, or compatible with, the enjoyment of uninterrupted good health. But we involuntarily breathe nearly *thirty thousand times* in the same length of time. We need, then, fresh supplies of pure air ten thousand times as often as it is necessary to partake of meals. Is it not apparent, then, that *man subsists more upon* AIR *than upon his* FOOD *and* DRINK?

The atmosphere which we so frequently inhale, and upon which our well-being so much depends, surrounds the earth to the height of about forty-five miles. The surface of the earth contains about two hundred millions of square miles, and it is estimated that there dwell upon it eight hundred millions of inhabitants. This gives to each individual about eleven cubic miles of air. But the air is breathed by the inferior animals as well as by man. It is also rendered impure by combustion. If by both of these causes ten times as much air is consumed as by man, there is still left one cubic mile of uncontaminated atmospheric air to every human being dwelling upon the surface of the earth. This would allow him to live more than twice the age allotted to man, without breathing any portion of the atmosphere a second time. And still, as if to avoid the possibility of evil to man on this account, the beneficent Creator has wisely so ordered, that while we do not interfere with the laws of Nature, there is not even the possibility of rebreathing respired air until it has been purified and restored to its natural and healthful state; for carbonic acid, the vitiating product of respiration, although immediately *fatal* to *animals*, constitutes the very *life* of *vegetation*. When brought in contact with the upper surface of the green leaves of trees and plants, and acted upon by the direct solar rays, this gas is decomposed, and its carbon is absorbed to sustain, in part, the life of the plant, by affording it one element of its food, while the oxygen is liberated and restored to the atmosphere. Vegetables and animals are thus perpetually interchanging kindly offices, and each flourishes upon that which is fatal to the other. It is in this way that the healthful state of the atmosphere is kept up. Its equilibrium seems never to be disturbed, or, if disturbed at all, it is immediately restored by the mutual exchange of poison for aliment, which is constantly going on between the animal and vegetable worlds. This interchange of kindly offices is constantly going on all over the earth, even in the highest latitudes, and in the very depths of winter; for air which has been respired is rarefied, and, when thrown from the lungs, *ascends*, and is thus not only out of our reach, whereby we are protected from respiring it a second time, but this (to us) deadly poison falls into the great aërial current which is constantly flowing from the polar to the tropical regions, where it is converted into vegetable growth. The oxygen which is exhaled in the processes of tropical vegetation, heated and rarefied by the vertical rays of the sun, mounts to the upper regions of the atmosphere, and, falling into a returning current, in its appointed time revisits the higher latitudes. So wisely has the Divine Author ordered these processes, that air, in its natural state[15] in any part of the world, does not contain more than *one half of one per cent.* of carbonic acid gas, although, as already stated, air which has been once respired contains *eight and a half per cent.* of this gas, which is at least seventeen times its natural quantity.

There are other agencies than carbonic acid gas which in civic life render the atmosphere impure. Of this nature is carbureted hydrogen gas, which is produced in various ways. This, says Dr. Comstock, is immediately destructive to animal life, and will not support combustion. It exists in stagnant water, especially in warm weather, and is generated by the decomposition of vegetable products. Dr. Arnott expresses the conviction that the immediate and chief cause of many of the diseases which impair the bodily and mental health of the people, and bring a considerable portion prematurely to the grave, is the poison of atmospheric impurity, arising from the accumulation in and around their dwellings of the decomposing remnants of the substances used for food and in their arts, and of the impurities given out from their own bodies. If you allow the sources of aërial impurity to exist in or around dwellings, he continues, you are poisoning the people; and while many die at early ages of fevers and other acute diseases, the remainder will have their health impaired and their lives shortened.

There are many instances on record where the progress of an epidemic has been speedily arrested by ventilation. A striking instance is given by the writer last quoted. "When I visited Glasgow with Mr. Chadwick," says he, "there was described to us one vast lodging-house, in connection with a manufactory there, in which formerly fever constantly prevailed, but where, by making an opening from the top of each room through a channel of communication to an air-pump common to all the channels, the disease had disappeared altogether. The supply of pure air obtained by that mode of ventilation was sufficient to dilute the cause of the disease, so that it became powerless."

Sulphureted hydrogen gas is also exceedingly poisonous to the lungs and to every part of the system. When pure, this gas is described as instantly fatal to animal life. Even when diluted with fifteen hundred times its bulk of air, it has been found so poisonous as to destroy a bird in a few seconds. "This gas," says Dr. Dunglison, in his Elements of Hygiene, "is extremely deleterious.[16] When respired in a pure state it kills instantly; and its deadly agency is rapidly exerted when put in contact with any of the tissues of the body, through which it penetrates with astonishing rapidity. Even when mixed with a portion of air, it has proved immediately destructive. Dr. Paris refers to the case of a chemist of his acquaintance, who was suddenly deprived of sense as he stood over a pneumatic trough in which he was collecting this gas. From the experiments of Dupuytren and Thenard, air that contains a thousandth part of sulphureted hydrogen kills birds immediately. A dog perished in air containing a hundredth part, and a horse in air containing a fiftieth part of it."

The preceding are far from being all the causes of atmospheric impurity. Besides these, there are numerous exhalations, as well as gases, that are poisonous. Some of these exhalations are more abundant in the night, and about the time of the morning and evening twilight. "Hence the importance," says a writer on health, "to those who are feeble, of avoiding the air at all hours except when the sun is considerably above the horizon."

Although the atmosphere, in its natural state, is not at all times perfectly pure, still it is comparatively so, and especially in the daytime. All, therefore, who would retain and improve their health, should inhale the open air as much as possible, even though they can not, like Franklin's Methusalem,[17] be always in it. This remark is applicable to both sexes, and to every age and condition of life.

The following, from the pen of an American author[18] who has written much and well on physical education, is pertinent to the subject under consideration: "We breathe bad air principally as the production of our own bodies. Here is the source of a large share of human wo; and to this point must his attention be particularly directed who would save himself from disease, and promote, in the highest possible degree, his health and longevity. We must avoid breathing over the carbonic acid gas contained in the tight or unventilated rooms in which we labor or remain for a long time, whether parlors, school-rooms, counting-rooms, bed-rooms, shops, or factories. The individual who lives most according to nature—who observes with most care the laws of life and health—must necessarily throw off much carbonic acid from his lungs, if not from his skin. It does not follow, however, that because this gas is formed we are obliged to inhale it. We may change our position, change our clothing, ventilate our rooms of all sorts, shake up our bed-clothing often and air our bed, and use clean, loose, and porous clothing by night and by day. We may thus very effectually guard against injuries from a very injurious agent.

"One thing should be remembered in connection with this subject which is truly encouraging. The more we accustom ourselves to pure air, the more easily will our lungs and nasal organs detect its presence. He who has redeemed his senses and restored his lungs to integrity, like him who has redeemed a conscience once deadened, is so alive to every bad impression made upon any of these, that he can often detect impurity around or within him, and thus learn to avoid it. It will scarcely be possible for such a person long to breathe bad air, or nauseous or unwholesome effluvia, without knowing it, and learning to avoid the causes which produce it. Such a person will not neglect long to remove the impurities which accumulate so readily on the surface of his body, or suffer himself to use food or drink which induces flatulence, and thus exposes either his intestines or his lungs, or the lungs of others, to that most extremely poisonous agent, sulphureted hydrogen gas. Nor will he be likely to permit the accumulation of filth, liquid or solid, around or in his dwelling. There are those whose senses will detect a very small quantity of stagnant water, or vinegar, or other liquids, or fruit, or changed food in the house, or even the presence of those semi-putrid substances, wine and cider. But some will indeed say that such integrity of the senses would be an annoyance rather than a blessing. On the same principle, however, would a high degree of conscientiousness in regard to right and wrong in moral conduct be a curse to us. If it be desirable to have our physical sense of right and wrong benumbed, it is so to have our moral sense benumbed also. Yet what person of sense ever complained of too tender a conscience, or too perfect a sense of right and wrong in morals?"

EXERCISE OF THE LUNGS.—Judicious exercise of the lungs, in the opinion of that eminent physiologist, Dr. Andrew Combe, is one of the most efficacious means which can be employed for promoting their development and warding off their diseases. In this respect the organs of respiration closely resemble the muscles and all other organized parts. They are made to be used, and if they are left in habitual inactivity, their strength and health are unavoidably impaired; while, if their exercise be ill-timed or excessive, disease will as certainly follow.

The lungs may be exercised *directly* by the use of the voice in speaking, reading aloud, or singing, and *indirectly* by such kinds of bodily or muscular exertion as require quicker and deeper breathing. In general, both ought to be conjoined. But where the chief object is to improve the lungs, those kinds which have a tendency to expand the chest and call the organs of respiration into play ought to be especially preferred. Rowing a boat, fencing, quoits, shuttlecock, the proper use of skipping the rope, dumb-bells, and gymnastics are of this description, and have been recommended for this purpose. All of them employ actively the muscles of the chest and trunk, and excite the lungs themselves to freer and fuller expansion. Climbing up a hill is, for the same reason, an exercise of high utility in giving tone and freedom to the pulmonary functions. Where, either from hereditary predisposition or accidental causes, the chest is unusually weak, every effort should be made, from infancy upward, to favor the growth and strength of the lungs, by the habitual use of such of these exercises as can most easily be practiced. The earlier they are resorted to, and the more steadily they are pursued, the more certainly will their beneficial results be experienced.

If the *direct* exercise of the lungs in practicing deep inspiration, speaking, reading aloud, and singing, is properly managed and persevered in, particularly before the frame has become consolidated, it will exert a very beneficial influence in expanding the chest, and giving tone and imparting health to the important organs contained in it. As a preventive measure, Dr. Clark, in his treatise on Consumption and Scrofula, recommends the full expansion of the chest in the following manner: "We desire the young person, while standing, to throw his arms and shoulders back, and, while in this position, to inhale slowly as much air as he can, and repeat this exercise at short intervals several times in succession. When this can be done in the open air it is most desirable, a double advantage being thus obtained from the practice. Some exercise of this kind should be adopted daily by all young persons, more especially by those whose chests are narrow or deformed, and should be slowly and gradually increased."

In this preventive measure recommended by Dr. Clark, some of our most eminent physiologists heartily concur. They also express the opinion that, for the same reason, even the crying and sobbing of children, when not caused by disease, contribute to their future health. Dr. Combe says, "The loud laugh and noisy exclamations attending the sports of the young have an evident relation to the same beneficial end, and ought, therefore, to be encouraged." But beneficial as the direct exercise of the lungs is thus shown to be, in expanding and strengthening the chest, its influence extends still further, and, as we have already seen, contributes greatly to promote the important process of digestion. If, therefore, the lungs be rarely called into active exercise, not only do *they* suffer, but an important aid to digestion being withdrawn, the *stomach* and *bowels* also become weakened, and indigestion and costiveness ensue.

The exercise of what has not unaptly been called Vocal Gymnastics, and the loud and distinct speaking enforced in many of our schools, not only fortify the vocal organs against the attacks of disease, but tend greatly to promote the general health. For this purpose, also, as well as for its social and moral influences, vocal music should be introduced into all our schools. That by these and like exercises deep inspirations and full expirations are encouraged, any one may become convinced who will attend to what passes in his own body while reading aloud a single paragraph.

There is danger of exercising the lungs too much when disease exists in the chest. At such times, not only speaking, reading aloud, and singing, but ordinary muscular exertion, ought to be refrained from, or be regulated by professional advice. When a joint is sore or inflamed, we know that motion impedes its recovery. When the eye is affected, we, for a similar reason, shut out the light. So, when the stomach is disordered, we respect its condition, and are more careful about diet. The lungs demand a treatment founded on the same general principle. When inflamed, they should be exercised as little as possible. All violent exercise ought, therefore, to be refrained from during at least the active stages of a cold; but colds may often be entirely prevented at the time of exposure by a proper exercise of the lungs.

In conversing with an eminent physician recently on this subject, he expressed the conviction that one of the most effectual methods of warding off a cold, when exposed by wet feet or otherwise, is to take frequent deep inhalations of air. By this means the carbonic acid, which the returning circulation deposits in the lungs, is not only more effectually disengaged, but, at the same time, the greater amount of oxygen that enters the lungs and combines with the blood quickens the circulation, and thus, imparting increased vitality to the system, enables it more effectually to resist any attack that may be induced by unusual exposure.

A late medical writer, who has become quite celebrated in this country for the successful treatment of pulmonary consumption,[19] expresses the opinion that, to the consumptive, air is a most excellent medicine, and "far more valuable than all other remedies." He thinks it "the grand agent in expanding the chest." In urging the importance of habitually maintaining an erect position, he expresses the conviction that "practice will soon make sitting or standing perfectly erect vastly more agreeable and less fatiguing than a stooping posture." To persons predisposed to consumption, these hints, he thinks, are of the greatest importance. While walking, he says, "the chest should be carried proudly erect and straight, the top of it pointing rather backward than forward." To illustrate the advantages of habitually maintaining this position, he refers to the North American Indians, who never had consumption, and who are remarkable for their perfectly erect posture while walking. "Next to this," he adds, "it is of vast importance to the consumptive to breathe well. He should make a practice of taking long breaths, sucking in all the air he can, and holding it in the chest as long as possible." He recommends the repetition of this a hundred times a day, and especially with those who have a slight cold or symptoms of weak lungs. When practiced in pure cold air, its advantages are most apparent. To increase the benefits resulting from this practice, he recommends the use of the "inhaling tube." He thinks that inhaling tubes made of silver or gold are much better than those made of wood or India-rubber. In this opinion I fully concur, for I think with him that gold and silver tubes will not so readily "contract any impure or poisonous matter." But there is another and a stronger reason why I prefer *silver*, and especially GOLD inhaling tubes, to those made of wood or India-rubber. *They would be more highly prized* and MORE FREQUENTLY USED.

The same writer entertains the belief that about one third of all the consumptions originate from weakness of the abdominal belts. He hence, in such cases, recommends the use of the "abdominal supporter." In order to favor an erect posture and an open chest, he also recommends the use of "shoulder-braces." He says the proper use of these, with other remedies, will "entirely prevent the possibility of consumption, from whatever cause." The inhaling-tube, together with the shoulder-braces and supporter when needed, he says are perfect preventives, and should not be neglected; for if the shoulders are kept off the chest, and the abdomen is well supported, and then an inhaling tube is faithfully used, "the lungs can never become diseased. Any person in this way, who chooses to take the trouble, can have a large chest and healthy lungs."

When persons have contracted disease they may require these *artificial helps*; but it should be borne in mind that an all-wise and beneficent Creator has kindly given to each of his creatures *two inhaling tubes*, admirably adapted to their wants. He has also furnished them with a set of *abdominal muscles* which, when properly used, have generally been found to supersede the necessity of artificial "supporters." He has, moreover, in the plenitude of his goodness, furnished each member of the human family with a good pair of *shoulder-braces*. It should also be borne in mind that Nature's shoulder-braces *improve by use*, while the artificial ones not only soon fail, but their very use generally impairs the healthy action of the natural ones; for these, like all other muscles, improve by use and become enfeebled by disuse. Parents and teachers, then, and all who have the care of the young, should encourage the correct use of Nature's inhaling tubes, shoulder-braces, and abdominal supporters; for in this way they have it in their power not only to supersede the necessity of resorting to artificial ones later in life, but of preventing much of human misery, and contributing to the permanent elevation of the race.

In the cultivation and expansion of the faculties of the mind, we act altogether upon *organized matter*—and this, too, of the most delicate kind—which, while it serves as the mediator between *body* and *spirit*, partakes so largely of the nature, character, and essential attributes of the *former*, that, without its proper physical growth and development, all the manifestations of the *latter* sink into comparative insignificance; so that, without a perfect organization of the *brain*, the mental powers must be proportionally paralyzed; without *its* maintaining a healthy condition, *they* must be rendered proportionally weak and inactive.[20] —Dr. J. L. Peirce.

It has already been stated that there exists such an intimate connection between physical, intellectual, and moral education, that, in order duly to appreciate the importance of either, we must not view it separate and alone merely, but in connection with both of the others. However much value, then, we may attach to physical education on its own account, considering man as a corporeal being, we shall have occasion greatly to magnify its importance as we direct our attention to the cultivation and development of his mental faculties. We have no means of becoming acquainted with the laws which govern independent mind; but that mind separate from body is, from its very nature, all-knowing and intelligent, is an opinion that has obtained to a considerable extent. Be this as it may, it does not immediately concern us in the present state. This much we know, that embodied mind acquires knowledge slowly, and with a degree of perfection depending upon the condition of the brain and the bodily organs of sense, through the medium of which mind communicates with the external world. We do not even know whether education modifies the mind itself; and, if at all, how it affects it in its disembodied state. Neither is it important that we should possess this knowledge. There is, however, much reason for believing that the mind of man in the future state will be permanently affected by, and enjoy the full benefit of, the preparatory training it has received in this life; that then, as now, it will be progressive in its attainments; and that the rapidity with which it will then acquire knowledge, and the nature of its pursuits, will depend upon the degree of cultivation, and the habits and character formed in this life.

From what we know of the beneficent and all-wise Creator, as manifested in his word and works, we have abundant reason for believing that our highest and enduring good will be best promoted by becoming acquainted with, and yielding a cheerful obedience to, the laws of organic mind. Whatever the effect of education upon independent mind may be, we may rest well assured that man's everlasting well-being in the future state will be most directly and certainly reached by a strict conformity to those laws which regulate mind in its present mode of being. It should be borne in mind, also, that just in proportion as man remains ignorant of those laws, or, knowing them, disregards them, will he fail to secure his best good in this life not only, but in that which is to come, to an extent corresponding with the influence which education may exert upon independent mind. In order, then, most successfully to carry forward the great work of intellectual and moral culture, and to secure to man the fullest benefits of education in the present life, and in that higher mode of being which awaits him in the future, we have only to acquaint him with the laws by which embodied mind is governed, and to induce him to yield a ready, cheerful, and uniform obedience to those laws. We shall therefore devote the following pages to an inquiry into the laws which must be observed by embodied mind in order to render it the fittest possible instrument for discovering, applying, and obeying the laws under which God has placed the universe, which constitutes the one great object of education, when considered in its widest and true sense.

All physiologists and philosophers regard the brain as the organ of the mind. Although it is not befitting here to give a particular description of this complicated organ, still it may be well further to premise that, by nearly universal consent, it is regarded as the immediate seat of the *intellectual* faculties not only, but of the passions and moral feelings of our nature, as well as of consciousness and every other mental act. It is also well established that the brain is the principal source of that nervous influence which is essential to vitality, and to the action of each and all of our bodily organs. As, then, its functions are the highest and most important in the animal economy, it becomes an object of paramount importance in education to discover the laws by which they are regulated, that by yielding obedience to them we may avoid the evils consequent on their violation.

Let no one suppose these evils are few or small; for, in the language of an eloquent writer, "the system of education which is generally pursued in the United States is unphilosophical in its elementary principles, ill adapted to the condition of man, practically mocks his necessities, and is intrinsically absurd. The high excellences of the present system, in other respects, are fully appreciated. Modern education has indeed achieved wonders. It has substituted things for names, experiment for hypothesis, first principles for arbitrary rules. It has simplified processes, stripped knowledge of its abstraction and thrown it into visibility, made practical results rather than mystery the standard by which to measure the value of attainment, and facts rather than conjecture its circulating medium."[21]

A sound original constitution may be regarded as the first condition of the healthy action of the brain; for, being a part of the animal economy, it is subject to the same general laws that govern the other bodily organs. When a healthy brain is transmitted to children, and their treatment from infancy is judicious and rational, its health becomes so firmly established that, in after life, its power of endurance will be greatly increased, and it will be enabled most effectually to ward off the insidious attacks of disease. On the other hand, where this organ has either inherited deficiencies and imperfections, or where they have been subsequently induced by early mismanagement, it becomes peculiarly susceptible, and frequently yields to the slightest attacks. The most eminent physiologists of the age concur in the opinion that, of all the causes which predispose to nervous and mental disease, the transmission of hereditary tendency from parents to children is the most powerful, producing, as it does, in the children, an unusual liability to those maladies under which their parents have labored.

When both parents are descended from tainted families, their progeny, as a matter of course, will be more deeply affected than where one of them is from a pure stock. This sufficiently accounts for the fact that hereditary predisposition is a more common cause of nervous disease in those circles that intermarry much with each other than where a wider choice is exercised. Fortunately, such is the constitution of society in this country, that there are fewer evils of this kind among us than are manifest in many of the European states, where intermarriages are restricted to persons of the same rank, as has already been illustrated by reference to the grandees of Spain, who have become a race of dwarfs intellectually as well as physically. But even in this country there are painful illustrations of the truth of the popular belief that when cousins intermarry their offspring are liable to be idiotic. The command of God not to marry within certain degrees of consanguinity is, then, in accordance with the organic laws of our being, and the wisdom of the prohibition is abundantly confirmed by observation.

What was said of hereditary transmission in the second chapter of this work applies here with increased force. It is of the highest possible importance that this subject should receive the especial attention of every parent, and of all who may hereafter sustain the parental relation; for posterity, to the latest generations, will be affected by the laws of hereditary transmission, whether those laws are understood and obeyed or not. The importance of this subject, already inconceivably vast, becomes infinitely momentous in view of the probability that the evils under consideration are not confined to this life, but must, from the nature of the case, continue to be felt while mind endures.

Unfortunately, it is not merely as a cause of disease that hereditary predisposition is to be dreaded. The obstacles which it throws in the way of permanent recovery are even more formidable, and can never be entirely removed. Safety is to be found only in avoiding the perpetuation of the mischief. When, therefore, two persons, each naturally of an excitable and delicate nervous temperament, choose to unite for life, they have themselves to blame for the concentrated influence of similar tendencies in destroying the health of their offspring, and subjecting them to all the miseries of nervous disease, melancholy, or madness.

There is another consideration that should be noticed here: it is this. Even where no hereditary defect exists, the state of the mother during pregnancy has an influence on the mental character and health of the offspring, of which even *few parents* have any adequate conception. "It is often in the maternal womb that we are to look for the true cause not only of imbecility, but of the different kinds of mania. During the agitated periods of the French Revolution, many ladies then pregnant, and whose minds were kept constantly on the stretch by the anxiety and alarm inseparable from the epoch in which they lived, and whose nervous systems were thereby rendered irritable in the highest degree compatible with sanity, were afterward delivered of infants whose brains and nervous systems had been affected to such a degree by the state of their parent, that, in future life, as children they were subject to spasms, convulsions, and other nervous affections, and in youth to imbecility or madness, almost without any exciting cause."[22]

Dr. Caldwell, too, an able and philanthropic advocate of an improved system of physical, intellectual, and moral education in this country, is very urgent in enforcing rational care, during the period of gestation, on the part of every mother who values the future health and happiness of her offspring. Among other things, he insists on mothers taking more active exercise in the open air than they usually do. He also cautions them against allowing a feeling of false delicacy to keep them confined in their rooms for weeks and months together. At such times especially the mind ought to be kept free from gloom or anxiety, and in that state of cheerful activity which results from the proper exercise of the intellect, and especially of the moral and social feelings.

But if seclusion and depression be hurtful to the unborn progeny, surely thoughtless dissipation and late hours, dancing and waltzing, together with irritability of temper and peevishness of disposition, can not be less injurious. Every female that is about to become a mother should treasure up the remark of that sensible lady, the Margravine of Anspach, who says, "when a female is likely to become a mother, she ought to be doubly careful of her temper, and, in particular, to indulge no ideas that are not cheerful and no sentiments that are not kind. Such is the connection between the mind and the body, that the features of the face are moulded commonly into an expression of the internal disposition; and is it not natural to think that an infant, before it is born, may be affected by the temper of its mother?" If these things are true—and they are as well authenticated as any physiological facts are or can be—then not only *mothers*, but all with whom they associate, and especially *fathers*, are interested in knowing these important physiological laws; and they should aim, from the very beginning, so to observe them as to secure to posterity, physically and mentally, the full benefits that are connected with cheerful obedience.

A due supply of properly oxygenated blood is another condition upon which the healthy action of the brain depends. Although it may not be easy to perceive the effects of slight differences in the quality of the blood, still, when these differences exist in a considerable degree, the effects are too obvious to be overlooked. Withdraw entirely the stimulus of arterial blood, and the brain ceases to act, and sensibility and consciousness become extinct. When carbonic acid gas is inhaled, the blood circulating through the lungs does not undergo that process of oxygenation which is essential to life, as has been explained in a preceding chapter. As the venous blood in this unchanged state is unfit to excite or sustain the action of the brain, the mental functions become impaired, and death speedily ensues, as in the case of a number of persons breathing a portion of confined air, or inhaling the fumes of charcoal. On the other hand, if oxygen gas be inhaled instead of common air, the blood becomes too much oxygenated, and, as a consequence, the brain is unduly stimulated, and an intensity of action bordering on inflammation takes place, which also soon terminates in death.

These are extreme cases, I admit; but their consequences are equally remarkable and fatal. The slighter variations in the state of the blood produce equally sure, though less palpable effects. Whenever its vitality is impaired by breathing an atmosphere so vitiated as not to produce the proper degree of oxygenation, the blood can only afford an imperfect stimulus to the brain. As a necessary consequence, languor and inactivity of the mental and nervous functions ensue, and a tendency to headache, fainting, or hysteria makes its appearance. This is seen every day in the listlessness and apathy prevalent in crowded and ill-ventilated school-rooms, and in the headaches and liability to fainting which are so sure to attack persons of a delicate habit, in the contaminated atmospheres of crowded theaters, churches, and assemblies of whatever kind. The same effects, although less strikingly apparent, are perhaps more permanently felt by the inmates of cotton manufactories and public hospitals, who are noted for being irritable and sensitive. The languor and nervous debility consequent on confinement in ill-ventilated apartments, or in air vitiated by the breath of many people, are neither more nor less than minor degrees of the process of poisoning, which was particularly explained in the preceding chapter, while treating upon the philosophy of respiration.

That it is not real debility which produces these effects, is apparent from the fact, that egress to the open air almost instantly restores activity and vigor to both mind and body, unless the exposure has been very long. There is an interesting but fearful illustration of the truth of this statement at the 96th page of this work, to which I beg leave to refer. Where the exposure has been very long continued, more time is of course required to re-establish the exhausted powers of the brain. Indeed, we may not, in such cases, hope for complete recovery; for when persons remain several hours a day in a vitiated atmosphere, for weeks and months together, both mind and body become permanently diseased. It is well known to every person who has given attention to the subject, that hitherto this has been the condition of *public schools*, generally, in every part of the United States, and throughout the civilized world. This has, perhaps, tended more than all other causes combined, to render the profession of teaching disreputable, and to constitute the very name of schoolmaster, or pedagogue, a hissing and a by-word. And why is this? I can account for it in but one way. The school teacher is subject to the *same organic laws as other men*; and, either on account of the ignorance or parsimony of his employers, he has been shut up with *their* children several hours a day, in narrow and ill-ventilated apartments, where, whatever else they may have done, their principal business has of necessity been *to poison one another to death*. And, as if not satisfied with this, when the teacher has ruined his health in our employment, and become a mere wreck, physically and mentally, *we despise him*. This is a double injustice, and *is* adding insult to injury. And the consequences are hardly less fatal to the children. The situation of the majority of our schools, when viewed in connection with the physiological laws already explained, sufficiently accounts for that irritability, listlessness, and languor which have been so often observed in both teachers and pupils. Both irritability of the nervous system and dullness of the intellect are unquestionably the direct and necessary result of a want of pure air. The vital energies of the pupils are thus prostrated, and they become not only restless and *indisposed to study*, but absolutely *incapable of studying*. Their minds hence wander, and they unavoidably seek relief in mischievous and disorderly conduct. This doubly provokes the already exasperated teacher, who can hardly look with complaisance upon good behavior, and who, from a like cause, is in the same irritable condition of both body and mind with themselves. He, too, must needs give vent to his irascible feelings some how. And what way is more natural, under such circumstances, than to resort to the use of the ferule, the rod, and the strap! We have already referred to a case, in which formerly fever constantly prevailed, but where disease disappeared altogether upon the introduction of *pure air*. Let the same prudential course be adopted in our schools, in connection with other appropriate means, and we shall readily see the superiority of the natural stimulus of oxygen over the artificial sedative of the rod.

The regular and systematic exercise of the functions of the brain is another condition upon which its healthy action depends. The brain is an organized part, and is subject to precisely the same laws of exercise that the other bodily organs are. If it is doomed to inactivity, its health decays, and the mental operations and feelings, as a necessary consequence, become dull, feeble, and slow. But let it be duly exercised after regular intervals of repose, and the mind acquires activity and strength. Too severe or too protracted exercise of the brain is as great a violation of the organic law just stated as inactivity is, and is sometimes productive of the most fearful consequences. By over-tasking this organ, either in the force or duration of its activity, its functions become impaired, and irritability and disease take the place of health and vigor.

So important is the law under consideration, and so essential to the health of the brain and to the welfare of man, that I deem it advisable to explain more particularly the consequences of both inadequate and excessive exercise.

We have seen that by disuse the muscles become emaciated and the bones soften. The blood-vessels, in like manner, become obliterated, and the nerves lose their characteristic structure. *The brain is no exception to this general rule.* Its tone is impaired by permanent inactivity, and it becomes less fit to manifest the mental powers with readiness and energy. Nor will this surprise any reflecting person, who considers that the brain, as a part of the same animal system, is nourished by the same blood, and regulated by the same vital laws as the muscles, bones, arteries, and nerves.

It is the withdrawal of the stimulus necessary to the healthy exercise of the brain, and the consequent weakening and depressing effect produced upon this organ, that renders solitary confinement so severe a punishment even to the most daring minds. It is a lower degree of the same cause that renders continuous seclusion from society so injurious to both mental and physical health. This explains why persons who are cut off from social converse by some bodily infirmity so frequently become discontented and morose, in spite of every resolution to the contrary. The feelings and faculties of the mind, which had formerly full play in their intercourse with their fellow-creatures, have no longer scope for sufficient exercise, and the almost inevitable result is irritability and weakness in the corresponding parts of the brain.

This fact is strikingly illustrated by reference to the deaf and blind, who, by the loss of one or more of the senses, are precluded from a full participation in all the varied sources of interest which their more favored brethren enjoy without abatement, and in whom irritability, weakness of mind, and idiocy are known to be much more prevalent than among other classes of people. "The deaf and dumb," says Andral, "presents, in intelligence, character, and the development of his passions, certain modifications, which depend on his state of isolation in the midst of society. He remains habitually in a state of half childishness, is very credulous, but, like the savage, remains free from many of the prejudices acquired in society. In him the tender feelings are not deep; he appears susceptible neither of strong attachment nor of lively gratitude; pity moves him feebly; he has little emulation, few enjoyments, and few desires. This is what is commonly observed in the deaf and dumb; but the picture is far from being of universal application; some, more happily endowed, are remarkable for the great development of their intellectual and moral nature; but others, on the contrary, remain immersed in complete idiocy."

Andral adds, that we must not infer from this that the deaf and dumb are therefore constitutionally inferior in mind to other men. "*Their powers are not developed, because they live isolated from society. Place them, by some means or other, in relation with their fellow-men, and they will become their equals.*" This is the cause of the rapid brightening up of both mind and features, which is so often observed in blind or deaf children when transferred from home to public institutions, and there taught the means of converse with their fellows.

I have myself witnessed several striking illustrations of the benefits resulting from mental culture in persons who have lost one or more of their senses. Among these I would especially instance the American Asylum at Hartford for the education and instruction of the deaf and dumb, and the Perkins Institution and Massachusetts Asylum for the Blind, located at South Boston, to the accomplished principals and teachers of both of which institutions I would acknowledge my indebtedness for valuable reports and the information of various kinds which they obligingly communicated to me at the time of my visits during the past summer.

Dr. Howe, the accomplished director of the Asylum for the Blind, after many years of experience and careful observation in this country and in Europe, expresses the conviction that *the blind, as a class, are inferior to other persons in mental power and ability*. The opinions put forth in almost every report of the institutions for the blind in this country, in almost all books on the subject, and even the doctor's earlier writings, may be brought to disprove this statement. He is now, nevertheless, fully convinced that it will be found true. This erroneous conviction, every where so prevalent, may be accounted for from the fact that none but intelligent parents of blind children could at first comprehend the possibility of their being educated, and even *they* would not think of trying the experiment except upon a child of more than ordinary ability. As soon, however, as the experiment proved successful, and institutions for the blind became generally known, the blind, without distinction—the bright and the backward, the bold and the timid—resorted to them, which gave an opportunity of judging of the *whole class*. The result is, that now, while the schools for the blind present a certain number of children who make more rapid progress in *intellectual studies* than the average of seeing children, they also present a much larger number who are decidedly inferior to them in both physical and mental vigor.

The loss of one sense makes us exercise the others so constantly and so effectually as to acquire a power quite unknown to common persons. This goes far to compensate the blind man who is in the pursuit of knowledge, and enables him to learn vastly more of *some* subjects than other men; but there are capacities of his nature which can never be developed. Perfect harmony in the exercise and development of his mental faculties he can never possess, any more than he can exhibit perfect physical beauty and proportion.

The proposition that the blind, *as a class*, are inferior in mental power and ability to ordinary persons, has been established beyond a doubt. Take an equal number of blind and seeing persons, of as nearly the same age and situation in life as may be, and it has been established by well authenticated data, that when all the blind have died, there will still be about half of the seeing ones alive. In other words, the chance of life among the blind is only about half what it is among the seeing. The standard of bodily health and vigor, then, being so much lower among the blind, the inevitable inference is that mental power and ability will be proportionably less also; for such is the dependence of the mind upon the body, that there can be no continuance of mental health and vigor without bodily health and vigor.

It is also true that *the deaf and dumb, as a class, are inferior to other persons in mental power and ability*. The general reasons for this are the same as those already given in the case of blind persons, and need not hence be repeated. The truth of this proposition is established beyond a doubt by the concurrent testimony of those who have had the greatest experience with this unfortunate class of persons both in this country and in Europe. The report of the directors of the American Asylum for the year 1845 shows that two pupils had died during the year. One of these had an affection of the lungs which terminated in consumption, and the disease of the other was dropsy on the brain. In a third, hereditary consumption was rapidly developing itself. Others, still, had been subject to more or less of bodily indisposition.

After speaking of the case of a young man in whom *hereditary consumption* had been rapidly developed, the following statement is introduced: "This great destroyer of our race is found extensively in Europe, as well as in our own country, to be a *common disease among the deaf and dumb*. It is brought on by scrofula, by fevers, by violent colds, and by various other causes; and there is often, no doubt, *a hereditary tendency to it in families connected by blood*". If this is the effect of the loss of one of the senses upon the *bodily health*, keeping in view the principle already stated, we shall naturally enough be led to inquire what the influence is upon the *health of the mind*. A careful examination of the educational statistics of several states has convinced me that an unusually large proportion of the deaf and dumb—and perhaps an equally large proportion of the blind, and especially those who have remained uneducated and unenlightened—have been visited with mental derangement, and have *lived and died insane*.

This is easily accounted for. Uneducated persons, who are deprived of one or more of the senses, are isolated from the world in which they live. The book of nature is open before them, but they are unable to peruse it. The simplest operations constantly going on around them are locked in mystery.

They are an enigma to themselves. Even those who are endowed with inquisitive minds are perplexed with the existing state of things. They know nothing of the physical organization of the planet we inhabit, of its political and civil divisions, and of the whole machinery of human society, and are profoundly ignorant of the past history and future destiny of the race to which they belong. It is not remarkable that mind so unnaturally and peculiarly circumstanced—with its usual inlets of knowledge so obstructed, and deprived of external objects to act upon—should prey upon itself, and thus superinduce insanity in its usual forms, and more especially when unaided and undirected by education.

Keeping the same principle in view, we shall not be surprised to find that *want of exercise* of the brain and nervous system, or, in other words, that inactivity of intellect and feeling, is a very frequent predisposing cause of every form of nervous disease, even with those who have not been deprived of any of their senses. For demonstrative evidence of this position, we have only to look at the numerous victims to be found among females of the middle and higher ranks, who have no call to exertion in gaining the means of subsistence, and no objects of interest on which to exercise their mental faculties, and who consequently sink into a state of mental sloth and nervous weakness, which not only deprives them of much enjoyment, but subjects them to suffering, both of body and mind, from the slightest causes.

In looking abroad upon society, we find innumerable examples of mental and nervous debility from this cause. When a person of some mental capacity is confined for a long time to an unvarying round of employment, which affords neither scope nor stimulus for one half of his faculties, and, from want of education or society, has no external resources, his mental powers, for want of exercise to keep up due vitality in their cerebral organs, become blunted, and his perceptions slow and dull. Unusual subjects of thought become to him disagreeable and painful. The intellect and feelings not being provided with interests external to themselves, must either become inactive and weak, or work upon themselves and become diseased.

But let the situation of such persons be changed; bring them, for instance, from the listlessness of retirement to the business and bustle of a city; give them a variety of imperative employments, and place them in society so as to supply to their cerebral organs that extent of exercise which gives health and vivacity of action, and in a few months the change produced will be surprising. Health, animation, and acuteness will take the place of former insipidity and dullness. In such instances, it would be absurd to suppose that it is the *mind itself* which becomes heavy and feeble, and again revives into energy by these changes in external circumstances. The effects arise entirely from changes in the state of the *brain*, and the mental manifestations and the bodily health have been improved solely by the improvement of its condition.

The evils arising from excessive or ill-timed exercise of the brain, or any of its parts, are numerous, and equally in accordance with the ordinary laws of physiology. When we use the eye too long or in too bright a light, it becomes bloodshot, and the increased action of its vessels and nerves gives rise to a sensation of fatigue and pain requiring us to desist. If we turn away and relieve the eye, the irritation gradually subsides, and the healthy state returns; but if we continue to look intently, or resume our employment before the eye has regained its natural state by repose, the irritation at last becomes permanent, and disease, followed by weakness of sight, or even blindness, may ensue, as often happens to glass-blowers, smiths, and others who are obliged to work in an intense light.

Precisely analogous phenomena occur when, from intense mental excitement, the brain is kept long in a state of excessive activity. The only difference is, that we can always see what happens in the eye, but rarely what takes place in the brain. Occasionally, however, cases of fracture of the skull occur, in which, part of the bone being removed, we *can see* the quickened circulation in the vessels of the brain as easily as in those of the eye. Sir Astley Cooper had a young gentleman brought to him who had lost a portion of his skull just above the eyebrow. "On examining the head," says Sir Astley, "I distinctly saw that the pulsation of the brain was regular and slow; but at this time he was agitated by some opposition to his wishes, and directly the blood was sent with increased force to the brain, and the pulsation became frequent and violent." Sir Astley hence concludes that, in the treatment of injuries of the brain, if you omit to keep the mind free from agitation, your other means will be unavailing.

A still more remarkable case is said to have occurred in the hospital of Montpellier in 1821. The subject of it was a female who had lost a large portion of her scalp, skull-bone, and dura mater. A corresponding portion of her brain was consequently bare, and subject to inspection. When she was in a dreamless sleep, her brain was motionless, and lay within the cranium; but when her sleep was imperfect, and she was agitated by dreams, her brain moved and protruded without the cranium. In vivid dreams the protrusion was considerable; and when she was awake and engaged in active thought or sprightly conversation, it was still greater.

In alluding to this subject, Dr. Caldwell remarks, that if it were possible, without doing an injury to other parts, to augment the constant afflux of healthy arterial blood to the brain, the mental operations would be invigorated by it. This position is illustrated by reference to the fact that when a public speaker is flushed and heated in debate, his mind works more freely and powerfully than at any other time. And why? Because his brain is in better tune. What has thus suddenly improved its condition? An increased current of blood into it, produced by the excitement of its own increased action. That the blood does, on such occasions, flow more copiously into the brain, no one can doubt who is at all acquainted with the cerebral sensations which the orator himself experiences at the time, or who witnesses the unusual fullness and flush of his countenance, and the dewiness, flashing, and protrusion of his eye.

Indeed, in many instances, the increased circulation in the brain attendant on high mental excitement reveals itself by its effects when least expected, and leaves traces after death which are but too legible. Many are the instances in which public men have been suddenly arrested in their career by the inordinate action of the brain induced by incessant toil, and more numerous still are those whose mental power has been forever impaired by similar excess.

It is generally known that the eye, when tasked beyond its strength, becomes insensible to light, and ceases to convey impressions to the mind. The brain, in like manner, when much exhausted, becomes incapable of thought, and consciousness is well-nigh lost in a feeling of utter confusion. At any time in life, excessive and continued mental exertion is hurtful; but in infancy and early youth, when the structure of the brain is still immature and delicate, permanent injury is more easily produced by injudicious treatment than at any subsequent period. In this respect, the analogy is complete between the brain and the other parts of the body, as we have already seen exemplified in the injurious effects of premature exercise of the bones and muscles. Scrofulous and rickety children are the most usual sufferers in this way. They are generally remarkable for large heads, great precocity of understanding, and small, delicate bodies. But in such instances, the great size of the brain, and the acuteness of the mind, are the results of morbid growth, and even with the best management, the child passes the first years of its life constantly on the brink of active disease. Instead, however, of trying to repress its mental activity, as they should, the fond parents, misled by the promise of genius, too often excite it still further by unceasing cultivation and the never-failing stimulus of praise; and finding its progress, for a time, equal to their warmest wishes, they look forward with ecstasy to the day when its talents will break forth and shed a luster on their name. But in exact proportion as the picture becomes brighter to their fancy, the probability of its becoming realized becomes less; for the brain, worn out by premature exertion, either becomes diseased or loses its tone, leaving the mental powers feeble and depressed for the remainder of life. The expected prodigy is thus, in the end, easily outstripped in the social race by many whose dull outset promised him an easy victory.

To him who takes for his guide the necessities of the constitution, it will be obvious that the modes of treatment commonly resorted to should in such cases be reversed; and that, instead of straining to the utmost the already irritable powers of the precocious child, leaving his dull competitors to ripen at leisure, a systematic attempt ought to be made, from early infancy, to rouse to action the languid faculties of the latter, while no pains should be spared to moderate and give tone to the activity of the former. But instead of this, the prematurely intelligent child is generally sent to school, and tasked with lessons at an unusually early age, while the healthy but more backward boy, who requires to be stimulated, is kept at home in idleness merely on account of his backwardness. A double error is here committed, and the consequences to the active-minded boy are not unfrequently the permanent loss both of health and of his envied superiority of intellect.

In speaking of children of this description, Dr. Brigham, in an excellent little work on the influence of mental excitement on health, remarks as follows: "Dangerous forms of scrofulous disease among children have repeatedly fallen under my observation, for which I could not account in any other way than by supposing that the brain had been excited at the expense of the other parts of the system, and at a time in life when nature is endeavoring to perfect all the organs of the body; and after the disease commenced, I have seen, with grief, the influence of the same cause in retarding or preventing recovery. I have seen several affecting and melancholy instances of children, five or six years of age, lingering a while with diseases from which those less gifted readily recover, and at last dying, notwithstanding the utmost efforts to restore them. During their sickness they constantly manifested a passion for books and mental excitement, and were admired for the maturity of their minds. The chance for the recovery of such precocious children is, in my opinion, small when attacked by disease; and several medical men have informed me that their own observations had led them to form the same opinion, and have remarked that, in two cases of sickness, if one of the patients was a child of superior and highly-cultivated mental powers, and the other one equally sick, but whose mind had not been excited by study, they should feel less confident of the recovery of the former than of the latter. This mental precocity results from an unnatural development of one organ of the body at the expense of the constitution."

There can be little doubt but that ignorance on the part of parents and teachers is the principal cause that leads to the too early and excessive cultivation of the minds of children, and especially of such as are precocious and delicate. Hence the necessity of imparting instruction on this subject to both parents and teachers, and to all persons who are in any way charged with the care and education of the young. This necessity becomes the more imperative from the fact that the cupidity of authors and publishers has led to the preparation of "children's books," many of which are announced as purposely prepared "for children from *two* to *three* years old!" I might instance advertisements of "Infant Manuals" of Botany, Geometry, and Astronomy!

In not a few isolated families, but in many neighborhoods, villages, and cities, in various parts of the country, children *under three years of age* are not only required to commit to memory many verses, texts of Scripture, and stories, but are frequently sent to school for six hours a day. Few children are kept back later than the age of *four*, unless they reside a great distance from school, and some not even then. At home, too, they are induced by all sorts of excitement to learn additional tasks, or peruse juvenile books and magazines, till the nervous system becomes enfeebled and the health broken. "I have myself," says Dr. Brigham, "seen many children who are supposed to possess almost miraculous mental powers, experiencing these effects and sinking under them. Some of them died early, when but six or eight years of age, but manifested to the last a maturity of understanding, which only increased the agony of separation. Their minds, like some of the fairest flowers, were 'no sooner blown than blasted;' others have grown up to manhood, but with feeble bodies and disordered nervous system, which subjected them to hypochondriasis, dyspepsy, and all the Protean forms of nervous disease; others of the class of early prodigies exhibit in manhood but small mental powers, and are the mere passive instruments of those who in early life were accounted far their inferiors."

This hot-bed system of education is not confined to the United States, but is practiced less or more in all civilized countries. Dr. Combe, of Scotland, gives an account of one of these early prodigies whose fate he witnessed. The circumstances were exactly such as those above described. The prematurely developed intellect was admired, and constantly stimulated by injudicious praise, and by daily exhibition to every visitor who chanced to call. Entertaining books were thrown in its way, reading by the fireside encouraged, play and exercise neglected, the diet allowed to be full and heating, and the appetite pampered by every delicacy. The results were the speedy deterioration of a weak constitution, a high degree of nervous sensibility, deranged digestion, disordered bowels, defective nutrition, and, lastly, *death*, at the very time when the interest excited by the mental precocity was at its height.

Such, however, is the ignorance of the majority of parents and teachers on all physiological subjects, that when one of these infant prodigies dies from erroneous treatment, it is not unusual to publish a memoir of his life, that other parents and teachers may see by what means such transcendent qualities were called forth. Dr. Brigham refers to a memoir of this kind, in which the history of a child, aged four years and eleven months, is narrated as approved by "several judicious persons, ministers and others, all of whom united in the request that it might be published, and all agreed in the opinion that a knowledge of the manner in which the child was treated, together with the results, would be profitable to both parents and children, and a benefit to the cause of education." This infant philosopher was "taught hymns before he could speak plainly;" "reasoned with" and constantly instructed until his last illness, which, "*without any assignable cause,*" put on a violent and unexpected form, and carried him off!

As a *warning to others* not to force education too soon or too fast, this case may be truly profitable to both parents and children, and a benefit to the cause of education; but *as an example to be followed,* it assuredly can not be too strongly or too loudly condemned. While I speak thus strongly, I am ready to admit that infant schools in which physical health and moral training are duly attended to are excellent institutions, and are particularly advantageous where parents, from want of leisure or from other causes, are unable to bestow upon their children that attention which their tender years require.

In youth, too, much mischief is done by the long daily periods of attendance at school, and the continued application of mind which the ordinary system of education requires. The law of exercise already more than once repeated, that *long-sustained action exhausts the vital powers of an organ,* applies as well to the brain as to the muscles. Hence the necessity of varying the occupations of the young, and allowing frequent intervals of active exercise in the open air, instead of enforcing the continued confinement now so common. This exclusive attention to mental culture fails, as might be expected, even in its essential object; for all experience shows that, with a rational distribution of employment and exercise, a child will make greater progress in a given period than in double the time employed in continuous mental exertion. If the human being were made up of nothing but a brain and nervous system, we might do well to content ourselves with sedentary pursuits, and to confine our attention entirely to the mind. But when we learn from observation that we have numerous other important organs of motion, sanguification, digestion, circulation, and nutrition, all demanding exercise in the open air, as alike essential to their own health and to that of the nervous system, it is worse than folly to shut our eyes to the truth, and to act as if we could, by denying it, alter the constitution of nature, and thereby escape the consequences of our own misconduct.

Reason and experience being thus set at naught by both parents and teachers in the education of their children, young people naturally grow up with the notion that no such influences as the laws of organization exist, and that they may follow any course of life which inclination leads them to prefer without injury to health, provided they avoid what is called dissipation. It is owing to this ignorance that young men of a studious or literary habit enter heedlessly upon an amount of mental exertion, unalleviated by bodily exercise or intervals of repose, which is quite incompatible with the continued enjoyment of a sound mind in a sound body. Such, however, is the effect of the total neglect of all instruction in the laws of the organic frame during early education, that it becomes almost impossible effectually to warn an ardent student against the dangers to which he is constantly exposing himself. Nothing but actual experience will convince him of the truth.

Numerous are the instances in which young men of the first promise have almost totally disqualified themselves for future useful exertion in consequence of long-protracted and severe study, who, under a more rational system of education, might have attained that eminence, the injudicious pursuit of which has defeated their own most cherished hopes, and ruined their general health. Such persons might be saved to themselves and to society by early instruction in the nature and laws of the animal economy. They mean well, but err from ignorance more than from headstrong zeal.

I shall conclude this chapter with a few rules relating to mental exercise, and the development and culture of the mind and brain. It is a law of the animal economy that two classes of functions can not be called into vigorous action at the same time without one or the other, or both, sooner or later sustaining injury. Hence the important rule never to enter upon continued mental exertion or to rouse deep feeling immediately after a full meal, otherwise the activity of the brain is sure to interfere with that of the stomach, and disorder its functions. Even in a perfectly healthy person, unwelcome news, sudden anxiety, or mental excitement, occurring after eating, will put an entire stop to digestion, and cause the stomach to loathe the sight of food. In accordance with this rule, we learn by experience that the very worst forms of indigestion and nervous depression are those which arise from excessive mental application, or turmoil of feeling and distraction of mind, conjoined with unrestrained indulgence in the pleasures of the table. In such circumstances, the stomach and brain react upon and disturb each other, till all the horrors of nervous disease make their unwelcome appearance, and render life miserable. The tendency to inactivity and sleep, which besets most animals after a full meal, shows repose to be, in such circumstances, the evident intention of Nature. The bad effects of violating this rule, although not in all cases immediately apparent, will most assuredly be manifest at a period less or more remote.

Dr. Caldwell, who has devoted much time and talent to the diffusion of sound physiological information and the general improvement of the race, and whose opportunities of observation have been very extensive, expressly states, that dyspepsy and madness prevail more extensively in the United States than among the people of any other nation. Of the amount of our dyspeptics, he says, no estimate can be formed; but it is immense. Whether we inquire in cities, towns, villages, or country places; among the rich, the poor, or those in moderate circumstances, we find dyspepsy more or less prevalent throughout the land.

The early part of the day is the best time for severe mental exertion. Nature has allotted the darkness of night for repose, and for the restoration by sleep of the exhausted energies of both body and mind. If study or composition be ardently engaged in toward the close of the day, and especially at a late hour of the evening, sound and invigorating sleep may not be expected until the night is far spent, for the increased action of the brain which always accompanies activity of mind requires a long time to subside. Persons who practice night study, if they be at all of an irritable habit of body, will be sleepless for hours after going to bed, and be tormented perhaps by unpleasant dreams, which will render their sleep unrefreshing. If this practice be long continued, the want of refreshing repose will ultimately induce a state of morbid irritability of the nervous system bordering on insanity. It is therefore of great advantage to engage in severer studies early in the day, and to devote the after part of the day and the evening to less intense application. It will be well to devote a portion of the evening, and especially the latter part of it, to light reading, music, or cheerful and amusing conversation. The excitement induced in the brain by previous study will be soothed by these influences, and will more readily subside, and sound and refreshing sleep will be much more likely to follow. This rule is of the utmost importance to those who are obliged to perform a great amount of mental labor. It is only by conforming to it, and devoting their mornings to study and their evenings to relaxation, that many of our most prolific writers have been enabled to preserve their health. By neglecting this rule, others of the fairest promise have been cut down in the midst of their usefulness.

Regularity is of great importance in the development and culture of the moral and intellectual powers, the tendency to resume the same mode of action at stated times being peculiarly the characteristic of the nervous system. It is this principle of our nature which promotes the formation of what are called habits. By repeating any kind of mental effort every day at the same hour, we at length find ourselves entering upon it, without premeditation, when the time approaches. In like manner, by arranging our studies in accordance with this law, and taking up each regularly in the same order, a natural aptitude is soon produced, which renders application more easy than it would be were we to take up the subjects as accident might dictate. The tendency to periodical and associated activity sometimes becomes so strong, that the faculties seem to go through their operations almost without conscious effort, while their facility of action becomes so much increased as ultimately to give unerring certainty where at first great difficulty was experienced. It is not so much the soul or abstract principle of mind which is thus changed, as the organic medium through which mind is destined to act in the present mode of being.

The necessity of judicious repetition in mental and moral education is, in fact, too little adverted to, because the principle on which it is effectual has not hitherto been generally understood. Practice is as necessary to induce facility of action in the organs of the mind as in those of motion. The idea or feeling must not only be communicated, but it must be represented and reproduced in different forms till all the faculties concerned in understanding it come to work efficiently together in the conception of it, and until a sufficient impression is made upon the organ of mind to enable the latter to retain it. Servants and others are frequently blamed for not doing a thing at regular intervals when they have been but once told to do so. We learn, however, from the organic laws, that it is presumptuous to expect the formation of a habit from a single act, and that we must reproduce the associated activity of the requisite faculties many times before the result will certainly follow, just as we must repeat the movement in dancing or skating many times before we become master of it.

We may understand a new subject by a single perusal, but we can fully master it only by dwelling upon it again and again. In order to make a durable impression on the mind, repetition is necessary. It follows, hence, that in learning a language or science, six successive months of application will be more effectual in fixing it indelibly in the mind, and making it a part of the mental furniture, than double or even treble the time if the lessons are interrupted by long intervals. The too common practice of beginning a study, and, after pursuing it a little time, leaving it to be completed at a later period, is unphilosophical and very injurious. The fatigue of study is thus doubled, and the success greatly diminished. Studies should not, as a general thing, be entered upon until the mind is sufficiently mature to understand them thoroughly, and, when begun, they should not be discontinued until they are completely mastered. By this means the mind becomes accustomed to sound and healthy action, which alone can qualify the student for eminent usefulness in after life. Much of the want of success in the various departments of industry, and many of the failures that are constantly occurring among business men, are justly attributable to the fits of attention and the irregular modes of study they became habituated to in their school-boy days. Hence the mischief of long vacations, and the evil of beginning studies before the age at which they may be understood. Parents and teachers should hence, at an early period, impress indelibly upon the minds of their children and pupils the ever true and practical sentiment, that *what is worth doing at all is worth doing well*. Although, at first, their progress may *seem* to be retarded thereby, still, in the end, it will contribute greatly to accelerate their real advancement, and in after life, whether employed in literary or business pursuits, will be a means of augmenting their happiness and increasing their prospect of success in whatever department of labor they may be engaged.

In physical education most persons seem well aware of the advantages of repetition. They know, for instance, that if practice in dancing, fencing, skating, and riding is persevered in for a sufficient length of time to give the muscles the requisite promptitude and harmony of action, the power will be ever afterward retained, although rarely called into use. But if we stop short of this point, we may reiterate practice by fits and starts without any proportional advancement. The same principle is equally applicable to the moral and intellectual powers which operate by means of material organs.

The impossibility of successfully playing the hypocrite for any considerable length of time, and the necessity of being in private what we wish to appear in public, spring from the same rule. If we wish to be ourselves polite, just, kind, and sociable, or to induce others to become so, we must act habitually under the influence of the corresponding sentiments, in the domestic circle, in the school-room, and in every-day life, as well as in the company of strangers and on great occasions. It is the private and daily practice of individuals that gives ready activity to the sentiments and marks the real character. If parents or teachers indulge habitually in vulgarities of speech and behavior in the family or in the school, and put on politeness occasionally for the reception and entertainment of strangers, their true character will shine through the mask which is intended to conceal it. The habitual association to which the organs and faculties have been accustomed can not thus be controlled. Parents hence, in addition to correct personal influence in the family, should provide for their children teachers whose habits and character are in all respects what they are willing their children should form. If they neglect to do this, the utmost they can reasonably expect is that their children will become what the teacher is.

The principle that repetition is necessary in order to make a durable impression on the organ of the mind, and thus constitute a mental habit, explains how natural endowments are modified by external situation. The extent to which this modification may be carried, and is actually carried in every community, is much greater than most persons are aware of. Take a child, for example, of average propensities, sentiments, and intellect, and place him among a class of people in whom the selfish faculties are exclusively exercised—a class who regard gain as the end of life, and look upon cunning and cheating as legitimate means, and who never express disapprobation or moral indignation against either crime or selfishness—and his lower faculties, being exclusively exercised, will increase in strength, while the higher ones, remaining unemployed, will become enfeebled. A child thus situated will, consequently, not only act as those around him do, but insensibly grow up resembling them in disposition and character; for, by the law of repetition, the organs of the selfish qualities will have acquired proportionally greater aptitude and vigor, just as do the muscles of the fencer or dancer. But suppose the same individual placed, *from infancy*, in the society of a superiorly endowed moral and intellectual people, the moral faculties will then be habitually excited, and their organs invigorated by repetition, till a greater aptitude will be induced in them, or, in other words, till a higher moral character will be formed. The natural endowments of individuals set limits to these modifications of character; but where original dispositions and tendencies are not strongly marked, the range is very wide.

In the cultivation of the brain and mental faculties, each organ should be exercised directly upon its own appropriate objects, and not merely roused or addressed through the medium of another organ. When we wish to teach the graceful and rapid evolutions of fencing, we do not content ourselves with merely giving directions, but our chief attention is employed in making the muscles themselves go through the evolutions, till, by frequent repetition and correction, they acquire the requisite quickness and precision of action. So, when we wish to teach music, we do not merely address the understanding and explain the qualities of sounds. We train the ear to an attentive discrimination of these sounds, and the hand or the vocal organs, as the case may be, to the reproduction of the motions which call them into existence. We follow this plan, because the laws of organization require the direct practice of the organs concerned, and we feel instinctively that we can succeed only by obeying these laws. The purely mental faculties are connected during life with material organs, and are hence subjected to precisely the same laws. If, therefore, we wish to improve these faculties—the reasoning powers, for example—we must exercise them regularly in tracing the cause and relations of things. In like manner, if our aim is the development of the sentiments of attachment, benevolence, justice, or respect, we must exercise each of them directly and for its own sake, otherwise neither it nor its organ will ever acquire promptitude or strength.

It is the brain, or organ of the mind, more than the abstract immaterial principle itself, that requires cultivation, or can, indeed, receive it in this life. Education hence operates invariably in subjection to the laws of organization. In improving the *external* senses, we admit this principle readily enough; but when we come to the *internal* faculties of thought and feeling, it is either denied or neglected. That the superior quickness of touch, sight, and hearing, consequent upon judicious exercise, is referable to increased facility of action in their appropriate organs, is readily admitted. But when we explain, on the same principle, the superior development of the reasoning powers, or the greater warmth of feeling produced by similar exercise in these and other internal faculties, few are inclined to listen to our proposition, or allow to it half the weight or attention its importance demands, although every fact in philosophy and experience concurs in supporting it. We see the mental powers of feeling and of thought unfolding themselves in infancy and youth in exact accordance with the progress of the organization. We see them perverted or suspended by the sudden inroad of disease. We sometimes observe every previous acquirement obliterated from the adult mind by fever or by accident, leaving education to be commenced anew, as if it had never been; and yet, with all these evidences of the organic influence, the proposition that the established laws of physiology, as applied to the brain, should be considered our best and surest guide in education, seems to many a novelty. Among the numerous treatises on education, there are very few volumes in which it is even hinted that these laws have the slightest influence over either intellectual or moral improvement.

As God has given us bones and muscles, and blood-vessels and nerves, for the purpose of being used, let us not despise the gift, but consent at once to turn them to account, and to reap health and vigor as the reward which he has associated with moderate labor. As he has given us lungs to breathe with and blood to circulate, let us at once and forever abandon the folly of shutting ourselves up with little intermission, whether engaged in study or other sedentary occupations, and consent to inhale, copiously and freely, that wholesome atmosphere which his benevolence has spread around us in such rich profusion. As he has given us appetites and organs of digestion, let us profit by his bounty, and earn their enjoyment by healthful exercise in some department of productive industry. As he has given us a moral and a social nature, which is invigorated by activity, and impaired by solitude and restraint, let us cultivate good feelings, and act toward each other on principles of kindness, justice, forbearance, and mutual assistance; and as he has given us intellect, let us exercise it in seeking a knowledge of his works and of his laws, and in tracing out the relation in which we stand toward him, toward our fellow-men, and toward the various objects of the external world. In so doing, we may be well assured we shall find a reward a thousand times more rich and pure, yea, infinitely more delightful and enduring, than we can hope to experience in following our own blind devices, regardless of his will and benevolent intentions toward us.

If the eye be obstructed, the ear opens wide its portals, and hears your very emotions in the varying tones of your voice; if the ear be stopped, the quickened eye will almost read the words as they fall from your lips; and if both be close sealed up, the whole body becomes like a sensitive plant—the quickened skin perceives the very vibrations of the air, and you may even write your thoughts upon it, and receive answers from the sentient soul within.—ANNUAL REPORT *of the Trustees of the Perkins Institution and Massachusetts Asylum for the Blind*, 1841.

He who formed man of the dust of the earth, and breathed into his nostrils the breath of life, has honored his material organs by associating them with the immaterial soul. In this life *the senses* constitute the great conveyances of knowledge to the human mind. It then becomes not only a legitimate object of inquiry, but one which commends itself to every human being, and especially to every parent and teacher, Can these senses be improved by human interference? And if so, how can that improvement be best effected?

The senses are the interpreters between the material universe without and the spirit within. Without the celestial machinery of sensation, man must have ever remained what Adam was before the Almighty breathed into his form of clay the awakening breath of life. The dormant energies of the mind can be aroused, and the soul can be put into mysterious communion with external nature only by the magical power of sensation.

The possession of all the corporeal senses, and their systematic and judicious culture by all proper appliances, are necessary in order to place man in such a relation to the material universe and its great Architect as most fully and successfully to cultivate the varied capabilities of his nature, and best to subserve the purposes of his creation. He who is deprived of the healthful exercise of one or more of his senses, or, possessing them all unimpaired, has neglected their proper culture, is, from the nature of the case, in a proportionate degree cut off from a knowledge of God as manifested in his works, and from that happiness which is the legitimate fruit of such knowledge.

Much light has been thrown upon this subject within a few years by the judicious labors of that class of practical educators who have devoted their lives to the amelioration of the condition of persons deprived of one or more of the senses. It is difficult to conceive the real condition of the minds of persons thus situated, and especially while they remain uneducated. He who is deprived of the sense of sight has the windows of his soul closed, and is effectually shut out from this world of light and beauty. In like manner, he who is deprived of the sense of hearing is excluded from the world of music and of speech. What, then, must be the condition of persons deprived of both of these senses? How desolate and cheerless! Yet some such there are.

While on a visit to the Asylum for the Blind, in Boston, a few months ago, I met two of this unfortunate class of persons—Laura Bridgman and Oliver Caswell. Laura has been several years connected with the institution.

Laura Bridgman, *the Deaf, Dumb, and Blind Girl.*—So remarkable is the case of this interesting girl, so full of interest, so replete with instruction, and in every way so admirably adapted to illustrate the subject of this chapter, that I proceed to give to my readers a sketch of the method pursued in her instruction, together with the results attendant upon it. My information in relation to her is derived from both personal acquaintance and the reports of her case, though principally from the latter source.

Laura was born in Hanover, New Hampshire, on the 21st of December, 1829. She is described as having been a very sprightly and pretty infant. During the first years of her existence she held her life by the feeblest tenure, being subject to severe fits, which seemed to rack her frame almost beyond the power of endurance. At the age of four years her bodily health seemed restored; but what a situation was hers! The darkness and silence of the tomb were around her. No mother's smile called forth her answering smile. No father's voice taught her to imitate his sounds. To her, brothers and sisters were but forms of matter which resisted her touch, but which hardly differed from the furniture of the house save in warmth and in the power of locomotion, and not even in these respects from the dog and the cat. But the immortal spirit implanted within her could not die, nor could it be maimed or mutilated; and, though most of its avenues of communication with the world were cut off, it began to manifest itself through the others. As soon as she could walk, she began to explore the room, and then the house. She thus soon became familiar with the form, density, weight, and heat of every article she could lay her hands upon. She followed her mother, and felt of her hands and arms, as she was occupied about the house, and her disposition to imitate led her to repeat every thing herself. She even learned to sew a little and to knit.

Her affections, too, began to expand, and seemed to be lavished upon the members of her family with peculiar force. But the means of communication with her were very limited. She could be told to go to a place only by being pushed, or to come to one by a sign of drawing her. Patting her gently on the head signified approbation, on the back disapprobation. She showed every disposition to learn, and manifestly began to use a natural language of her own. She had a sign to express her idea of each member of the family, as drawing her fingers down each side of her face to allude to the whiskers of one, twirling her hand around in imitation of the motion of a spinning-wheel for another, and so on. But, although Laura received all the aid a kind mother could bestow, she soon began to give proof of the importance of language in the development of human character. By the time she was seven years old the moral effects of her privation began to appear, for there was no way of controlling her will but by the absolute power of another, and at this humanity revolts.

At this time, Dr. Samuel G. Howe, the distinguished and successful director of the asylum, learned of her situation, and hastened to see her. He found her with a well-formed figure, a strongly-marked nervous-sanguine temperament, a large and beautifully shaped head, and the whole system in healthy action. Here seemed a rare opportunity of trying a plan for the education of a deaf and blind person, which the doctor had formed on seeing Julia Brace at Hartford. The parents readily consented to her going to the institution in Boston, where Laura was received in October, 1837, just before she had completed her eighth year. For a while she was much bewildered. After waiting about two weeks, and until she became acquainted with her new locality, and somewhat familiar with the inmates, the attempt was made to give her a knowledge of arbitrary signs, by which she could interchange thoughts with others. One of two methods was to be adopted. Either the language of signs, on the basis of the natural language she had already commenced herself, was to be built up, or it remained to teach her the purely arbitrary language in common use. The former would have been easy, but very ineffectual. The latter, although very difficult, if accomplished, would prove vastly superior. It was therefore determined upon.

The *blind* learn to read by means of raised letters, which they gain a knowledge of by the sense of feeling. *The ends of the fingers*, resting upon the raised letters, thus constitute, in part, *the eyes of the blind*. This, although apparently difficult, becomes comparatively easy when the blind person possesses the *sense of hearing*, and is thus enabled to become acquainted with spoken language. On the contrary, the *deaf*, and consequently *dumb*, are unable to acquire a knowledge of spoken language so as to use it with any degree of success. In their education, hence, the *language of signs*, which can be addressed to the eye, is substituted for spoken language. In communicating with one another, by means of the *manual alphabet*, they substitute positions of the hand, which they can both make and see, for letters and words, which they can neither pronounce nor hear.

To be deprived of either sight or hearing was formerly regarded as an almost insuperable obstacle in the way of education. Persons deprived of both these senses have heretofore been considered by high legal authorities,[23] as well as by public opinion, as occupying, of necessity, a state of irresponsible and irrecoverable idiocy. By the education of the remaining senses, however, this formidable and heretofore insuperable barrier has been overleaped, or, rather, the obstacle has been met and overcome. The experiment has been successfully tried, once and again, in our own country. The deaf and blind mute has not only acquired a knowledge of reading and writing, and of the common branches of education, but has been enabled successfully to prosecute the study of natural philosophy, of mental science, and of geometry. The accomplishment of all this has resulted from the successful cultivation of the sense of touch or of feeling. The raised letter of the blind has been used for written language, and the manual language of the mute, taken by the *finger-eyes* of the blind, has been successfully substituted for spoken language.

Laura's mind dwelt in darkness and silence. In order, therefore, to communicate to her a knowledge of the arbitrary language in common use, it was necessary to combine the methods of instructing the blind and the deaf. The first experiments in instructing her were made by taking articles in common use, such as knives, forks, spoons, keys, etc., and pasting upon them labels with their names printed in *raised letters*. These she felt of very carefully, and soon, of course, distinguished that the crooked lines *s p o o n* differed as much from the crooked lines *k e y*, as the spoon differed from the key in form. Small detached labels, with the same words printed upon them, were then put into her hands, and she soon observed that they were similar to those pasted on the articles. She showed her perception of this similarity by laying the label *k e y* upon the key, and the label *s p o o n* upon the spoon. When this was done she was encouraged by the natural sign of approbation—patting on the head.

The same process was then repeated with all the articles which she could handle, and she very easily learned to place the proper labels upon them. After a while, instead of labels, the individual letters were given to her, on detached bits of paper. These were at first arranged side by side, so as to spell *b o o k*, *k e y*, &c. They were then mixed up, and a sign was made for her to arrange them herself, so as to express the words *b o o k*, *k e y*, etc., and she did so.

The process of instruction, hitherto, had been mechanical, and the success attending it about as great as that in teaching a very knowing dog a variety of tricks. The poor child sat in mute amazement, and patiently imitated every thing her teacher did. Presently the truth began to flash upon her; her intellect began to work; she perceived that here was a way by which she could herself make up a sign of any thing that was in her own mind, and show it to another mind, and at once her countenance lighted up with a human expression! her immortal spirit eagerly seizing upon a new link of union with other spirits! Dr. Howe says he could almost fix upon the moment when this truth dawned upon her mind and spread its light to her countenance. He saw at once that nothing but patient and persevering, but judicious efforts were needed in her instruction, and that these would most assuredly be crowned with success.

It is difficult to form a just conception of the amount of labor bestowed upon Laura thus far. In communicating with her, spoken language could not be used, for she was destitute of hearing. Neither are signs of any use when addressed to the eyes of the blind. When, therefore, it was said that "a sign was made," we are to understand by it that the action was performed by her teacher, she feeling of his hands, and then imitating the motion. The next step in the process of her instruction was to procure a set of metal types, with the different letters of the alphabet cast upon their ends; also a board, in which were square holes, into which she could set the types so that the letters on the end could alone be felt above the surface. Then, on any article being handed to her whose name she had learned—a pencil or a watch, for instance—she would select the component letters and arrange them on her board, and read them with apparent pleasure.

When she had been exercised in this way for several weeks, and until her knowledge of words had become considerably extensive, the important step was taken of teaching her how to represent the different letters by the position of her fingers, instead of the cumbrous apparatus of the board and types. This she accomplished speedily and easily, for her intellect had begun to work in aid of her teacher, and her progress was rapid.

Six months after Laura had left home her mother went to visit her. The scene of their meeting was full of interest. The mother stood some time gazing with overflowing eyes upon her unfortunate child, who, all unconscious of her presence, was playing about the room. Presently Laura ran against her, and at once began feeling of her hands, examining her dress, and trying to find out if she knew her; but, not succeeding in this, she turned away as from a stranger, and the poor woman could not conceal the pang she felt at finding her beloved child did not know her. She then gave Laura a string of beads which she used to wear at home. These were at once recognized by the child, who gave satisfactory indications that she understood they were from home. The mother now tried to caress her; but Laura repelled her, preferring to be with her acquaintances.

Other articles from home were then given to Laura, and she began to look much interested; she examined the stranger much closer, and gave the doctor to understand she knew they came from Hanover; she now even endured her mother's caresses, but would leave her with indifference at the slightest signal. After a while, on the mother taking hold of her again, a vague idea seemed to flit across Laura's mind that this could not be a stranger; she therefore felt of her hands very eagerly, while her countenance assumed an expression of intense interest; she became very pale, and then suddenly red; hope seemed struggling with doubt and anxiety, and never were contending emotions more strongly painted upon the human face. At this moment of painful uncertainty, the mother drew Laura close to her side, and kissed her fondly, when at once the truth flashed upon the child, and all distrust and anxiety disappeared from her face. With an expression of exceeding joy, Laura nestled to the bosom of her parent, and yielded herself to her fond embraces. After this the beads were all unheeded, and the playthings which were offered to her were utterly disregarded. Her playmates, for whom she but a moment before left the stranger, now vainly strove to pull her from her mother. The meeting and subsequent parting showed alike the affection, the intelligence, and the resolution of the child as well as of her mother.

The following facts are drawn from the report made of her case at the end of the year 1839, after she had been a little more than two years under instruction. Having mastered the manual alphabet of the deaf mutes, and having learned to spell readily the names of every thing within her reach, she was then taught words expressive of positive qualities, as hardness and softness. This was a very difficult process. She was next taught those expressions of relation to place which she could understand. A ring, for example, was taken and placed *on* a box; then the words were spelled to her, and she repeated them from imitation. The ring was afterward placed *on* a hat, desk, etc. In a similar manner she learned the use of *in*, *into*, etc. She would illustrate the use of these and other words as follows: She would spell *o n ,* and then lay one hand *on* the other; then she would spell *i n t o ,* and inclose one hand *within* the other.

Laura very easily acquired a knowledge and use of active verbs, especially those expressive of *tangible action*, as to walk, to run, to sew, to shake. In acquiring a knowledge of language, she used the words with which she had become acquainted in a general sense, and according to the order of *her sense of ideas*. Thus, in asking some one to give her bread, she would first use the word expressive of the leading idea, and say, *Bread, give, Laura*. If she wanted water, she would say, *Water, drink, Laura*.

Having acquired the use of substantives, adjectives, verbs, prepositions, and conjunctions, it was thought time to make the experiment of trying to teach her to *write*, and to show her she might communicate her ideas to persons not in contact with her. It was amusing to witness the mute amazement with which she submitted to the process; the docility with which she imitated every motion, and the perseverance with which she moved her pencil over and over again in the same track, until she could form the letter. But when at last the idea dawned upon her that by this mysterious process she could make other people understand what she thought, her joy was boundless! Never did a child apply more eagerly and joyfully to any task than she did to this; and in a few months she could make every letter distinctly, and separate words from each other.

At this time Laura actually wrote, unaided, a legible letter to her mother, in which she expressed the idea of her being well, and of her expectation of going home in a few weeks. It was, indeed, a very rude and imperfect letter, couched in the language which a prattling infant would use. Still, it shadowed forth and expressed to her mother the ideas that were passing in her own mind. She had attained about the same command of language as common children three years of age. But her power of expression was, of course, by no means equal to her power of conception; for she had no words to express many of the perceptions and sensations which her mind doubtless experienced. In the spring of 1840, when she had been under instruction about two and a half years, returning fatigued from her journey home, she complained of a pain in her side, and on being asked what caused it, she replied as follows: "Laura did go to see mother, ride did make Laura side ache, horse was wrong, did not run softly." Her improvement in the use of language was very rapid, and she soon became, in some respects, quite a critic. When one of the girls had the mumps, Laura learned the name of the disease; soon after she had it herself, but she had the swelling only on one side; and some one saying to her, "You have got the mumps," she replied quickly, "*No, no; I have mump.*"

About this time Laura learned the difference between the present and past tense of the verb. And here her simplicity rebukes the clumsy irregularities of our language. She learned *jump, jumped—walk, walked*, etc., until she had an idea of the mode of forming the imperfect tense of regular verbs; but when she came to the word *see*, she insisted that it should be *seed* in the imperfect; and upon going down to dinner, she asked if it was *eat, eated*; but being told it was *eat*, ATE, she seemed to try to express the idea that this transposition of the letters was not only wrong, but ludicrous, for she laughed heartily. She continued this habit of forming words analogically.

When she had become acquainted with the meaning of the word restless, she seemed to understand that *less* at the end of a word means without, destitute of, or wanting, as rest-less, fruit-less; also that *ful* at the end of a word expresses abundance of what is implied by the primitive, as bliss-ful, play-ful. This is clearly illustrated in the following expressions. One day, feeling weak, she said, "I am very strongless." Being told this was not right, she said, "Why, you say restless when I do not sit still." Then she said, "I am very weakful."

My primary object in referring to Laura has been to illustrate, in a striking manner, the practicability of the education of the senses to an extent not heretofore generally known. To such an extent has the sense of touch been cultivated in her, that her fingers serve as very good substitutes for both eyes and ears. I will mention one or two instances which strikingly illustrate the acuteness of Laura's sense of touch. When I was at the institution a few months ago, she was told a person was present whom she had never met, and who wished an introduction to her. She reached her hand, expecting to meet a *stranger*. By mistake (for her teachers design never to allow her to be deceived), she took the hand of another gentleman, whom she recognized immediately, though she had never met him but twice before. She recognizes her acquaintances in an instant by touching their hands or their dress, and there are probably hundreds of individuals who, if they were to stand in a row, and hold out each a hand to her, would be recognized by that alone. The memory of these sensations is very vivid, and she will readily recognize a person whom she has once thus touched. Many cases of this kind have been noticed; such as a person shaking hands with her, and making a peculiar pressure with one finger, and repeating this on his second visit, after a lapse of many months, being instantly known by her. She has been known to recognize persons with whom she had thus simply shaken hands but once, after a lapse of six months. But this is hardly more wonderful than that one should be able to recall impressions made upon the mind through the organ of sight, as when we recognize a person of whom we have had but one glimpse a year before; but it shows the exhaustless capacity of those organs which the Creator has bestowed, as it were, in reserve against accidents, and which we too commonly allow to lie unused and unvalued.

OLIVER CASWELL.—Had I not devoted so much space to this subject already, it would be interesting to consider the case of Oliver, who, like Laura, is deaf, dumb, and blind. His experience is full of interest, though less striking than that already presented. His progress in learning language, and in acquiring intellectual knowledge, is comparatively slow, because he has not that fineness of fiber and that activity of temperament which enable Laura to struggle so successfully against the immense disadvantages under which they both labor. Oliver is a boy of rather unfavorable organization; he had been deaf and blind from infancy; he received no instruction until he was twelve years old, and consequently lost the most precious years for learning; he has nevertheless been taught to express his thoughts both by the finger language and by writing; he has also become acquainted with the rudiments of the common branches of education, and is intelligent and morally responsible. His case proves, therefore, very clearly, that the success of the attempt made to instruct Laura Bridgman was not owing solely to her uncommon capacity.

Oliver's natural ability is small, and his acquired knowledge very limited; but his sense of right and wrong, his obedience to moral obligations, and his attachment to friends, are very remarkable.[24] He never willfully violates the rights or injures the feelings of others, and seldom shows any signs of temper when his own seem to be invaded. He even bears the teasing of little boys with gentleness and patience. He is very tractable, and always obeys respectfully the requests of his teacher. This shows the effect which kind and gentle treatment has had upon his character, for when he first went to the institution in Boston he was sometimes very willful, and showed occasional outbursts of temper which were fearfully violent. "It seems hardly possible," says Dr. Howe, "that the gentle and affectionate youth, who loves all the household and is beloved by all in return, should be the same who a few years ago scratched and bit, like a young savage, those who attempted to control him."

We regard it as a fact fully established that the sense of touch may be cultivated to a much greater extent than most persons are aware of. The same remark will apply to the cultivation of all the senses. We shall consider them separately.

THE SENSE OF TOUCH.—The remarks already made apply chiefly to this sense. The nerves that supply it proceed from the anterior half of the spinal cord. This sense is most delicate where there are the greatest number of nervous filaments, and those of the largest size. The hands, and especially the fingers, have a most delicate and nice sense of touch, though the sense is extended over the whole body, in every part of which it is less or more acute. In this respect, then, this sense is unlike the others, which are confined to small spaces, as we shall see when we come to consider them. The action of the sensitive nerves depends upon the state of the brain, and the condition of the system generally. In sound and perfect sleep, when the brain is inactive, ordinary impressions made upon the skin are unobserved. Fear and grief diminish the impressibility of this tissue, while hope and joy increase it. The quantity and quality of the blood also influence sensation. If this vital fluid becomes impure, or its quantity is diminished, the sensibility of the skin will be impaired thereby. Whatever affects the general health affects the healthy action of this sense. It is also much affected by sudden changes in temperature. If the skin is wounded while under the influence of cold, the pain will be slight. By carrying this chilling influence too far, the surface becomes entirely destitute of sensation. This is produced by the contraction of the blood-vessels upon the surface. On the contrary, when the chilled extremities are suddenly exposed to heat, the rapid enlargement of the contracted blood-vessels excites the nerves unduly, which causes the pain experienced on such occasions.

The sensibility of the nerves depends much upon the habits of persons. Suppose two boys go out to play when the thermometer stands at the freezing point, and that one of them has been accustomed to exercise in the open air, and to practice daily ablution, while the other one has been confined most of the time to a warm room, and has been accustomed to wash only his hands and face. The skin of the former, other things being equal, will be active and healthy, while that of the latter will be enfeebled and diseased. The organs of touch diffused over the body at the surface will be very differently affected in these two boys, and the perceptions of their minds will be alike dissimilar. One will be roused to action, and will feel just right for some animating game. Both body and mind will be elastic and joyous. He will bound like the roe, make the welkin ring with his merry shout, and return to the bosom of his family with a gladdened heart, ready to impart and receive pleasure, while the other boy will be too keenly affected by the contact of the air, and think it too cold to stay out of doors. He will thrust his hands into his pockets, and curl himself up like one decrepit with age. His teeth will chatter and his whole frame tremble. Of course, very different reflections will be awakened in his mind. He will hurry back to the fireside, thinking winter a very dismal season, and will be apt to fret himself and all about him, because of the confinement from which he has not the resolution to break out.

The sensibility of the cutaneous nerves in these two cases depends upon the habits of the persons. If the latter would practice frequent ablutions, and excite a healthy action in the skin by friction and exercise, and conform to other laws of health, he would experience all that gladness of heart, and elasticity of body and mind, which the other is supposed to enjoy. Hence the advantages resulting from a strict conformity to the laws of health in this particular as well as in others that are generally regarded as more important.

The general law that the exercise of a faculty increases its power is applicable to the senses. We have referred to the blind, who read as rapidly as seeing persons by passing their fingers over raised letters, the sense of touch being substituted by them for that of vision. Nor is the education of this sense useful to the blind merely. It may frequently be appealed to with great advantage by all who have cultivated it. The miller, for example, can judge more accurately of the quality of flour and meal, by passing some between his fingers than by the exercise of vision. The cloth-dresser, also, by the aid of this sense, not only marks the nicest shades of texture in examining cloths of different qualities, but in many instances learns to distinguish *colors* by the sense of touch with perhaps greater accuracy than is common with seeing persons.

THE SENSE OF TASTE.—The sense of taste bears the greatest resemblance to the sense of feeling. The upper surface of the tongue is the principal agent in tasting, though the lips, the palate, and the internal surface of the cheeks participate in this function, as does the upper part of the œsophagus. The multitude of points called papillæ, scattered over the upper surface of the tongue, constitute the more immediate seat of this sense. It is in these sensitive papillæ that the ramifications of the gustatory or tasting nerves terminate. When fluids are taken into the mouth, and especially those whose taste is pungent, these papillæ dilate and erect themselves, and the particular sensation produced is transmitted to the brain through the medium of the minute filaments of the gustatory nerves.

In order fully to gratify the taste in eating dry, solid food, it is necessary that the food be first reduced to a liquid state, or, at least, that it be thoroughly moistened. Nature has made full provision for this in furnishing the mouth with salivary glands, whose secretions are most abundant when engaged in masticating dry, hard substances. These quickened secretions contribute to gratify the taste and increase the pleasure of eating, and, at the same time, materially aid in the important processes of mastication and digestion. Nature, also, with her accustomed bounty, has furnished man with a great variety of articles for food. By this means the various tastes of different persons may be gratified, although, in many instances, those articles of food which are most agreeable to some persons are extremely disagreeable to others.

Many persons can not eat the most nourishing food, as fruits, butter, etc., because to them the taste of these articles is disagreeable. But this is very easily accounted for, as in the mouth the food mixes with various fluids that differ in different persons, and in the same person at different times. These fluids, and particularly the saliva, assist in the formation and change of taste. This accounts not only for the different tastes of different persons, but also for the varying taste of the same persons, and for that fickleness of taste which is so common in sickness, when the fluids of the mouth, in a disordered and deranged state, mix with the food, and produce the disagreeable taste so often complained of at such times, and which, moreover, occasionally create a permanent dislike for food that was previously much relished.

This sense was given to men and animals to guide them in the selection of their food, and to enable them to guard against the use of articles that would be injurious if introduced into the stomach. In the inferior animals, the sense of taste still answers the original design of its bestowment; but in man, it has been abused and perverted by the use of artificial stimulants, which have created an acquired taste that, in most persons, is very detrimental to health. This sense is so modified by habit, that, not unfrequently, articles which were at first exceedingly offensive, become, at length, highly agreeable. It is in this manner that many persons, whose sense of taste has been impaired or perverted, have formed the disgusting and ruinous habits of smoking and chewing tobacco, and of using stimulating and intoxicating drinks. But these pernicious habits, and all similar indulgences, lessen the sensibility of the gustatory nerve, and ultimately destroy the natural relish for healthful food and drink. By this means, also, the digestive powers become disordered, and the general health is materially impaired. All persons, then, should seek to preserve the natural integrity of this sense, and to restore it immediately to healthy action when at all depraved, for upon this depends much of health and longevity, of happiness and usefulness.

This sense may be rendered very acute by cultivation, as is illustrated by persons who are accustomed to taste medicines, liquors, teas, etc. It ought, however, to be chiefly exercised in partaking of those simple articles of food and drink which are most conducive to health. In its natural state it prefers these, and if depraved it will soon recover a healthy tone, if not continually tempted by stimulating substances. This is beautifully illustrated in thousands of instances all over our country by persons who were once accustomed to use strong drink, but who have substituted for it sparkling water, a beverage prepared by God himself to nourish and invigorate his creatures, and beautify his footstool.

THE SENSE OF SMELL.—The sense of taste has received a faithful companion in that of smell. The beneficent Creator, with that wisdom which characterizes all his works, has very wisely placed the organ of this sense just above the mouth, in order that the scent of many things that are hurtful may warn us from partaking of them before they reach the mouth. The air-passages of the nose, in which this sense is located, are lined with a thin skin, called the mucous membrane, which is continuous with the lining membrane of the parts of the throat and of the external skin. Upon this membrane the olfactory nerve ramifies. The odoriferous particles of matter that float in the air come in contact with these fine and sensitive nerves as the air rushes through the nostrils, and the impression is conveyed to the brain by the olfactory nerve. The mucous membrane, upon which this ramifies, is of considerable extent in man. In the lower animals it is less or more extensive, according to the degree of acuteness of this sense. This membrane is full of little glands that are continually giving off thick mucus, and especially when the membrane is inflamed. There is a small canal leading from the eyes to the nose, through which a fluid, that also forms tears, is constantly passing when the passage is clear. It is the office of this fluid to moisten and thin the mucus of the nose. When this mucous is too abundant, as in some stages of a cold, and especially if it becomes dry from the closing of the canal leading from the eyes, or from any other cause, as fever, the sense of smell will be greatly impaired, if not entirely suspended. It is, indeed, not unfrequently permanently injured in this way, and sometimes is irrecoverably lost.

The sensation of smell, it should be borne in mind, is produced by a kind of odoriferous vapor, very fine and invisible, that flies off from nearly all bodies. The air which contains this vapor is drawn into the nose, and is in this way brought into contact with the very delicate nerves of smell that ramify the membrane which lines the air-passages of this organ. It is only when the exceedingly small particles of which the odor of various bodies is composed come in contact with the minute ramifications of the olfactory nerve that this sensation is produced. In order to protect these sensitive nerves, as well as to prevent the introduction into the lungs of injurious substances, the air-passages of the nose are furnished with hairy appendages, which are less or more abundant according to the size of these passages. These intercept any foreign substances that enter the nose, and thus irritate the mucous membrane, and cause a quick and powerful contraction of the diaphragm, by which the offending matter is immediately expelled. This phenomenon, which is called sneezing, depends upon a connection of the olfactory with the respiratory nerves.

This sense not only comes in to the aid of taste in enabling man and the lower animals to select proper food, and avoid that which is injurious, but it also gives us positive and varied pleasure by the inhalation of agreeable odors, while, at the same time, it enables us to avoid an infectious atmosphere, and all objects whose odors are offensive and hurtful.

It is true that man can accustom himself to nearly all kinds of odor, even to those that at first are very disagreeable. He indeed not unfrequently so vitiates the sense of smell as actually to prefer those scents which, to persons who have preserved the integrity of this sense, are regarded as exceedingly offensive, and even filthy. But why, let me ask, did the Creator give us the sense of smell? Was it to be thus perverted? No, indeed: it was, without doubt, that we might enjoy the refreshing fragrance of flowers and herbs, of food and drink; and also that we might distinguish between air that is pure and healthful, and that which is impure and infectious. As most articles of food which are agreeable to the smell are wholesome, and as those which are disagreeable are generally unwholesome, so, also, those states of the atmosphere which are grateful to this sense are salubrious, and those odors which are pleasant are healthful, while air which is ungrateful will generally be found injurious to health, as will also all those odors which are unpleasant to this sense when in a healthful state. He who has had occasion to enter a crowded court-room, lecture-room, church, or assembly-room of whatever kind, which has been occupied for a considerable time without adequate ventilation, can not fail to remember the unwelcome impression made upon his nasal organs when first he inhaled the vitiated atmosphere within, though by degrees he might have become accustomed to it, did he remain, so as ultimately to become well-nigh insensible to its noisome influence. But let such and all others be well assured that, however offensive such a fetid atmosphere may be to the smell, it is equally injurious to the health. And let those who, having returned from a morning walk or healthful exercise in a salubrious atmosphere, have had occasion to revisit the small and unventilated lodging-room in which they spent a restless night without refreshing sleep, perceive, in the sickening smell, a sufficient cause for all their pains and aches, and wonder how they survived such a gross violation of the organic laws.

All of the senses may be improved by education. The sense of smell constitutes no exception to this rule. Let none be discouraged, then; for the more we accustom our lungs and nasal organs to pure air, the more will they require it, and the more readily will they detect the presence of the least impurity.

This sense becomes very acute in deaf persons, and even more so in the case of those that are blind. The reason is obvious; for, as they are led of necessity to rely upon it more than persons who have all the senses, it becomes thereby developed, and is enabled more accurately to judge of the properties of whatever is submitted to its scrutiny. Seeing persons rarely partake of any article of food, and especially of any thing new, without first smelling it, and blind persons never; for this is the only means by which they can judge of its wholesomeness or unwholesomeness without tasting it.

Whatever stupefies the brain, impairs the healthy action of the nerve of smell, or thickens the membrane that lines the nasal cavities, and thus diminishes the sensibility of the nerves ramified upon it, injures this sense. All these effects are produced by the habitual use of snuff, which, when introduced into the nose, diminishes the sensibility of the nerves, and thickens the lining membrane. By its use the air-passages through the nostrils sometimes become completely obstructed. It is on this account that most habitual snuff-takers are compelled to open their mouths in order to breathe freely. It has been well said, that if Nature had intended that the nose should be used as a snuff-hole, she would doubtless have put it on the other end up.

THE SENSE OF HEARING.—The external ear, although curiously shaped, is not the most important part of the organ whose function it is to take cognizance of sounds. In the transmission of sound to the brain, the vibrations of the air produced by the sonorous body are collected by the external ear, and conducted through the auditory canal to the drum of the ear, which is so arranged that it may be relaxed or tightened like the head of an ordinary drum. That its motion may be free, the air contained within the drum has free communication with the external air by an open passage, called the Eustachian tube, leading to the back of the mouth. This tube is sometimes obstructed by wax, when a degree of deafness ensues. But when the obstruction is removed in the effort of sneezing or otherwise, a crack or sudden noise is generally experienced, accompanied usually with an immediate return of acute hearing.

The ear-drum performs a two-fold office; for while it aids in the transmission of sound from without to the internal ear, it at the same time modifies the intensity of sound. This softening of the sound is effected by the relaxation of a muscle when sounds are so acute as to be painful; but when listening to low sounds, the drum is rendered tense by the contraction of this muscle, and the sounds become, by this means, more audible. The vibrations made on the drum are transmitted by the tympanum—an irregular bony cavity—to the internal ear, which is filled with a watery fluid. In this fluid the filaments of the auditory nerve terminate, which receive and transmit the sound to the brain.

The ear has the power of judging of the direction from which sound comes, as is strikingly exemplified in the fact that when horses or mules march in company at night, those in front direct their ears forward, and those in the rear turn them backward, while those in the center turn them laterally or across, the whole troop seeming to be actuated by a feeling to watch the common safety. This is also illustrated by four or six horse teams, and is a fact with which coachmen are familiar. It is further illustrated by the dog, and many other animals. The external ear of man is likewise furnished with muscles; and savages are said to have the power of moving or directing their ears at pleasure, like a horse, to catch sounds as they come from different directions; but few men in civilized life retain this power.

The acuteness of this sense in men and animals, other things being equal, depends upon the size of the ear. In timid animals, as the hare and the rabbit, the ear is very large. They are thus apprized of the approach of an enemy in time to flee to a place of safety.

The ear-trumpet—which is a tube wide at one end, where the sound enters, and narrow at the other, where the ear is applied—is constructed on this principle, its sides being so curved that, according to the law of reflection, all the sound which enters it is brought to a focus in the narrow end. It thus increases many fold the intensity of a sound which reaches the ear through it, and enables a person who has become deaf to common conversation to mix again with pleasure in society. The concave hand held behind the ear answers in some degree the purpose of an ear-trumpet.

The Ear of Dionysius, in the dungeons of Syracuse, was a notorious instance of a sound-collecting surface. The roof of the prison was so formed as to collect the words, and even whispers, of the unhappy prisoners, and to direct them along a hidden conduit to where the tyrant sat listening.

Acuteness of hearing requires the healthy action of the brain, and particularly of that portion of it from which the auditory nerve proceeds, combined with perfection in the structure and functions of the different parts of the ear. The best method, then, of retaining and improving the hearing, is to observe well the general laws of health, and particularly to avoid every thing that will in the least impair the structure or healthy action of the parts immediately concerned in the exercise of this function. Inflammatory fevers, affections of the brain, and injuries upon the head, are among the more common causes of imperfect hearing. Hence the impropriety of striking children upon the head in correcting them, whether in the family or in the school. The instances are not few in which deafness, and the impairing of the mental faculties, have resulted from that barbarous practice familiarly known as "boxing the ears." This inhuman practice is likely to result in injury to the drum of the ear, either in thickening this membrane, or in diminishing its vibratory character. Inflammation of the ear-drum, either acute or chronic, is the common cause of its increased thickness. How often this is produced by blows, the reader may judge. Diminution of the vibratory character of the ear-drum may result from an accumulation of wax upon its outer surface. In such cases chronic inflammation of the parts is not unfrequently the result of the injudicious practice of attempting its removal by introducing the heads of pins into the ear.

This wax, it should be known, is designed to subserve an important end; for the tube leading from the external ear, being, like the nose, constantly open, is liable to the entrance of foreign bodies, such as dust, insects, and the like. But, fortunately, it is not left without the means of defense; for on its inside there are numerous fine bristles, which, interlacing each other, interpose a barrier to the entrance of every thing but sound. Moreover, between the roots of these hairs there are numerous little glands, that secrete a nauseous, bitter wax, which, by its offensiveness, either deters insects from entering, or entangles them and prevents their advance in case they do enter. This wax, then, is very serviceable. But its usefulness does not stop here. When the ear becomes dry from a deficiency of it, the hearing becomes imperfect, as also when it is thin and purulent. This wax not unfrequently becomes hard and obstructs the tube, causing less or more deafness. But this form of deafness may be easily cured, even though it has existed for years; for, having softened the accumulations of viscid wax by dropping animal oil into the ear, they may be removed by the injection of warm soap-suds, which is an effectual and safe remedy.

The sense of hearing is perhaps as susceptible of cultivation as any of the senses. The Indian in the forest, who is accustomed to listen to the approach of his enemies or of his prey, acquires such acuteness of hearing as to be able to detect sounds that would be inaudible to persons living amid the din of civilized life. The blind, also, who of necessity are led to rely more upon this sense than seeing persons, excel in the acuteness of their hearing. They recognize their acquaintances by the exercise of this sense as readily as persons usually do by that of sight, an attainment which very few seeing persons make, and yet one that is perhaps within the reach of ninety-nine persons in every hundred. The blind judge with great accuracy the distance of persons in conversation, of carriages in motion, and of all sonorous bodies whose vibrations reach their ears. They even estimate with remarkable correctness the distance and height of buildings by the reflection or interception of sound. It is in consequence of the acuteness of this sense, acquired by careful cultivation, that the blind, as a class, have become so generally and justly distinguished for their pre-eminence in instrumental music. This enables them also to cultivate vocal music with more than ordinary success.

The due cultivation of the sense of hearing will contribute vastly to promote our intellectual and moral well-being. If it be true, as we are told it is by those who have been engaged in teaching both the deaf and the blind, that the absence of hearing is even a more formidable impediment to the communication of knowledge than that of sight, we must infer that all imperfections of the organ of hearing itself, or in the manner of using it, must correspondingly lessen the accuracy of the knowledge we receive through that organ. The meaning of language very often is conveyed not so much by the words themselves as in the tones of voice in which the words are uttered. If, therefore, the hearing be indistinct, or there be no habit formed of careful attention to the inflections of sound, the impressions received from what we hear must often be inaccurate. Our speech, too, will be far less agreeable, and be inefficient, even if it be not positively inarticulate. We owe it to others, no less than to ourselves, then, to cultivate the powers of the voice—the common instrument that God has given us for the interchange of thought, sentiment, and feeling, and which, though so common, is the most perfect of all instruments for the transmission of sound. Yet how deplorably is it neglected! how shamefully is it misused! It can be fully developed and made what it is capable of being only through the influence of the ear. If this organ be neglected, the voice must needs be imperfect. And the voices of many persons are through life imperfect and disagreeable, because they were not carefully trained in early life to articulate distinctly, much less to utter *musical* sounds. The opinion is confidently expressed by those who are best qualified to decide the matter, that nearly all children might be taught to sing, if proper attention were paid early enough to the use they make of their ears and their organs of sound. The careful training of these should be considered an indispensable part of a school-teacher's as well as of a parent's duty.

The ear will find appropriate discipline in distinguishing, without aid from the eye, the causes of various sounds, as the opening of a door, the shutting of a knife, the dropping of various coins, the moving of different articles of furniture, etc. It may also find appropriate exercise in determining the direction from which various sounds proceed; in recognizing acquaintances by their natural voices, and in detecting the counterfeit voices of companions; in arranging and classifying the elementary sounds of the language, and in determining all the different musical tones; in judging of the genus and species of birds by their chirping, of the distance and nature of sonorous bodies of various kinds, etc., etc. These are some of the direct means of improving this sense: others will suggest themselves to the thoughtful reader.

THE SENSE OF SIGHT.—The sense of sight, which is the most refined and admirable of all the senses, still remains to be considered. The senses generally serve as interpreters between the material universe without and the spirit within. But it is more especially by the sense of sight that we are enabled to hold converse with the external world. Without it we should be deprived of a large portion of the pleasures of life not only, but even of the means of maintaining our existence. It is through the sense of vision that the wisdom, power, and benevolence of the Deity are chiefly manifested to us.

I shall describe the apparatus of vision only so far as is necessary in order to subserve my leading object, which is the preservation and improvement of this sense, and the means of rendering it tributary to intellectual and moral culture. The eye, which is the organ of vision, is an optical instrument of the most perfect construction. It is surrounded by *coats,* which contain refracting mediums, called *humors.* There are three coats, called the *sclerotic,* the *choroid,* and the *retina*; and three humors, called the *aqueous,* the *crystalline,* and the *vitreous.*

The *sclerotic* or outer coat, called also the white of the eye, is an opaque, fibrous membrane. It has almost the firmness of leather, possesses little sensibility, and is rarely exposed to inflammation or other diseases. It invests the eye on every side except the front, and besides maintaining its globular form and preserving its internal and delicate structure, serves for the attachment of those muscles which move this organ. The opening in the fore part of this opaque coat is filled by the transparent *cornea,* which resembles a watch crystal in shape, and is received into a groove in the front part of the sclerotic coat in the same manner that a watch-glass is received into its case. But for this arrangement light could not gain admission to the eye.

The *choroid coat,* which constitutes the second investing membrane of the eye, is of a dark brown color upon its outer surface, and of a deep black within. The internal surface of this membrane secretes a dark substance resembling black paint, upon which the retina is spread out, and which is of great importance in the function of vision, as it seems to absorb the rays of light immediately after they have struck upon the sensible surface of the retina.

The *retina,* which is the third and innermost membrane of the eye, is the expansion of the optic nerve, and constitutes the immediate seat of vision. Such is the arrangement of the humors of the eye, and so perfectly are they adapted to the functions they are called upon to perform, that in the healthy state of this organ, the light entering the pupil is so refracted as to paint upon the retina an exact image of the objects from which it proceeds. The optic nerve, whose expansion forms the retina, receives this image and transmits it to the mind.

Arnott has well remarked, that "a whole printed sheet of a newspaper may be represented on the retina on less surface than that of a finger nail; and yet not only shall every word and letter be separately perceivable, but even any imperfection of a single letter. Or, more wonderful still, when at night an eye is turned up to the blue vault of heaven, there is portrayed on the little concave of the retina the boundless concave of the sky, with every object in its just proportions. There a moon in beautiful miniature may be sailing among her white-edged clouds, and surrounded by a thousand twinkling stars, so that to an animalcule supposed to be within and near the pupil, the retina might appear another starry firmament with all its glory."

Besides these three coats, and the cornea which constitutes about one fifth of the anterior portion of the outer coat, it is necessary to notice the *iris*, so called from its variety of color in different persons, and upon which alone the color of the eye depends. The iris is a circular membrane situated just behind the cornea, and is attached to one of the coats at its circumference. In its center is a small round hole, called the *pupil*; and sometimes spoken of familiarly as the sight of the eye, as no light can enter the eye except through it. The iris possesses the power of dilating and contracting, so as to admit more or less light, as it may be needed. This change in the size of the pupil is effected by two sets of muscular fibers. The first set converge from the circumference of the iris to the circular margin of the pupil, and constitute the *radiated muscle*. The outer ends of these fibers are attached to the sclerotic coat, which is unyielding; hence, when they contract, the pupil *enlarges* to receive more light. The other set is composed of circular fibers, which go round in the iris from the border to the pupil, and constitute the *orbicular muscle*, the contraction of which *diminishes* the size of the pupil. When too much light enters the eye, the excited and sensitive retina immediately gives warning of the danger, and the nerves, which are plentifully distributed to the iris, stimulate the orbicular muscle to contract, and the radiated one to relax, by which the size of the pupil is lessened. But when the light which enters the pupil is insufficient to transmit a distinct image of objects to the brain, the orbicular muscle relaxes, and the radiated one contracts, so as to enlarge the pupil. The contraction of the pupil is readily seen when a person passes from a darkened room into a bright sunlight, or when a light is first brought into a room in the twilight of evening. Any person may notice this contraction in his own eye by beholding himself in a glass immediately after passing from a dark to a well-lighted room. So, also, when a person looks at an object near the eye, the pupil contracts, but when he looks at an object more remote, it dilates. The muscles of the iris are somewhat under the control of the will; for most persons can contract or dilate the pupil, in some degree, at pleasure. Some persons possess this faculty to a great extent.

The three *humors of the eye* have been compared to the glasses of a telescope, and the coats to the tube, which keeps them in their places. The *aqueous* humor is situated in the fore part of the eye, and is divided by the iris into what are called the anterior and posterior chambers of the eye. The *crystalline* humor, or lens, is situated immediately behind the aqueous humor, a short distance back of the pupil, and is a perfectly transparent double convex lens, closely resembling in shape the common burning glass. This resemblance does not stop here; for this lens, like the burning glass, possesses the property of converging the rays of light which fall upon it, and bringing them to a focus. When this lens becomes so opaque as to obstruct the passage of light, either partially or entirely, a person is said to have a *cataract*. This can be cured only by a surgical operation. The *vitreous* humor, situated back of the other two, forms the principal part of the globe of the eye. It differs from the aqueous in one important particular. When that is discharged in extracting the crystalline lens for cataract or otherwise, it will be restored again in a few hours, and the eye will continue to perform its function. But if this be discharged by accident, the eye is irrecoverably lost. This, however, does not often occur; for, as we shall presently see, the eye is admirably fortified.

The eye is a perfect optical instrument, infinitely surpassing all specimens of human skill. This is true, view it in what light we may. It not only possesses the power of so adjusting its parts as to adapt it to the examination of objects at different distances, and in light of different degrees of intensity, but we are enabled to direct it at will to objects above, beneath, or around us.

The various motions of the eye are produced by six little muscles. These are attached at one extremity to the immovable bones of the orbit, while at the other extremity they are inserted into the sclerotic coat, four of them near its junction with the cornea, by broad, thin tendons, which give to the white of the eye its pearly appearance. These muscles are so arranged by the matchless skill of the Architect as to enable the beholder to direct the eye to any object he chooses, and to hold it there for any length of time that is compatible with the laws by which muscular exercise should be regulated. By the slight or intense action of four of these, called the straight muscles, the eye is less or more compressed, and the relative positions of its humors are by this means so nicely adjusted as to enable us to view objects near by or at a distance. The other two are called oblique muscles, one of which, with its long tendon passing through a cartilaginous loop, acts upon the principle of the fixed pulley, and turns the eye in a direction contrary to its own action. When the external muscle becomes too short, the eye turns out; but if the internal muscle is unduly contracted, the eye turns inward, toward the nose. One eye is sometimes turned up or down, but this is of less frequent occurrence.

It would be interesting to notice the protecting organs of the eye, consisting of the *orbit,* which is a deep bony socket, in which the eye securely rests; of the *eye-brows,* which are two projecting arches, covered with hair, and so arranged as to prevent the moisture that accumulates upon the forehead, in free perspiration, from flowing into the eye; of the *eye-lids,* which are two movable curtains for the protection of the eye, and which secrete a fluid that moistens and lubricates it; of the *lachrymal gland,* with its ducts, which keeps the eye constantly moist, and whose secretions go on while we wake and when we sleep, etc., etc.; but the preceding must suffice.

With this brief description of the apparatus of vision, we proceed to the consideration of the means of preserving and improving this sense, and of rendering it tributary to intellectual and moral culture.

The rule requiring that *action should alternate with rest,* which has been so often stated, and which applies to all the organs of both body and mind, should be especially observed in relation to the eye. This organ requires exercise, and light is its appropriate stimulus; but injury is the inevitable consequence of keeping it too constantly employed, or too intently fixed for a long time on any object. Whenever the eye is fixed for any length of time upon an object which it distinguishes with difficulty, it experiences a painful sensation, which is a sure indication that it has been overtaxed. The sight is also impaired when the eye is too little used, or when its natural stimulus is shut out, as is strikingly illustrated in the case of persons confined in dungeons. A distinguished oculist has said that many men daily impair or destroy their eyes by immoderate use, and that not a few have done the same by too little use of them.

The exposure of the eyes to *sudden transitions from weak to strong light* is very injurious. This may be regarded as one of the must prolific causes of weakness of sight. The injury is generally gradual, it is true, but it is none the less fatal on that account. The immediate sensation of pain, when a strong light is brought into a dark room, should be a sufficient warning to avoid such sudden extremes. The iris dilates and contracts, and thus enlarges or diminishes the size of the pupil as the light that fails upon the eye is faint or strong; but this dilation and contraction are not instantaneous. There are numerous instances on record in which total blindness has resulted from a sudden transition from darkness to the brilliancy of day. The habit of looking at a bright light of any kind, and especially of watching flashes of lightning, which is practiced by many, is exceedingly dangerous. The practice which many students and others indulge in, of resting their eyes as the twilight of evening advances, and allowing the pupil to dilate until it is quite dark, and then suddenly introducing a bright light, is a palpable violation of this rule, and one that is sure, sooner or later, sensibly to injure the eyes. The exposure of the eyes suddenly to a strong light upon waking from sleep, and all sudden changes of whatever kind from darkness to intense light, should be carefully avoided by persons who would preserve their sight unimpaired.

The strength of light used should be regulated *according to the powers of the eye*. This is a general, though a very important rule. Both the amount and the distribution of light should be such as to produce no unpleasant sensations. The eye possesses a certain degree of adaptation to light, according as it is intense or feeble. Some eyes require a stronger light than others, but all eyes are injured by being used in light that is too intense or too feeble. Reading by a strong sunlight, and by moon or star light, may be adduced as illustrations which are alike painful and injurious.

Too little light is well-nigh as injurious as too much, as he can not fail to have noticed who has had occasion to travel a difficult road in a dark night. The injury, in such cases, is two-fold; for while, on the one hand, the radiated muscle of the iris is unduly contracted for a length of time, in order sufficiently to enlarge the pupil to render objects visible, the sensitive retina, on the other hand, is overtaxed to gain a knowledge of them in too feeble light. The pain which the strained eye thus experiences is only an indication and a warning to the individual of the permanent injury he is inflicting upon this delicate organ.

Rooms should be well and evenly lighted. The irregular and flickering light of common lamps and candles is very injurious, and should be avoided in the study, and in all mechanical pursuits where the eye is much taxed. The best oculists concur in the opinion that reflected and concentrated light are highly injurious. Several cases of actual blindness are recorded as having occurred within a few years from exposure to concentrated light, and weakness of sight that has unfitted the individual for usefulness through life has often been thus produced. The rays of the sun are considered as peculiarly injurious when reflected from an opposite building or wall, or even when they pass through a window, and, descending to the floor, are thence reflected to the eyes. What, then, shall we say of the habit of constructing school-rooms in such a manner that perhaps a majority of the scholars are obliged to write and study at desks upon which the direct rays of the sun shine for a considerable portion of the day unbroken unless it be by a passing cloud! And yet thousands of school-houses are situated in such a manner as to create this very necessity all over our country. At a moderate estimate, the eyes of one hundred thousand children are taxed in this manner in the schools of the United States every passing year. A vast amount of discomfort and unhappiness is produced in this way that might easily be avoided, would parents and teachers take the trouble. Any exposure of this kind should be immediately obviated, either by blinds, or by curtains of some soft color. A few newspapers are much better than nothing. The desks and furniture should be of such a color that the eye may repose upon them with agreeable sensations. Nature is clothed with drapery whose color is refreshing to the eye; and it is false taste, as well as false philosophy, which attempts to dazzle in order to please it.

The use of side lights is injurious. The eye will accommodate itself to light of different degrees of intensity within a limited range, but both eyes should be exposed to an equal degree of light. The sympathy between the eyes is so great, that if the pupil of one eye is dilated by being kept in the shade, as must, of course, be the case where the light is on one side, the eye which is exposed can not contract itself sufficiently for protection, and is almost inevitably injured.

When viewing objects, we should avoid, as far as possible, *all oblique positions of the eye.* By neglecting this rule, an unnatural and permanent contraction of the muscle is liable to be produced, as is illustrated in the numerous instances of strabismus, or cross-eye, which are every where too common.

We should accustom the eye to viewing objects at different distances. The muscles upon which the form of the eye and the size of the pupil depend are subject to the general laws of muscular action. Their strength and flexibility, which are increased by healthful exercise, are impaired by disuse. Hence students who have neglected this rule, and have accustomed themselves for a long time to view objects near by, lose the power of adjusting the eye so as to view things at a distance. As a consequence, they become near-sighted, and put on glasses, when, by a proper use of the eye, their vision might have been preserved unimpaired many long years. I know some students upon whom this habit became so firmly fixed before they were twenty years of age, that they felt compelled to put on glasses, but who, unwilling to contract so pernicious a habit in early life, commenced a course of discipline in accordance with the suggestions here given. By perseverance, their eyes not only recovered their former healthful action, but became so improved that they now possess the sense of vision unimpaired not only, but in a very high state of cultivation.

Persons become near or long sighted as the objects to which they are accustomed to direct the eye are near or remote. This is illustrated in the case of students, watch-makers, and engravers, who are accustomed to examine minute objects near the eye, and, as a consequence, become near-sighted; and of surveyors, hunters, and sailors, who, being accustomed to view objects at a distance, become long-sighted. By a proper discipline of the eye, persons may attain and retain the power of viewing objects near by and at a distance, as is illustrated in the case of those gunsmiths who are accustomed to manufacture guns, and to try them in shooting at a mark at a great distance. The preceding principles being borne in mind in their various applications. I need, perhaps, state but one more rule.

He who would secure clear and distinct vision, must observe all those rules which are necessary to keep the body in health. The sympathy of the eyes with all the other organs of the body is wonderful and intimate. There is no other organ whose strength depends so much on the general vigor of the system. Strict temperance in eating and drinking may be regarded as an indispensable requisite for the preservation of healthy eyes. To this may be attributed the clear heads of the ancient philosophers, who, unlike most students of the present day, exercised their bodies and limbs as well as their minds. Their works are not the production of congested brains, for these were not oppressed with blood belonging to other parts of the body. They studied and thought, and exercised both body and mind in the open air, and thus observed the laws of health. But among the multitudes of close students of the present day, who complain of weakness of the eyes, the misfortune is generally attributable to an almost total neglect of the first principles of health.

While we reproach and loathe the man whose eyes are red and weeping with the effects of intemperate drinking, we cordially pity purblind students, as in some sense martyrs to the cause of learning. Dr. Reynolds, a distinguished American oculist, administers a rebuke to such which we fear is too often merited: "A closer examination of their history presents a very different result. Our sympathy may grow cool if we regard them with a physiologic eye. It is a love of the flesh, more than a love of the spirit, that too often clouds their vision. It is too much food, crowding with unnecessary blood the tender vessels of the retina. It is too little exercise, allowing these accumulated fluids to settle down into fatal congestion. It is positions wholly at variance with the freedom of the circulation, and various other imprudences, which are the results of carelessness or unjustifiable ignorance. 'The day laborer may eat what he will, provided it is wholesome, and his eyes will not suffer. But let the student, who is called upon to devote not only his eyes, but his brain, to severe labor, live upon highly nutritious food, and such as is difficult of digestion, and we shall soon see how his vision will be impaired, through the vehement and persevering determination of blood to the head, which such a course must inevitably occasion.' So speaks Beer, whose extensive opportunities of observation have perhaps never been exceeded. The daily practice of every observing oculist is filled with coincident experience."

Among the prevalent habits of students by which the eyes are injured, the same writer mentions the irritation produced by rubbing them on awaking in the morning, a practice which has in some cases occasioned permanent and incurable disease; reading while the body is in a recumbent position; using the eyes too early after the system has been affected with serious disease; exercising them too much in the examination of minute objects; the popular plan of *using green spectacles*, and *the use of tobacco.*

Light which is sufficient for distinct vision, and which falls over the shoulder in an oblique direction, from above, upon the book or study table, is generally regarded, and with great propriety, as best suited to the eyes. Some oculists prefer to have the light fall over the *left* shoulder.

The acuteness of this sense and the extent of its cultivation are very much greater in some individuals and classes of men than in others. This is a fact that has been remarked by observing persons. Its consequences should not be overlooked, for they are neither few nor unimportant. Those persons who have been long accustomed, either by the necessity of their situation, the example of those about them, or the judicious care of parents and teachers, to observe attentively the relations of parts, the symmetry of forms, or the shades of color, have eyes that are perpetually soliciting their minds to notice some beautiful or grand perceptions. Wherever they turn, they espy some new, and, therefore, curious arrangement of the elements of shape, some striking combination of light and shade, or some delicious peculiarity of coloring. The multiplicity and variety of their perceptions must and do increase the number of their thoughts, or give to their thoughts greater compass and definiteness. Such persons are likely to become poets, or painters, or sculptors, or architects. At any rate, they will appreciate and enjoy the productions of others who have devoted themselves to these delightful arts. And will not such persons be most readily awakened to descry and adore the power, the skill, and the beneficence of the Great Architect who reared the stupendous fabric of the universe, who devised the infinite variety of forms which diversify creation, and whose pencil has so profusely decked every work with myriads of mingling dyes, resulting all from a few parent colors? To an unpracticed eye, the beauties and wonders of creation are all lost. The surface of the earth is a blank, or, at best, but a confused and misty page. Such an eye passes over this scene of things, and makes no communication to the mind that will awaken thought, much less enkindle the spirit of devout adoration, and fill the soul with love to Him "whose universal love smiles every where."

Mr. May speaks no less sensibly than eloquently when he says, "I may be extravagant in my estimation of the importance of the culture of the eye and the ear, but so it is, that while I have been reading the writings of the Hebrew Prophets, and of those other gifted bards who communed so intently with nature and with nature's God, it has seemed to me impossible that any one could enter fully into all the tenderness, beauty, and sublimity of their language, or receive into his heart all its peculiarity of meaning, unless his own eye had been used to trace the skill of that hand which framed and fashioned every thing that is, and to descry the delicacy of that pencil which has painted all the flowers of the field, nor unless his own ear has learned to perceive the melody and harmony of sounds."

We can discipline the sight directly, and to a very great extent; and we can have the satisfaction of perceiving the progressive improvement of the faculty. For this purpose, every school should be furnished with appropriate apparatus. A set of measures is indispensable. I will illustrate by an example. For the benefit of the primary department connected with a seminary of learning that was formerly for several years under my supervision, I constructed a set of rules for linear measurement. Their breadth and thickness were uniform, each being an inch wide and half an inch thick. The set consisted of nine rules, whose lengths were as follows: four were each one foot long; one, a foot and a half long; two, two feet; one, two and a half feet; and one, three feet. Every rule had a small hole bored through each end. I had also a number of small pins turned just the right size to fit these holes. I have since submitted to several hundred teachers, in institutes and elsewhere, my mode of combining and using these measures; and from the deep interest which a large number of intelligent parents and teachers in different localities have manifested in the subject, I venture to refer to it in this connection. I first tried the experiment ten years ago, with a class of about twenty children from four to seven years of age. Several of these could not read, and some of them had not learned the alphabet. The children were first led to observe carefully the length of these several rules, until they could determine at sight the length of each. For several of the first lessons some of them would misjudge. They would, for instance, call a two foot rule one and a half or two and a half feet long. In such cases their judgments were immediately corrected by the application of two one foot rules. They were then led to observe with care, tables, desks, etc., and to estimate their length, and were afterward permitted to measure them, and discover the degree of accuracy in their decisions. After obtaining the opinions of the children in relation to the length or height of an object, I would measure it myself in the presence of the class. When the class became a little experienced, we examined the length, breadth, and height of rooms, of houses, and of churches; and then the distance of objects less or more remote, correcting or confirming their estimates by the application of the rule or measure, which gave a permanent interest to the exercise. By exercising the class in this manner, not to exceed half an hour a day, they would, at the end of the first quarter, judge of each other's height, of the height of persons generally, of the length of various objects, of the size of buildings, and of the dimensions of yards, gardens, and fields, with greater accuracy than the average of adult persons, as was tested by actual measurement in some instances where there was a disagreement in opinion.

By holding these rules in different positions, the children readily became familiar with the meaning and practical application of the terms perpendicular, horizontal, and oblique. They would also tell which term is applicable to the different parts of the stove-pipe; to the different parts of the furniture of the school-room; to the floor, sides of the room, roof, etc.; and to all objects with which they were familiar.

But the reader may inquire, what is the use of the holes and the pins? By pinning two rules together, one resting upon the other, and then turning one of them around, the class will readily gain a correct idea of the use of the term *angle*; also of the terms acute angle, right angle, and obtuse angle. By pinning three of these rules together at their ends, the children not only *see*, but can *handle* the simplest form of geometrical figures. When this figure is *defined*, they are enabled permanently to possess themselves of the meaning of the word *triangle*, by the simultaneous exercise of *three senses*. By combining rules of the same and different lengths, they become familiar with equilateral, isosceles, scalene, right, and obtuse angled triangles. By combining, in this way, such a set of rules as I have described, the child readily becomes familiar with the names and many of the properties of more than half a score of geometrical figures, with less effort on the part of the teacher than would be required to teach the child the names of the same number of letters. These exercises, then, may well precede the learning of the alphabet, or, at least, proceed simultaneously with it. By this means the child's interest in the school is increased; his senses are cultivated; he is enabled better to fix his attention; he progresses more rapidly and thoroughly in his juvenile studies, and at the same time lays the foundation for future excellence in penmanship and drawing, and other useful arts.

The child may also be taught to discriminate the varieties of green in leaves and other things; of yellow, red, and blue, in flowers and paints; and to distinguish not only the shades of all the colors, but their respective proportions in mixtures of two or more. Many persons, for want of such early culture, have grown to years without the ability of distinguishing between colors, as others have who have neglected the culture of the ear without the ability of distinguishing between tunes.

Drawing, whether of maps, the shape of objects, or of landscapes, is admirably adapted to discipline the sight. Children should be encouraged carefully to survey and accurately to describe the prominent points of a landscape, both in nature and in picture. Let them point out the elevations and depressions; the mowing, the pasture, the wood, and the tillage land; the trees, the houses, and the streams. Listen to their accounts of their plays, walks, and journeys, and of any events of which they have been witnesses. In these and all other exercises of the sight, children should be encouraged to be strictly accurate; and whenever it is practicable, the judgment they pronounce and the descriptions they give should, if erroneous, be corrected by the truth. Children can not fail to be interested in such exercises; and even where they have been careless and inaccurate observers, they will soon become more watchful and exact.

It is by the benign influences of education only that the senses can be improved. And still their culture has been entirely neglected by perhaps the majority of parents and teachers, who in other respects have manifested a commendable degree of interest in this subject. That by judicious culture the senses may be educated to activity and accuracy, and be made to send larger and purer streams of knowledge to the soul, has been unanswerably proved by an accumulation of unquestionable testimony. Most persons, however, allow the senses to remain uneducated, except as they may be cultivated by fortuitous circumstances. Eyes have they, but they see not; ears have they, but they hear not; neither do they understand. It is not impossible, nor perhaps improbable, that he who has these two senses properly cultivated will derive more unalloyed pleasure in spending a brief hour in gazing upon a beautiful landscape, in examining for the same length of time a simple flower, or in listening to the sweet melody of the linnet as it warbles its song of praise, than those who have neglected the cultivation of the senses experience during their whole lives!

This subject commends itself to all who regard their individual happiness, or who desire to render their usefulness as extensive as possible. Upon parents, teachers, and clergymen, who are more immediately concerned in the correct education of the rising generation, its claims are imperative. Let them be met, in connection with other appropriate means now in use and hereafter to be put in requisition, and our schools can not fail to become increasingly attractive; truancy, hence, will be less frequent, and the benign influences resulting from the correct education of the *whole man* will inspire the benevolent and philanthropic to renewed and increased efforts to secure the right education of *all men*, a condition upon which the maximum of human happiness depends.

CHAPTER VII.

THE NECESSITY OF MORAL AND RELIGIOUS EDUCATION.

The exaltation of talent, as it is called, above virtue and religion, is the curse of the age. Education is now chiefly a stimulus to learning, and thus men acquire power without the principles which alone make it a good. Talent is worshiped; but if divorced from rectitude, it will prove more of a demon than a god.—CHANNING.

Religion ought to be the basis of education, according to often-repeated writings and declamations. The assertion is true. Christianity furnishes the true basis for raising up character; but the foundation must be laid in a very different manner from that which is commonly practiced. * * * We can, indeed, scarcely conceive of the purity, the self-denial, and the power that might be given to human character by systematic development.—LALOR.

We have now reached a department of our subject of surpassing importance, for however judiciously physical and intellectual cultivation may have been conducted, if we make a mistake here, all is lost. Knowledge is *power*, it is true; but we should bear in mind that it is potent for evil as well as for good; and that, whether its effects be good or ill, depends entirely upon the dispositions and sentiments by which it is impelled and guided. Numerous have been the instances illustrative of the fact that the greatest scourges of our race are men of gigantic *cultivated* intellect. Where knowledge but qualifies its possessor for inflicting misery, ignorance would indeed be bliss.

I find my views on this important subject so admirably expressed in the writings of some of the most eminent men of the age, that I feel it both a privilege and a duty to enforce the sentiments I would inculcate by the introduction of their testimony.

Dr. Humphrey observes,[25] that "it must strike every one who is capable of taking a just and comprehensive view of the subject, that the common idea of a good education—of such an education as every child in the state ought to receive—is exceedingly narrow and defective. Most men leave out, or regard as of very little importance, some of the essential elements. They seem to forget that the child has a *conscience* and a *heart* to be educated as well as an *intellect*. If they do not lay too much stress on mental culture, which, indeed, is hardly possible, they lay by far too little upon that which is moral and religious. They expect to elevate the child to his proper station in society, to make him wise and happy, an honest man, a virtuous citizen, and a good patriot, by furnishing him with a comfortable school-house, suitable class-books, competent teachers, and, if he is poor, paying his quarter bills, while they greatly underrate, if they do not entirely overlook, that high moral training, without which knowledge is the power of doing evil rather than good. It may possibly nurture up a race of intellectual giants, but, like the sons of Anak, they will be far readier to trample down the Lord's heritage than to protect and cultivate it.

"Education is not a talismanic word, but an *art*, or rather a *science*; and, I may add, the most important of all sciences. It is the right, the proper training of the *whole man*, the thorough and symmetrical cultivation of all his noble faculties. If he were endowed with a mere physical nature, he would need, he would *receive* none but a physical training. On the other hand, if he were a purely intellectual being, intellectual culture would comprehend all that could be included in a perfect education. And were it possible for a moral being to exist without either body or intellect, there would be nothing but the heart or affections to educate. But man is a complex, and not a simple being. He is neither all body, nor all mind, nor all heart. In popular language, he has three natures, a corporeal, a rational, and a moral. These three, mysteriously united, are essential to constitute a perfect man; and as they all begin to expand in very early childhood, the province of education is to watch, and assist, and shape the development; to train, and strengthen, and discipline neither of them alone, but each according to its intrinsic and relative importance.

"When it is said that 'man is a religious being,' we should carefully inquire in what respects he is so. In a guarded and limited sense the proposition is undoubtedly true. Terrible as was the shock which his moral nature received by 'the fall,' it was not wholly buried in the ruins. Though blackened and crushed to the effacing of that glorious image in which he was created, his moral susceptibilities were not destroyed. The capacity of being restored, and of infinite improvement in knowledge and virtue, was left. In the lowest depths of ignorance and debasement, the human soul feels that it must have some religion, some support, some refuge 'when flesh and heart fail.' There is a natural dread of annihilation, a longing after immortality, a starting back from the last leap in the dark. Men, if they have not true religion, will cling to the greatest absurdities as substitutes. Hence the pagan world is full of idols. Tribes and nations seemingly destitute of all moral sense, nevertheless have 'gods many and lords many.' If there are any cold-blooded, incorrigible atheists in the world, you must look for them not in heathen lands. You must go where the altars of the true God have been thrown down. In this view, *man is a religious being*. He has a moral nature. He is susceptible of deep and controlling religious impressions. He can, at a very early period of life, be made to see and feel the difference between right and wrong—between good and evil. He can, while yet a child, be influenced by hope and by fear—by reason, by persuasion, and by the word of God; and all this shows that religion was intended to be a prominent part of his education. There can be no mistake in this. It is plainly the will of God that the moral as well as the intellectual faculties should be cultivated. Every child, whether in the family or the school, is to be treated by those who have the care of him as a moral and accountable being. His religious susceptibilities invite to the most diligent culture, and virtually enjoin it upon every teacher. The simple study of man's moral nature, before we open the Bible, unavoidably leads to the conclusion that any system of popular education must be extremely defective which does not make special prevision for this branch of public instruction.

"Even if there had been no fatal lapse of our race—if our children were not naturally depraved, nor inclined to evil in the slightest degree, still they would need religious as well as physical and intellectual guidance and discipline. It is true, the educator's task would be infinitely easier and pleasanter than it now is, but they would need instruction. They would enter the world just as ignorant of their immortal destiny as of letters. They would have every thing to learn about the being and perfections of God; every thing about his rightful claims as their Creator, Preserver, and moral Governor; and every thing touching their duties and relations to their fellow-men. Moreover, there is every reason to believe that moral and religious training would be necessary *to strengthen the principle of virtue* in the rising generation, and confirm them in habits of obedience and benevolence. As, notwithstanding their bodies are perfect bodies, and their minds perfect minds at their creation, no member or faculty being wanting, still they need all the helps of education; so, if they had a perfectly upright moral nature, they would need the same helps. There is no more reason to think, had sin never entered into the world, every child would have grown up to the 'fullness of the stature of a perfect man' in a religious sense, without an appropriate education, than that he would have become a scholar without it. But the little beings that are all the while springing into life around us to be educated are the sinful offspring of apostate parents. How deeply depraved, how strongly inclined to sin from the cradle, this is not the place to inquire. All agree that they show an early bias in the wrong direction; and that, left to grow up without moral culture and restraint, the great majority would go far astray, and become bad members of society. This is sufficient for our present argument. The evil bias must be counteracted. For the safety of the state, as well as for their own sakes, all its children must be brought under the forming and sanative influence of religious education. No adequate substitute was ever devised, or ever can be. 'Train up a child in the way he should go, and when he is old he will not depart from it.' This is divine; and the opposite is equally true. Train up a child in the way he should *not* go, or—which comes to about the same thing—leave him to take the wrong way of his own accord, and when he is old he will not depart from that. His tread will be heavier and heavier upon the broad and beaten track. 'Men do not gather grapes of thorns, nor figs of thistles.' 'Can the Ethiopian change his skin, or the leopard his spots? Then may those also do good who are accustomed to do evil.'

"Moral and religious training ought, undoubtedly, to be commenced in every family much earlier than children are sent to school, and no parent can throw off upon the schoolmaster the responsibility of bringing them up in the 'nurture and admonition of the Lord.' He must himself teach them the good way, and lead them along in it by his own example. But few parents, however, have the leisure and ability to do all that is demanded in this vitally essential branch of education. All are entitled to the aid of their pastors and religious teachers; and every good shepherd will feel a tender concern for the lambs of his flock, and will feed them with the sincere milk of the word both in the sanctuary and at the fireside. But the work should not stop here. There ought to be a co-operation of good influences in all the seminaries of learning, and especially in the primary schools. This co-operation would be necessary if moral and religious household instruction were universally given, and if all the children of the state regularly attended public worship, and enjoyed the benefits of catechetical and Sabbath-school teaching. But those who would banish religion from our admirable systems of popular education by the plea that it belongs exclusively to the family and the Church, ought to remember what multitudes of children this exclusion would deprive of their birth-right as members of a Christian community. There are tens of thousands in our own heaven-blessed New England, and hundreds of thousands in these United States, who receive no religious instruction whatever at home, and whose parents are connected with no religious denomination. What is to be done? We can neither compel ignorant and graceless fathers and mothers to teach their children the fear of the Lord, nor to send them to any place of worship or Sabbath-school. I ask again, what is to be done? These neglected children are in the midst of us. Our cities swarm with them. They are scattered every where over our beautiful hills and valleys. Grow up they will among our own children, without principle and without morals, to breathe mildew upon the young virtues which we have sown in our families, and to prey upon the dearest interests of society, unless somebody cares for their moral and religious education. And where shall they receive this education, if not in the school-house? You will find them there, if in any place of instruction, and multitudes of them you can reach nowhere else.

"A more Utopian dream never visited the brain of a sensible man than that which promises to usher in a new golden age by the diffusion and thoroughness of what is commonly understood by popular education. With all its funds, and improved school-houses, and able teachers, and grammars, and maps, and black-boards, such an education is essentially defective. Without moral principle at bottom to guide and control its energies, education is a sharp sword in the hands of a practiced and reckless fencer. I have no hesitation in saying, that if we could have but one, moral and religious culture is even more important than a knowledge of letters; and that the former can not be excluded from any system of popular education without infinite hazard. Happily, the two are so far from being hostile powers in the common domain, that they are natural allies, moving on harmoniously in the same right line, and mutually strengthening each other. The more virtue you can infuse into the hearts of your pupils, the better they will improve their time, and the more rapid will be their proficiency in their common studies. The most successful teachers have found the half hour devoted to moral and religious instruction more profitable to the scholar than any other half hour in the day; and there are no teachers who govern their schools with so much ease as this class. Though punishment is sometimes necessary where moral influence has done its utmost, the conscience is, in all ordinary cases, an infinitely better disciplinarian than the rod. When you can get a school to obey and to study because it is right, and from a conviction of accountability to God, you have gained a victory which is worth more than all the penal statutes in the world; but you can never gain such a victory without laying great stress upon religious principle in your daily instructions.

"There is, I am aware, in the minds of some warm and respectable friends of popular education, an objection against incorporating religious instruction into the system as one of its essential elements. It can not, they think, be done without bringing in along with it the evils of sectarianism. If this objection could not be obviated, it would, I confess, have great weight in my own mind. It supposes that if any religious instruction is given, the distinctive tenets of some particular denomination must be inculcated. But is this at all necessary? Must we either exclude religion altogether from our common schools, or teach some one of the many creeds which are embraced by as many different sects in the ecclesiastical calendar? Surely not. There are certain great moral and religious principles in which all denominations are agreed; such as the ten commandments, our Savior's golden rule—every thing, in short, which lies within the whole range of duty to God and duty to our fellow-men. I should be glad to know what sectarianism there can be in a schoolmaster's teaching my children the first and second tables of the moral law; to 'love the Lord their God with all their heart, and their neighbor as themselves;' in teaching them to keep the Sabbath holy, to honor their parents, not to swear, nor drink, nor lie, nor cheat, nor steal, nor covet. Verily, if this is what any mean by sectarianism, then the more we have of it in our common schools the better. 'It is a lamentation, and shall be for a lamentation,' that there is so little of it. I have not the least hesitation in saying, that no instructor, whether male or female, ought ever to be employed who is not both able and willing to teach morality and religion in the manner which I have just alluded to. Were this faithfully done in all the primary schools of the nation, our civil and religious liberties, and all our blessed institutions, would be incomparably safer than they are now. The parent who says, I do not send my child to school to learn religion, but to be taught reading, and writing, and grammar, knows not 'what manner of spirit he is of.' It is very certain, that such a father will teach his children any thing but religion at home; and is it right that they should be left to grow up as heathens in a Christian land? If he says to the schoolmaster, I do not wish you to make my son an Episcopalian, a Baptist, a Presbyterian, or a Methodist, very well. That is not the schoolmaster's business. He was not hired to teach sectarianism. But if the parent means to say, I do not send my child to school to have you teach him to fear God and keep his commandments, to be temperate, honest, and true, to be a good son and a good man, then the child is to be pitied for having such a father; and with good reason might we tremble for all that we hold most dear, if such remonstrances were to be multiplied and to prevail.

"In this connection I can not refrain from earnestly recommending the daily reading of the Scriptures, and prayer,[26] in all our schools, as eminently calculated to exert a powerful moral influence upon the scholars. It is melancholy to think what swarms of children are growing up even in Massachusetts—and what multitudes of them in every one of these United States—who will seldom, if ever, hear the voice of prayer if they do not hear it in the schools, and to whom the Bible will remain a sealed book if it be not opened there. I would not insist that *every* primary teacher should be absolutely required to open or close the school daily with prayer. Great and good as I think the influence of such an arrangement would be, it might be impossible, at present, to find a sufficient number of instructors otherwise well qualified who are fitted to lead in this exercise. The number, however,

I believe is steadily increasing. It is probably too late for me, but I hope that some of you, gentlemen, may live to see the time when the voice of prayer, and of praise too, will be heard in every school-house of the land. Could I know that this would be the case, it would give me a confidence in the perpetuity of our civil and religious liberties which I should exceedingly rejoice to cherish as I pass off from the stage."

It would seem that these patriotic sentiments, enforced by such persuasive eloquence by this venerable man, can hardly fail to find a permanent lodgment in every truly American bosom. The great principles of natural and revealed religion, in which all are agreed, ought to be inculcated in our common school-books,[27] just as every teacher ought orally to instill these principles into the minds of his pupils. That will be a happy day, especially to the children of ignorant and vicious parents, when they shall learn more of that "fear of the Lord which is the beginning of knowledge" in the school-house than they have ever yet done. Nor is it discovered that the practice of teaching morals according to the Christian code, and using the Bible for that purpose, the great majority adopting it, is any infringement whatever on the religious rights and liberty of any individual.

The anecdote of the Indian touching this subject may arrest the attention of some reader who would otherwise peruse these paragraphs without profit, and fix indelibly in his mind the sentiment I would inculcate, and I therefore insert it. The Indian inquires of the white man what religion he professes. The white man replies, "*Not any.*" "*Not any?*" says the Indian, in astonishment; "then you are *just like my dog*; he's got no religion." We have *men* enough like the Indian's dog, without teaching our *children* to be like him.

The French, in the days of the Revolution, voted God from his throne. They abolished the Sabbath, and declared that Christianity was a nullity. They set apart one day in ten, not for religion, but for idleness and licentiousness. History informs us that the goddess of Reason, personified by a naked prostitute, was drawn in triumph through the streets of Paris, and that the municipal officers of the city, and the members of the National Convention of France, joined publicly in the impious parade. We need not wonder, then, that even the forms of religion were destroyed, and that licentiousness and profligacy walked forth unveiled. How unlike this is the state of things in these United States! We are professedly a Christian nation. We recognize the existence of a superior and superintending power in all our institutions.

The New World was early sought by a Christian people, that fled from oppression in order to find a home where they might worship God unmolested, and bequeath to posterity the same inestimable privilege and inalienable right. In the days of the Revolution, Washington and his coadjutors were accustomed to invoke the blessing of the God of battles; and without His favor, they looked not for victory. In the Congress of this Great Nation, and in our State Legislatures, we are accustomed to acknowledge our dependence upon God in employing chaplains with whom we unite in daily devotions.

The Constitution of the United States requires that all legislative, executive, and judicial officers in the United States, and in the several states, shall be bound by oath or affirmation to support the Constitution. The Constitution of each of the several states requires a similar oath or affirmation; and some of them further provide that, in addition to the oath of office, all persons appointed to places of profit or trust shall, before entering upon the same, subscribe a declaration of their faith in the Christian religion.

In our Penitentiaries even, we employ chaplains for the social, moral, and religious improvement of criminals confined within them; for our object is, not merely to *deter others* from vice by the punishment of offenders, but, if possible, *to reform the offenders themselves*, and, bringing them back to virtue, make them useful members both of Christian and of civil society. Should we not, then, recognize God in our common schools—the primary training-places of our country's youth—by reading His word, and familiarizing the juvenile mind of the nation with the precepts of the Great Teacher, whose code of morals is acknowledged, even by infidels, to be infinitely superior to any of human origin? And should we not humbly invoke His aid in our efforts to learn and to do his will? and His blessing to attend those efforts? A Paul may plant, and Apollos water; but God giveth the increase.

The instruction in our common schools, I repeat, should be Christian, but not sectarian. There is sufficient common ground which all true believers in Christianity agree in, to effect an incalculable amount of good, if honestly and faithfully taught. Which of the various religious sects in our country would take exceptions to the inculcation of the following sentiments, and kindred ones expressed in every part of the Scriptures?

"Thou shalt love the Lord thy God with all thy heart, and with all thy soul, and with all thy mind. This is the first and great commandment. And the second is like unto it, Thou shalt love thy neighbor as thyself." "As ye would that men should do to you, do ye also to them likewise." "Love your enemies, bless them that curse you, do good to them that hate you, and pray for them which despitefully use you and persecute you."

If there is a single instance in which a sect of professing Christians would take exceptions to the inculcation of these and kindred sentiments in all the schools of our land, I have yet to learn it. On the contrary, I have received and accepted invitations from scores of clergymen, representing not less than eight different denominations, to address their congregations on the subject of "Moral and Religious Education in Common Schools;" and, having expressed the sentiments herein advocated, I have, in every instance, received letters of approval and encouragement; and their hearty prayers and active co-operation have confirmed me in the belief that they are ready and willing to "work together" upon this common platform, in advancing the interests of this glorious cause.

I have spoken of the Christian religion as the most important branch of a common school education. The cultivation of the intellectual faculties alone constitutes no sufficient guaranty that the subject of it will become either a virtuous man, a good neighbor, or a useful citizen. But where physical education has been properly attended to, if we combine with the cultivation of the intellectual faculties of a child a good moral and religious education, we have the highest and most unquestionable authority for believing that, in after life, he will "do justly, love mercy, and walk humbly with God."

"The Bible, in several expressive texts," says Dr. Stowe,[28] "gives emphatic utterance to the true principle of all right education. For example, 'The fear of the Lord is the beginning of wisdom, and a knowledge of the Holy is understanding.' Religion must be the basis of all right education; and an education without religion is an education for perdition. Religion, in its most general sense, is the union of the soul to its Creator; a union of sympathy, originating in affection, and guided by intelligence. The word is derived from the Latin terms *re* and *ligo,* and signifies to *tie again,* or *reunite*. The soul, sundered from God by sin, by grace is *reunited* to Him; and this is *religion*."

I might present many and substantial reasons why instruction in the principles of religion should be given in our common schools and in all our institutions of learning, and why those heaven-given principles should be exemplified wherever taught.

The nature of the human mind requires it, as is clearly shown by the writer last quoted. "The mind is created, and God is its creator. Every mind is conscious to itself that it is not self-existent or independent, but that its existence is a derived one, and its condition one of entire, uniform, unceasing dependence. This feeling is as truly a part of the essential constitution of the mind as the desire for food is of the body, and it never can be totally suppressed. If it ever seems to be annihilated, it is only for a very brief interval; and any man who would persist in affirming himself to be self-existent and independent, would be universally regarded as insane. The sympathy which attracts the sexes toward each other is not more universal nor generally stronger than that inward want which makes the whole human race feel the need of God; and, indeed, the feelings are, in many respects, so analogous to each other, that all ancient mysteries of mythology, and the Bible itself, have selected this sympathy as the most expressive, the most unvarying symbol of the relation between the soul and God.

"Till men can be taught to live and be healthy and strong without food; till some way is discovered in which the social state can be perpetuated and made happy, with a total separation of the sexes; till the time arrives when these things can be done, we can not expect to relieve the human mind from having some kind of religious faith. This being the fact, a system of education which excludes attention from this part of the mental constitution is as essentially incomplete as a system of military tactics that has no reference to fighting battles; a system of mechanics which teaches nothing respecting machinery; a system of agriculture that has nothing to do with planting and harvesting; a system of astronomy which never alludes to the stars; a system of politics which gives no intimation on government; or any thing else which professes to be a system, and leaves out the very element most essential to its existence. The history of all ages, of all nations, and of all communities is a continued illustration of this truth. Where did the nation ever exist untouched either by religion or superstition? which never had either a theology or a mythology? When you find a nation that exists without food of some sort, then you may find a nation that subsists without religion of some sort; and never, *never* before. How unphilosophical, how absurd it is, then, to pretend that a system of education may be complete, and yet make no provision for this part of the mental constitution! It is one of the grossest fooleries which the wickedness of man has ever led him to commit. But it is not only unphilosophical and foolish, it is also exceedingly mischievous; for where religion is withheld, the mind inevitably falls to superstition, as certainly as when wholesome food is withheld the sufferer will seek to satisfy his cravings with the first deleterious substance which comes within his reach. The only remedy against superstition is sound religious instruction. The want exists in the soul. It is no factitious, no accidental or temporary want, but an essential part of our nature. It is an urgent, imperious want; it must and will seek the means of satisfaction, and if a healthful supply be withheld, a noxious one will be substituted."

THE BIBLE IN SCHOOLS.—Having taken the liberty of recommending the devotional reading of the Scriptures in all the public schools as eminently calculated to make them what they ought to be—nurseries of morality and religion as well as of good learning I am now prepared to express the strong conviction, to adopt the language of Dr. Humphrey, "*that the Bible ought to be used in every primary school as a class-book.* I am not ignorant of the objections which even some good men are wont to urge against its introduction. The Bible, it is said, is too sacred a volume to be put on a level with common school-books, and to be thumbed over and thrown about by dirty hands. This objection supposes that if the Bible is made a school-book, it must needs be put into such rude hands; and that it can not be daily read in the classes without diminishing the reverence with which it ought to be regarded as the book of God. But I would have it used chiefly by the older scholars, who, if the teachers are not in the fault, will rarely deface it. A few words now and then, reminding them of its sacred contents, will be sufficient to protect it from rough and vulgar usage.

"The objection that making the Bible a common school-book would detract from its sacredness in the eyes of the children, and thus blunt rather than quicken their moral susceptibilities, is plausible; but it will not, I am confident, bear the test of examination and experience. What were the Scriptures given us for, if not to be read by the old and the young, the high and the low? Is the common use of any good thing which a kind Providence intended for all, calculated to make men underrate it? The best of Heaven's gifts, it is true, are *liable* to be perverted and abused; but ought this to deter us from using them thankfully and properly? We, the descendants of the Puritans, are so far from regarding the Bible as too sacred for common use, that, however we may differ among ourselves in other respects, we cordially unite in efforts to put the sacred treasure in the hands of all the people. It is one of our cardinal principles, as Protestants, that the more they read the Scriptures the better. Are we right or are we wrong here? Let us bring the question to the test of experience. Who are the most moral and well-principled class in the community? those who have been accustomed from childhood to read the Bible, till it has become the most familiar of all books, or those who read it but little? Of two schools, of equal advantages in other respects, which is best regulated and most easily governed? which has most of the fear of God in it, the deepest reverence for his word, that where the Bible is read or from which it is excluded? It is easy for ingenious men to reason plausibly, and tell us that such and such injurious effects *must* follow from making sacred things too familiar to the youthful mind; but who ever heard of such effects following from the use of the Bible as a school-book? It will be time enough to listen to this objection when a solitary example can be adduced to sustain it.

"How do all other men out of the Protestant communion, Papists, Mohammedans, Jews, and Gentiles, reason and act in the education of their children? Do they discard their sacred books from the schools as too holy for common and familiar use? No. They understand the influence of such reading far too well, and are too strongly attached to their respective religions to exclude it. The Romanists, indeed, forbid the use of the Scriptures to the common people; but the Missal and the Breviary, which they hold to be quite as sacred, are their most familiar school-books. A large portion of the children's time is taken up with reading the lessons and reciting the prayers; and what are the effects? Do they become disgusted with the Missal and Breviary by this daily familiarity? We all know the contrary. The very opposite effect is produced. It is astonishing to see with what tenacity children thus educated cling to the superstitions and absurdities of their fathers; and it is because their religion is wrought into the very texture of their minds, in the schools as well as in the churches. Go to Turkey, to Persia, to all the lands scorched and blighted by the fiery train of the Crescent, and what school-books will you find but portions of the Koran? Pass to Hindostan, and there you will find the Vedas and Shasters wherever any thing like popular education is attempted. Enter the great empire of China, and, according to the best information we can obtain, their sacred books are the school-books of that vast and teeming population. Inquire among the Jews, wherever in their various dispersions they have established schools, and what will you find but the Law and the Prophets, the Targums and the Talmud.

"Now when and where did ever Protestant children grow up with a greater reverence for the Bible, a stronger attachment to their religion, than Jewish, Mohammedan, and Pagan children cherish for their school-books, to the study of which they are almost exclusively confined, in every stage of their education? It is opposing theory, then, to great and undeniable facts, to say that using the Christian Scriptures in this manner would detract from their sacredness in the eyes of our children. If this is ever the case, it must be where the teacher himself is a Gallio, and lacks those moral qualifications which are essential to his profession. Another objection which is sometimes brought against the use of the Bible is, that considerable portions of it—though all true, and important as a part of our great religious charter—are not suitable for common and promiscuous reading. My answer is, we do not suppose that any instructor would take all his classes through the whole Bible, from Genesis to Revelation. The genealogical tables, and some other things, he would omit of course, but would always find lessons enough to which the most fastidious could make no objection.

"The way is now prepared to take an affirmative attitude, and offer some reasons in favor of using the Bible as a school-book. In the first place, *it is the cheapest school-book in the world*. It furnishes more reading for *fifty cents* than can be obtained in common school-books for *two dollars*. This difference of cost is, to the poor, an important consideration. With large families on their hands, they often find it extremely difficult to meet the demands of teachers and committees for new books. Were the Scriptures generally introduced, they would take the place of many other reading-books which parents are now obliged to purchase at four-fold expense. This would be a cogent argument on the score of economy, even if the popular school-books of this year were sure of maintaining their ground the next. But so busy is the press in bringing forward new claimants to public favor, that they rapidly supplant each other, and thus the burden is greatly increased.

"In the next place, *the Bible furnishes a far greater variety of the finest reading-lessons than any other book whatever*. This is a point to which my attention has been turned for many years, and the conviction grows upon me continually. There is no book in which children a little advanced beyond the simplest monosyllabic lessons will learn to read faster, or more readily catch the proprieties of inflection, emphasis, and cadence, than the Bible. I would by no means put it into the hands of a child to spell out and blunder over the chapters before he has read any thing else. The word of God ought not to be so used by mere beginners. But it contains lessons adapted to all classes of learners, after the first and simplest stage. Let any teacher who has never made the trial put a young class into the first chapter of John, and he will be surprised to find how easy the reading is, and with what pleasure and manifest improvement they may be carried through the whole Gospel; and as few are too young to read with advantage in the Bible, so none are too old. It is known to every body, that the very best reading lessons in our most popular school-books for the higher classes are taken from the Scriptures. Just open the Sacred Volume with reference to this single point, and turn over its thousand pages. As a history, to interest, instruct, and improve the youthful mind, what other book in the world can compare with it? Where else will you find such exquisitely finished pieces of biography? such poetry? such genuine and lofty eloquence? such rich and varied specimens of tenderness, pathos, beauty, and sublimity? I regret that I have not room for a few quotations. I can only refer, in very general terms, to the history of the creation; of Joseph and the forty years' wandering in the wilderness; to the book of Job; to the Psalms of David; to Isaiah; to the Gospels; and to the visions of John in the Isle of Patmos.

"Now if the primary qualities of a good school-book are to teach the art of reading, and to communicate instruction upon the most interesting and important subjects, I have no hesitation in saying that the Bible stands pre-eminently above every other. If I were again to become a primary instructor, or to teach the art of reading in any higher seminary than the common school-house, I would take the Bible in preference to any twenty 'Orators' or 'English Readers' that I have ever seen. Indeed, I would scarcely want any other. Milton and Shakspeare I would not reject, but I would do very well without them, for they are both surpassed by Isaiah and John. Let enlightened teachers, and members of any of the learned professions, read over aloud, in their best manner, such portions of Scripture as they may easily select, and see if they have ever found any thing better fitted to bring out and discipline the voice, and to express all the emotions in which the soul of true eloquence is bodied forth. Why do the masters of oratory, who charm great audiences with their recitations, take so many of their themes from the Bible? The reason is obvious. They can find none so well suited to their purpose. And why should not the common schools, in which are nurtured so many of the future orators, and rulers, and teachers of the land, have the advantage of the best of all reading-lessons? Moreover, since so much of the sense of Scripture depends upon the manner in which it is read, why should not the thousands of children be taught the art in school, who will never learn it at home? The more I study the Bible, the more does it appear to me to excel all other reading-books. You may go on improving indefinitely, without ever making yourself a perfect scriptural reader, just as you might, with all the help you can command, spend your whole life in the study of any one of its great truths without exhausting it. Let it not be said that we have but few instructors who are capable of entering into the spirit of the Sacred Volume, so as to teach their scholars to read it with propriety. Then let more be educated. It ought to be one of the daily exercises in our Normal Schools, and other seminaries for raising up competent teachers, to qualify them for this branch of instruction."

I remark again, that were the Bible made a school-book throughout the commonwealth and throughout the land, *an amount of scriptural knowledge would be insensibly treasured up, which would be of inestimable value in after life.* Every observing teacher must have been surprised to find how much the dullest scholar will learn by the ear, without seeming to pay any attention to what others are reading or reciting. The boy that sits half the time upon his little bench nodding or playing with his shoe-strings, will, in the course of a winter, commit whole pages and chapters to memory from the books he hears read, when you can hardly beat any thing into him by dint of the most diligent instruction. Indeed, I have sometimes thought that children in our common schools learn more by the ear, without any effort, than by the study of their own class-books; and I am quite sure this is the case with the most of the younger scholars. Let any book be read for a series of years in the same school, and half of the children will know most of it by heart. Wherever there are free schools—and the free school system is now becoming extensively adopted in every part of the United States—the great mass of the children are kept at school from four or five years of age, to nine or ten, through the year; and in the winter season, from nine or ten to fifteen or sixteen. The average of time thus devoted to their education is from eight to ten years. Now let the Bible be read daily as a class-book during all this time, in every school, and how much of it will, without effort, and without interfering in the least with other studies, be committed to memory. And who can estimate the value of such an acquisition? What pure morality; what maxims of supreme wisdom for guidance along the slippery paths of youth, and onward through every stage of life; what bright examples of early piety, and of its glorious rewards, even in the present world; what sublime revelations of the being and perfections of God; what incentives to love and serve him, and to discharge with fidelity all the duties which we owe to our fellow-men! and all these enforced by the highest sanctions of future accountability. Let any man tell, if he can, how much all this store of divine knowledge, thus insensibly acquired, would be worth to the millions of children who are growing up in these United States of America. They might not be at all sensible of its value at the time, but how happily and safely would it contribute to shape their future opinions and characters, both as men and as citizens.

Another cogent reason for using the Bible as a common school-book is, that *it is the firmest basis, and, indeed, the only sure basis of our free institutions, and, as such, ought to be familiar to all the children in the state from their earliest years.* While it recognizes the existence of civil governments, and enjoins obedience to magistrates as ministers of God for the good of the people, it regards all men as free and equal, the children of one common Father, and entitled to the same civil and religious privileges. I do not believe that any people could ever be enslaved who should be thoroughly and universally educated in the principles of the Bible.

It was no less truly than eloquently said by Daniel Webster, in his Bunker Hill address, that "the American colonists brought with them from the Old World a full portion of all the riches of the past in science and art, and in morals, religion, and literature. The *Bible* came with them. And it is not to be doubted that to the *free* and *universal* use of the Bible it is to be ascribed that in that age men were much indebted for right views of civil liberty. The Bible is a book of faith and a book of doctrine; but it is also a book which teaches man his individual responsibility, his own dignity, and equality with his fellow-men."

These sentiments of the great American statesman are worthy to be engraved in golden capitals upon the monument under whose shade they were uttered! Yes, it was the free and universal use of the Bible which made our Puritan fathers what they were; and it is because, in these degenerate times, multitudes of children will be taught to read it nowhere else, that I am so anxious to have it read as a school-book. One other, and the only additional reason which I shall suggest, is that, as the Bible is *infinitely the best,* so it is the only decidedly *religious book* which can be introduced into our popular systems of early education. So jealous are the different sects and denominations of each other, that it would be hardly possible to write or compile a religious school-book with which all would be satisfied. But here is a book prepared to our hands, which we all receive as the inspired record of our faith, and as containing the purest morality that has ever been taught in this lower world. Episcopalians can not object to it, because they believe it teaches the doctrines and polity of their own church; and this is just what they want. Neither Congregationalists, Presbyterians, Baptists, Methodists, Universalists, nor any other denomination, can object to it for the same reason. Every denomination believes, so far as it differs from the rest, that the Bible is on its side, and, of course, that the more it is read by all, the better.

For me to object to having the Bible read as a common school-book on account of any doctrine which those who differ from me suppose it to teach, would be virtually to confess that I had not full confidence in my own creed, and was afraid it would not bear a scriptural test. It seems to me an infinite advantage, for which we are bound devoutly to thank the Author of all good, that he has given us a religious book of incomparable excellence, which we may fearlessly put into the hands of all the children in the state, with the assurance that it is able to make them "wise unto salvation," and will certainly make them better children, better friends, and better members of society, so far as it influences them at all. But some persons who highly approve of daily scriptural reading in common schools are in favor of using *selections* rather than the whole Bible. I should certainly prefer this, provided the selections are judiciously made, to excluding the Scriptures altogether; but I think there are weighty and obvious reasons why the *whole* Bible should be taken rather than a part. The whole is cheaper than half would be in a separate volume; and when the whole is introduced, "without note or comment," there can be no possible ground for sectarian jealousy.

Doctors of divinity not only, but the most eminent statesmen in the country, hold the views here presented. The bold and noble stand taken by the Legislature of New York more than ten years ago (1838), has revived the hopes and infused fresh courage into the minds of those who believe that the safety and welfare of our country are essentially dependent on the prevalence of a "*religious* morality and a *moral* religion." The representatives of this great state, whose system of education is becoming increasingly an object of imitation in all the rest, at one and the same session doubled the amount of the public money for the purpose of improving the education given in the common schools—which, to the praise of that state, be it said, are *now free*—and in reply to the petition of sundry persons, praying that all religious exercises and the use of the Bible might be prohibited in the public schools, decided by a vote of *one hundred and twenty-one* to ONE! that the request of the petitioners be not granted. For the purpose of corroborating the doctrines of this volume, I will introduce a paragraph from the report of the Hon. Daniel D. Barnard on the occasion referred to, which was sustained by the noble, unequivocal, and almost unanimous testimony of the representatives of the most powerful member of the American states.

"Moral instruction is quite as important to the object had in view in popular education as intellectual instruction; it is indispensable to that object. But, to make instruction effective, it should be given according to the best code of morals known to the country and the age; and that code, it is universally conceded, is contained in the Bible. Hence the Bible, as containing that code, so far from being arbitrarily excluded from our schools, ought to be in common use in them. Keeping all the while in view the object of popular education, the fitting of the people by *moral* as well as by *intellectual* discipline for self-government, no one can doubt that any system of instruction which overlooks the training and informing of the moral faculties must be wretchedly and fatally defective. Crime and intellectual cultivation merely, so far from being dissociated in history and statistics, are unhappily old acquaintances and tried friends. To neglect the moral powers in education is to educate not quite half the man. To cultivate the intellect only is to unhinge the mind and destroy the essential balance of the mental powers; it is to light up a recess only the better to see how dark it is. And if this is all that is done in popular education, then nothing, literally nothing, is done toward establishing popular virtue and forming a moral people."

This is but a specimen of an invaluable document, which does honor to the heart and head of him who penned it, and to the Legislature of the commonwealth by which it was adopted by almost unparalleled unanimity.

The Hon. Samuel Young, the eminently distinguished superintendent of common schools in the same state, in a report made in 1843, inculcates sentiments which so well accord with my own views of the importance of weaving scriptural reading into the very warp and woof of popular education, that I gladly add his testimony. "I regard the New Testament as in all respects a suitable book to be daily read in our common schools, and I earnestly recommend its general introduction for this purpose. As a mere reading-book, intended to convey a practical knowledge of the English language, it is one of the best text-books in use; but this, although of great use to the pupils, is of minor importance when the moral influences of the book are duly considered. Education consists of something more than mere instruction. It is that training and discipline of all the faculties of the mind which shall symmetrically and harmoniously develop the future man for usefulness and for happiness in sustaining the various relations of life. It must be based upon knowledge and virtue; and its gradual advancement must be strictly subordinated to those cardinal and elementary principles of morality, which are nowhere so distinctly and beautifully inculcated as in that book from whence we all derive our common faith. The nursery and family fireside may accomplish much; the institutions of religion may exert a pervading influence; but what is commenced in the hallowed sanctuary of the domestic circle, and periodically inculcated at the altar, must be daily and hourly recognized in the common schools, that it may exert an ever-present influence, enter into and form a part of every act of life, and become thoroughly incorporated with the rapidly expanding character. The same incomparable standard of moral virtue and excellence, which is expounded from the pulpit and the altar, and which is daily held up to the admiration and imitation of the family circle, should also be reverently kept before the mind and the heart in the daily exercises of the school."

I will add the testimony of another whom we all delight to honor. Never were sentiments uttered more worthy to be remembered and repeated through all generations, than those which fell from the Father of his Country in his Farewell Address to the American people. "Of all the dispositions and habits which lead to political prosperity, religion and morality are indispensable supports. In vain would that man claim the tribute of patriotism who should labor to subvert these great pillars of human happiness, these firmest props of the duties of men and citizens. The mere politician, equally with the pious man, ought to respect and cherish them. A volume could not trace all their connections with private and public felicity. Let it simply be asked. Where is the security for property, for reputation, for life, if a sense of religious obligation desert the oaths which are the instruments of investigation in courts of justice? And let us with caution indulge the supposition that *morality* can be maintained *without religion*. Whatever may be conceded to the influence of refined education on minds of peculiar structure, reason and experience both forbid us to expect that national morality can prevail in exclusion of religious principles." How noble, how elevated, how just these parting words.

Washington was an enlightened Christian patriot, as well as a great general and a wise statesman. The oracles which he consulted in all his perils, and in the perils of his country, were the oracles of God.[29] No one of the fathers of the Revolution knew better than he did that religion rests upon the Bible as its main pillar, and that as a knowledge and belief of the Bible are essential to true religion, so they are to private and public morality. I can not doubt, says the venerable President of Amherst College, that could the greatest among the great men of his day add a codicil to his invaluable legacy, it would be, "Teach your children early to read and love the Bible.

Teach them to read it in your families; teach them in your schools; teach them everywhere, that the first moral lesson indelibly enstamped upon their hearts may be to 'fear God and keep his commandments.' 'The fear of the Lord, that is wisdom; and to depart from evil is understanding.'"

How few are aware of what the Bible has done for mankind, and still less of what it is destined to accomplish. "Quench its light, and you blot out the brightest luminary from these lower heavens. You bring back 'chaos and old night' to reign over the earth, and leave man, with all his immortal energies and aspirations, to 'wander in the blackness of darkness forever.' It was by constantly reading it that our Puritan fathers imbibed that unconquerable love of civil and religious liberty which sustained them through all the 'perils of the sea and perils of the wilderness.' It was from the Bible they drew those free and admired principles of civil government that were so much in advance of the age in which they lived. It was this book by which they 'resolved to go till they could find some better rule.'"

The Bible has built all our churches, and colleges, and school-houses; it has built our hospitals and retreats for the insane, the deaf, and the blind; it has built the House of Refuge, the Sailors' Home, and the Home for the Friendless. To it we are indebted for our homes, for our property, and for all the safeguards of our domestic relations and happiness. It is under its broad shield that we lie down in safety, without bolts or bars to protect us. It has given us our free constitutions of civil government, and with them all the statutes and ordinances of a great and independent people, whose territory extends from the Atlantic to the Pacific. It is the industry, sobriety, and enterprise, which nothing but the Bible could ever inspire and sustain, that have dug our canals, and built our thousand factories, and "clothed the hills with flocks, and covered over the valleys with corn;" that have laid down our railways and established telegraph lines, bringing the East into the neighborhood of the West, and enabling the North to hold converse with the South. The Bible has directly and indirectly done all this for us, and infinitely more. Let not, then, the book which has given to us sweet homes, and happy families, and systems of public instruction, and has thus constituted us a great and prosperous people—the book which diminishes our sorrows and multiplies our joys, and gives to those who obey its precepts a "hope big with immortality"—let not this book be excluded from the common schools of our country. In the name of patriotism, of philanthropy, and of our common Christianity, let me, in behalf of the millions of youth in our country who will otherwise remain ignorant of it, ask that, whatever else be excluded from our schools, there be retained in them this Book of books, the BIBLE.

CHAPTER VIII.

THE IMPORTANCE OF POPULAR EDUCATION.

Education, as the means of improving the mural and intellectual faculties, is, under all circumstances, a subject of the most imposing consideration. To rescue man from that state of degradation to which he is doomed unless redeemed by education; to unfold his physical, intellectual, and moral powers, and to fit him for those high destinies which his Creator has prepared for him, can not fail to excite the most ardent sensibility of the philosopher and philanthropist. A comparison of the savage that roams through the forest with the enlightened inhabitant of a civilized country would be a brief but impressive representation of the momentous importance of education.—*Report of School Commissioners, New York,* 1812.

He who has carefully perused the preceding chapters of this work is already aware that we regard the subject of popular education as one of paramount importance. The object of devoting a chapter to the special consideration of this subject at this time is, if possible, to remove from the mind any remaining doubts in relation to it. The reader will bear in mind that we regard education as having reference to the *whole man*—the body, the mind, and the heart; and that its object, and, when rightly directed, its effect, is to make him a complete creature after his kind. To his frame it should give vigor, activity, and beauty; to his intellect, power and thoughtfulness; and to his heart, virtue and felicity.

We shall be the better prepared to appreciate the importance and necessity of a judicious system of training and instruction if we consider that, in its absence, every individual will be educated by circumstances. Let it be borne in mind, then, that all the children in every community will be educated somewhere and somehow; and that it devolves upon citizens and parents to determine whether the children of the present generation shall receive their training in the *school-house* or in the *streets*; and if in the former, whether in good or poor schools.

In the discharge of my official duties in this state, I had occasion to visit two counties in 1846 in which there were no organized common schools.[30] They were not, however, without places of instruction, for in the shire town of each of those counties there were a billiard-room, bar-rooms, and bowling-alleys. I was forcibly impressed with the remark of an Indian chief residing in one of those counties. As he was passing along the streets one day, he discovered a second bowling-alley in process of erection. He paused, and, surveying it attentively, remarked to those at work upon it as follows: "You have here another long building going up rapidly; and," he added, "*is this the place where our children are to be educated?*" Such keen and well-merited rebuke rarely falls from human lips. Those two bowling-alleys, with their bars—indispensable appendages—were thronged from six o'clock in the morning until past midnight, six days in the week. They were, moreover, the very places where many of the youth of that village were receiving their education. And who were their teachers? Idlers, tipplers, gamblers, profane persons, Sabbath-breakers. Mark well this truth: *as is the teacher, so will be the school*. Those pupils will graduate, it may be, at our poor-houses, at our county jails, or at the state penitentiary. These debasing and corrupting appendages of civilization spent not all their influence upon the white man; and this is what gave pungency to the withering satire of the chief. They were at once working the ruin of the red man and of his pale neighbor.

The rudest nations or individuals can not be said to be wholly without education. Even the wildest savage is taught by his superiors not only the best mode of procuring food and shelter known to his race, but also the most adroit manner of defending himself and destroying his enemy. But we use the term in a higher, broader, and more capacious sense, as having reference to the whole man, and the whole duration of his being. A volume might be filled in stating and illustrating the advantages of education. We have only space to state and elucidate a few propositions. We remark, then, first, that

EDUCATION DISSIPATES THE EVILS OF IGNORANCE.

Ignorance is one principal cause of the want of virtue, and of the immoralities which abound in the world. Were we to take a survey of the moral state of the world as delineated in the history of nations, or as depicted by modern voyagers and travelers, we should find abundant illustration of the truth of this remark. We should find, in almost every instance, that ignorance of the character of the true God, and false conceptions of the nature of the worship and service he requires, have led, not only to the most obscene practices and immoral abominations, but to the perpetration of the most horrid cruelties.—Dr. Dick.

The evils of ignorance are not few in number nor small in magnitude. The whole history of the world justifies the statement that ignorant and uncultivated mind is prone to sensuality and cruelty. In what countries, let me ask, are the people most given to the lowest forms of animal gratification, and most regardless of the lives and happiness of others? Is it not in pagan lands, over which moral and intellectual darkness broods, and where men are vile without shame, and cruel without remorse? And if from pagan we pass to Christian countries, we shall find that those in which education is least prevalent are the very ones in which there is the most immorality, and the greatest indifference to the sufferings of animated and sentient beings. Spain—in which, until recently, there was but one newspaper printed, and in which only about one in thirty five of the people are instructed in schools—has a population about equal to that of England and Wales. Popular education in the latter countries, although much behind several of the other European states, is still greatly in advance of what it is in Spain, and there is an equally marked difference in the state of morals in the people of these countries. In England and Wales the whole number of convictions for murder in the year eighteen hundred and twenty-six was *thirteen*, and the number convicted for wounding, etc., with intent to kill, was *fourteen*; while in Spain, the number convicted during the same year was, for murder, *twelve hundred and thirty-three*! and for maiming with intent to kill, *seventeen hundred and seventy-three*! or a more than one hundred fold greater number than in the former countries. Facts like these speak volumes in favor of the elevating influences of popular education, while they show most conclusively the low and degraded condition to which people will sink in countries in which education is neglected.

Spain affords an apt illustration of the truth of the statement just made, that ignorant and uncultivated people are prone to sensuality and cruelty. Scenes of cruelty and blood constitute the favorite amusement of the Spaniards, their greatest delight being in bull-fights. An eye-witness describes the manner in which they conduct themselves during these appalling scenes in the following language. "The intense interest which they feel in this game is visible throughout, and often loudly expressed. An astounding shout always accompanies a critical moment. Whether it be the *bull* or *man* who is in danger, their joy is excessive; but their greatest sympathy is given to the feats of the BULL! If the picador receives the bull gallantly and forces him to retreat, or if the matadore courageously faces and wounds the bull, they applaud these acts of science and valor; but if the bull overthrow the horse and his rider, or if the matadore miss his aim and the bull seems ready to gore him, their delight knows no bounds. And it is certainly a fine spectacle to see thousands of spectators rise simultaneously, as they always do when the interest is intense. The greatest and most crowded theater in Europe presents nothing half so imposing as this. But how barbarous, how brutal is the whole exhibition! Could an English audience witness the scenes that are repeated every week in Madrid, a universal burst of '*shame*!' would follow the spectacle of a horse gored and bleeding, and actually treading upon his own entrails while he gallops round the arena. Even the appearance of the goaded bull could not be borne, panting, covered with wounds and blood, lacerated by darts, and yet brave and resolute to the end.

"The spectacle continued two hours and a half, and during that time there were seven bulls killed and six horses. When the last bull was dispatched, the people immediately rushed into the arena, and the carcass was dragged out amid the most deafening shouts."—*Spain in 1830,* vol. i., p. 191.

The same writer, after describing another fight, in which one bull had killed three horses and one man, and remained master of the arena, remarks, that "this was a time to observe the character of the people. When the unfortunate picador was killed, in place of a general exclamation of horror and loud expressions of pity, the universal cry was 'Que es bravo ese toro! ('Ah, the admirable bull!') The whole scene produced the most unbounded delight; the greater the horror, the greater was the shouting, and the more vehement the expressions of satisfaction. I did not perceive a single female avert her head or betray the slightest symptom of wounded feeling."—Vol. i., p. 195.

A correct system of public instruction develops a character widely different from that here brought to light. Instead of a love for vicious excitement, it cultivates a taste for simple and innocent pleasures, and gives to its subjects a command over their passions, and a disposition habitually to control them. It acquaints them with their duty, and enables them to find their highest pleasure in its discharge. They order their pursuits and choose their employments with reference to their own advantage, it is true; but still, a higher, and the controlling motive with them is, the promotion of the best good of the community in which they live. In short, their supreme desire is to co-operate with the beneficent Creator in advancing the permanent interests of the whole human family; in themselves obeying, and leading others to obey, all the laws which God has ordained for the government and well-being of his creatures.

Education, we said, dissipates the evils of ignorance. But in this country we hardly know what popular ignorance is. The most illiterate among us have derived many and inestimable advantages from our systems of public instruction. Occasionally persons are found among us who can neither read nor write. But even such persons insensibly imbibe ideas and moral influences from the more cultivated society about them which, in countries less favored, are denied to multitudes. Individuals who have had no early advantages for learning, who have never even entered a school-house, but have grown up amid a generally intelligent population, trained by the institutions established by our fathers, have in many instances acquired a mental character and influence which, but for these fortuitous circumstances, they could not have attained. The very excellence of our systems of education in many states of the Union, and the vital and pervading influence of the schools upon the public mind, reaching as they do, and improving even those that remain ignorant of letters, do not allow us to see the full extent of our obligation to them. This remark applies to all civilized countries where any systems of general education are adopted, but perhaps not to so great an extent in any other country as in our own.

The evils which flow from ignorance are deplorable enough in the case of individuals, although, as we have seen, the disastrous consequences are limited in the case of those who live surrounded by an intelligent community. But the general ignorance of large numbers and entire classes of men, unreached by the elevating influence of the educated, acting under the unchastened stimulus of the passions, and excited by the various causes of discontent which are constantly occurring in the progress of human affairs, is not unfrequently productive of scenes, the contemplation of which makes humanity shudder. The following extract from a foreign journal affords a pertinent illustration of the evils which flow from popular ignorance. It relates to the outrages committed by the peasantry in a part of Hungary in consequence of the ravages of the cholera in that region.

"The suspicion that the cholera was caused by poisoning the wells was universal among the peasantry of the counties of Zips and Zemplin, and every one was fully convinced of its truth. The first commotion arose in Klucknow, where, it is said, some peasants died in consequence of taking the preservatives; whether by an immoderate use of medicine, or whether they thought they were to take chloride of lime internally, is not known. This story, with a sudden and violent breaking out of the cholera at Klucknow, led the peasants to a notion of the poisoning of the wells, which spread like lightning. In the sequel, in the attack of the estate of Count Czaki, a servant of the chief bailiff was on the point of being murdered, when, to save his life, he offered to disclose something important. He said that he received from his master two pounds of poisonous powder, with orders to throw it into the wells, and, with an ax over his head, took oath publicly, in the church, to the truth of his statement. These statements, and the fact that the peasants, when they forcibly entered the houses of the landowners, every where found chloride of lime, which they took for the poisonous powder, confirmed their suspicions, and drove the people to madness. In this state of excitement, they committed the most appalling excesses. Thus, for instance, when a detachment of thirty soldiers, headed by an ensign, attempted to restore order in Klucknow, the peasants, who were ten times their number, fell upon them; the soldiers were released, but the ensign was bound, tortured with scissors and knives, then beheaded, and his head fixed on a pike as a trophy. A civil officer in company with the military was drowned, his carriage broken, and, chloride of lime being found in the carriage, one of the inmates was compelled to eat it till he vomited blood, which again confirmed the notion of poison. On the attack of the house of the lord at Klucknow, the countess saved her life by piteous entreaties: but the chief bailiff, in whose house chloride of lime was unhappily found, was killed, together with his son, a little daughter, a clerk, a maid, and two students who boarded with him. So the bands went from village to village; wherever a nobleman or a physician was found, death was his lot; and in a short time it was known that the high constable of the county of Zemplin, and several counts, nobles, and parish priests, had been murdered. A clergyman was hanged because he refused to take an oath that he had thrown poison into a well; the eyes of a countess were put out, and innocent children cut to pieces. Count Czaki, having first ascertained that his family was safe, fled from his estate at the risk of his life; but he was stopped at Kirtchtrauf, pelted with stones, and wounded all over, torn from his horse, and only saved by a worthy merchant who fell on him, crying, 'Now I have got the rascal.' He drew the count into a neighboring convent, where his wounds were dressed, and a refuge afforded him. His secretary was struck from his horse with an ax, but saved in a similar manner, and in the evening conveyed with his master to Leutschau."[31]

A little knowledge on the part of the peasantry would have prevented these horrible scenes. Had they learned even the elements of physiology and chemistry, they would have known that cleanliness is essential to health at all times, and that during the prevalence of a malignant epidemic it is doubly needful. They would have known, also, that chloride of lime is not a medicine to be taken internally, but that it is very useful for disinfecting offensive apartments, and that its tendency, when properly used, would be to counteract the cause of the disease which they so much dreaded.

Among all nations, and in all ages of the world, ignorance has not only debarred mankind from many exquisite and sublime enjoyments, but has created innumerable unfounded alarms, which greatly increase the sum of human misery. In the early ages of the world, a total eclipse of the sun or of the moon was regarded with the utmost consternation, as if some unusual catastrophe had been about to befall the universe. Believing that the moon in an eclipse was sickening or dying, through the influence of enchanters, the trembling spectators had recourse to the ringing of bells, the sounding of trumpets, the beating of brazen vessels, and to loud and horrid exclamations, in order to break the enchantment, and to drown the muttering of witches, that the moon might not hear them. Nor are such foolish opinions and customs yet banished from the world.

Comets, too, with their blazing tails, were long regarded, and still are by many, as harbingers of divine vengeance, presaging famines and inundations, or the downfall of princes and the destruction of empires. The northern lights have been frequently gazed at with similar apprehensions, whole provinces having been thrown into consternation by the fantastic coruscations of these lambent meteors. Some pretend to see in these harmless lights armies mixing in fierce encounter and fields streaming with blood, while others behold states overthrown, earthquakes, inundations, pestilences, and the most dreadful calamities. Because some one or other of these calamities formerly happened soon after the appearance of a comet or the blaze of an aurora, therefore they are considered either as the causes or the prognostics of such events.

Popular ignorance has given rise to the practice of *judicial astrology*; an art which, with all its foolish notions so fatal to the peace of mankind, has been practiced in every period of time. Under a belief that the characters and the fates of men are dependent on the various aspects of the stars and conjunctions of the planets, the most unfounded apprehensions, as well as the most delusive hopes, have been excited by the professors of this fallacious science. Such impositions on the credulity of mankind are founded on the grossest absurdity and the most palpable ignorance of the nature of things; still, in the midst of the light of science which the present century has shed upon the world, the astrologer meets with a rich support[32] even in the metropolis of Great Britain; and soothsayers, if not astrologers, get great gain by their craft in various portions of the United States. The extensive annual sale of hundreds of thousands of copies of almanacs that abound in astrological predictions in the United States and in Great Britain, and the extent to which they are consulted, affords a striking proof of the belief which is still attached to the doctrines of this fallacious science, and of the ignorance and credulity from which such a belief proceeds.

Shooting stars, fiery meteors, lunar rainbows, and other atmospherical phenomena, have likewise been considered by some as ominous of impending calamities, but they are regarded in a very different light by scientific observers. The most sublime phenomenon of shooting stars of which the world has furnished any record was witnessed throughout the United States on the morning of the 13th of November, 1833. This astonishing exhibition covered no inconsiderable portion of the earth's surface. The first appearance was every where that of fire-works of the most imposing grandeur, covering the entire vault of heaven with myriads of fire-balls resembling sky-rockets; but the most brilliant sky-rockets and fire-works of art bear less relation to the splendors of this celestial exhibition than the twinkling of the most tiny star to the broad glare of the noonday sun. Their coruscations were bright, gleaming, and incessant, and they fell thick as the flakes in the early snows of December. The whole heavens seemed in motion, and suggested to some the awful grandeur of the image employed in the Apocalypse upon the opening of the sixth seal, when "the stars of heaven fell unto the earth, even as a fig-tree casteth her untimely figs when she is shaken of a mighty wind."

While these scenes of grandeur were viewed with unspeakable delight by enlightened scientific observers, the ignorant and superstitious were overpowered with horror and dismay. The description which a gentleman of South Carolina gave of the effect produced by this phenomenon upon his ignorant blacks will apply well to many hardly better informed white persons. "I was suddenly awakened," said he, "by the most distressing cries that ever fell upon my ears. Shrieks of horror and cries of mercy I could hear from most of the negroes of three plantations, amounting in all to about six or eight hundred. While earnestly listening for the cause, I heard a faint voice near the door calling my name: I arose, and, taking my sword, stood at the door. At this moment I heard the same voice still beseeching me to rise and saying, 'O! my God, the world is on fire!' I then opened the door, and it is difficult to say which excited me most, the awfulness of the scene or the distressed cries of the negroes. Upward of one hundred lay prostrate on the ground, some speechless, and some with the bitterest cries, but most with their hands raised, imploring God to save the world and them. The scene was truly awful, for never did rain fall much thicker than the meteors fell toward the earth; east, west, north, and south, it was the same."

Those harmless meteors, the *ignes fatui*, which hover above moist and fenny places in the night-time, emitting a glimmering light, have been regarded by the ignorant as malicious spirits endeavoring to deceive the bewildered traveler and lead him to destruction. The plaintive note of the mourning dove, the ticking noise of the little insect called the death-watch, the howling of a dog in the night-time, the meeting of a bitch with whelps, or a snake lying in the road, the breaking of a looking-glass, and even the falling of salt from the table, and the curling of a fiber of wick in a burning candle, together with many other equally harmless incidents, have been regarded with apprehensions of terror, being considered as unfailing signs of impending disasters or of approaching death.

Dr. Dick remarks, that in the Highlands of Scotland—and it should be borne in mind that the Scotch are, as a nation, better instructed, and more moral and religious in their habits, than any other people in Europe—the motions and appearances of the clouds were, not long ago, considered ominous of disastrous events. On the evening before new year's day, if a black cloud appeared in any part of the horizon, it was thought to prognosticate a plague, a famine, or the death of some great man in that part of the country over which it seemed to hang; and in order to ascertain the place threatened by the omen, the motions of the clouds were often watched through the whole night. In the same country, the inhabitants regard certain days as *unlucky*, or ominous of bad fortune. The day of the week on which the third of May falls is deemed unlucky throughout the year.

With a very slight change, a part of this description would apply well to our own country, even up to the present time. How many thousands of days are lost annually in the United States in consequence of superstitious fears in relation to setting out upon a journey, entering upon a new pursuit of any kind, or even beginning to plant or plow on Friday, the unlucky day of the Americans. How many persons have had misfortunes attend them all their lives because they were born, or christened, or married on Friday! How many houses have been burned because they were begun, raised, or moved into on Friday! How many steamboats and vessels have been burned or wrecked because they were launched or sailed on Friday! And yet, strange as it may seem, this is the very day on which Columbus set sail on a voyage that resulted in the discovery of the New World.

Many people, and in some instances whole communities, always commence plowing, sowing, and reaping on Tuesday, though by this rule the most favorable weather for these purposes is frequently lost. Others, again, will not, on any account, perform certain kinds of labor on Friday. The age of the moon is also much attended to in many parts of the world. Among the vulgar Highlanders, an opinion prevails, that if a house takes fire while the moon is in the decrease, the family will from that time decline in its circumstances and sink into poverty. In this country, equally unfounded and ridiculous opinions are entertained. Passing by the more commonly received opinions that if swine are killed in the old of the moon, the pork will shrink in the pot; that seed sown at this time will be less likely to do well, etc., etc., I will mention one or two instances of opinions which, although equally well founded, are less commonly received, and which may therefore more forcibly impress the popular mind. A few years ago, I spent some months in a neighboring state, in a community where the belief was commonly entertained that shingles should not be laid nor stakes driven in the old of the moon, because the former would be more likely to warp, and the latter to be thrown by the frost. The same and kindred opinions are extensively held in various portions of the United States.

These are a few, and but a very few, of the superstitious notions and vain fears by which the great majority of the human race, in every age and country, have been enslaved, as he who will take the pains to peruse Dr. Dick's admirable treatise on the improvement of society by the diffusion of knowledge can not fail to be convinced. That such absurd notions should ever have prevailed is a most grating and humiliating thought, when we consider the noble faculties with which man is endowed. That they still prevail to a great extent, even in our own country, is a striking proof that as yet we are, as a people, but just emerging from the gloom of intellectual darkness. The prevalence of such opinions is to be regretted, not only on account of the groundless alarms they create, but chiefly on account of the false ideas they inspire with regard to the nature of the Supreme Ruler of the universe, and of his arrangements in the government of the world. He whose mind is enlightened with true science perceives throughout all nature the most striking evidences of benevolent design, and rejoices in the benignity of the Great Parent of the universe, discovering nothing in the arrangements of the Creator, in any department of his works, which has a direct tendency to produce pain to any intelligent or sensitive being. The superstitious man, on the contrary, contemplates the sky, the air, the waters, and the earth as filled with malicious beings, ever ready to haunt him with terror or to plot his destruction. The former contemplates the Deity directing the movements of the material world by fixed and invariable laws, which none but himself can counteract or suspend. The latter views these movements as continually liable to be controlled by capricious and malignant beings to gratify the most trivial passions. How very different, of course, must be their conceptions and feelings respecting the attributes and government of the Supreme Being! While the one views him as the infinitely wise and benevolent Father, whose paternal care and goodness inspire confidence and affection, the other must regard him, in a certain degree, as a capricious being, and offer up his adorations under the influence of fear.

These and like notions have also an evident tendency to habituate the mind to false principles and processes of reasoning which unfit it for legitimate conclusions in its researches after truth. They manifestly chain down the understanding, and unfit it for the appreciation of those noble and enlarged views which revelation and modern science exhibit of the order, extent, and economy of the universe. It is lamentable to reflect that so many thousands of beings endowed with the faculty of reason, who can not by any means be persuaded of the motion of the earth, and the distances and magnitudes of the heavenly bodies, should swallow, without the least hesitation, opinions ten thousand times more improbable. Notwithstanding the mathematical certainty of the truth of the Copernican system of astronomy, I have never yet become extensively acquainted with any community in which I have not found many persons professing a respectable degree of intelligence, and even official members of orthodox churches, who entirely discredit its sublime teachings; and yet some of these very persons find little difficulty in believing that an old woman can transform herself into a hare, and wing her way through the air on a broomstick. What contracted notions such persons must have of the almightiness of the Deity, and of the infinite depth of meaning of the following and like passages of Scripture: The heavens declare the glory of God, and the firmament showeth his handy work. Day unto day uttereth speech, and night unto night showeth knowledge.—*Ps.* xix., 1-2.

It has been already remarked, that the whole history of the world justifies the statement that ignorant and uncultivated mind is prone to sensuality and cruelty. Spain and Hungary were referred to in illustration. We are now prepared to remark, what is worse still, that where such superstitious notions as we have been considering are held, even by persons who are somewhat educated, they almost invariably lead to the perpetration of deeds of cruelty and injustice. Many of the barbarities committed in pagan countries, both in their religious worship and their civil polity, and most of the cruelties inflicted on the victims of the Romish Inquisition, have flowed from this source.[33] Nor are the annals of Great Britain and the United States deficient in examples of this kind. About the commencement of the last century, the belief in witchcraft, which was almost universal throughout Christendom, was held in both of these countries. The laws of England, which admitted its existence and punished it with death, were adopted by the Puritans of New England, and in less than twenty years from the founding of the colony, one individual was tried and executed for the supposed crime. Half a century later the delusion broke out in Salem. A minister, whose daughter and niece were subject to convulsions accompanied by extraordinary symptoms, supposing they were bewitched, cast his suspicions on an Indian woman who lived in the house, and who was whipped until she confessed herself a witch; and the truth of the confession, although obtained in this way, was not doubted. During the same year more than fifty persons were terrified into the confession of witchcraft, twenty of whom were put to death. Neither age, sex, nor station afforded any safeguard against a charge for this supposed crime. Women and children not only were its victims, but magistrates were condemned, and a clergyman of the highest respectability was among the executed. So late as 1722 a woman was burned for witchcraft in Scotland, which was among the last executions in that country.

It appears that these superstitious notions, so far from being innocent and harmless speculations, lead to the most deplorable results; they ought, therefore, to be undermined and thoroughly eradicated by all persons who wish to promote the happiness and well-being of general society. This duty is especially incumbent upon parents and teachers, and can be effected only by rendering correct early education universal. Ignorance of the laws and economy of nature is the one great source of these absurd opinions. They have not only no foundation in nature or experience, but are directly opposed to both. In proportion, then, as we advance in our researches into

Nature's economy and laws, shall we perceive their futility and absurdity. As in other cases, take away the cause, and the effect will be removed.

Education will dissipate all these evils. It is true that an acquaintance with a number of dead languages, with Roman and Grecian antiquities, with the subtleties of metaphysics, with pagan mythology, and with politics and poetry, may coexist with these superstitions, as was true in the case of the late Dr. Samuel Johnson, who believed in ghosts and in the *second sight*. However important in other respects these departments of an extensive and varied education may be, they do not form an effectual barrier against the admission of superstitious opinions. In order to do this, the mind must be directed to the study of the material universe, to contemplate the various appearances it presents, and to mark well the uniform results of those invariable laws by which it is governed. In particular, the attention should be directed to those discoveries which have been made by philosophers in the different departments of nature and art during the last two centuries. For this purpose, the study of natural history, as recording the various facts respecting the atmosphere, the waters, the earth, and animated beings, combined with the study of natural philosophy and astronomy, as explaining the causes of the phenomena of nature, will have a happy tendency to eradicate from the mind superstitious and false notions, and at the same time will present to view objects of delightful contemplation. Let a person be once thoroughly convinced that nature is uniform in her operations, and governed by regular laws impressed by an all-wise and benevolent Being, and he will soon be inspired with confidence, and will not easily be alarmed at any occasional phenomena which at first sight might appear as exceptions to the general rule.

Let persons be taught, for example, that eclipses are occasioned merely by the shadow of one opaque body falling upon another; that they are the necessary result of the inclination of the moon's orbit to that of the earth; that, if these orbits were in the same plane, there would be an eclipse of the sun and of the moon every month, the former occurring at the change, and the latter at the full of the moon; that the times when they do actually take place depend on the new or full moon happening at or near the points of intersection of the orbits of the earth and moon, and that other planets which have moons experience eclipses of a similar nature. Let them also be taught that the *comets* are regular bodies belonging to our system, which finish their revolutions and appear and disappear in stated periods of time; that the northern lights, though seldom seen in southern climes, are frequent in the regions of the North, and supply the inhabitants with light in the absence of the sun, and have probably a relation to the magnetic and electric fluids; that the *ignes fatui* are harmless lights, formed by the ignition of a certain species of gas produced in the soils above which they hover; and that the notes of the death-watch, so far from being presages of death, are ascertained to be the notes of *love* and presages of hymeneal intercourse among these little insects.

Let rational information of this kind be imparted to people generally, and they will learn to contemplate nature with tranquillity and composure. A more beneficial effect than this will at the same time be produced, for those very objects which were formerly beheld with alarm will now be converted into sources of enjoyment, and be contemplated with emotions of delight.

To remove the groundless apprehensions which arise from the fear of invisible and incorporeal beings, let persons be instructed in the various optical illusions to which we are subject, arising from the intervention of fogs, and the indistinctness of vision in the night-time, which makes us frequently mistake a bush that is near us for a large tree at a distance, and let them be taught that under the influence of these illusions a timid imagination will transform the indistinct image of a cow or a horse into a terrific phantom of a monstrous size. Let them also be taught, by a selection of well-authenticated facts, the powerful influence of the imagination in creating ideal forms, especially when under the dominion of fear; the effects produced by the workings of conscience when harassed by guilt; let them be taught the effects produced by lively dreams, by strong doses of opium, by drunkenness, hysteric passions, madness, and other disorders that affect the mind. Let the experiments of optics, and the striking phenomena produced by electricity, galvanism, magnetism, and the different gases, be exhibited to their view, together with details of the results which have been produced by various mechanical contrivances. In fine, let their attention be directed to the foolish, whimsical, and extravagant notions attributed to apparitions, and to their inconsistency with the wise and benevolent arrangements of the Governor of the universe.

There is no rational foundation for entertaining any doubts but that, could such instructions as I have suggested be universally given, the effect would be the banishment of superstitions of the nature contemplated from among mankind; *for they have uniformly produced this effect on every mind which has been thus enlightened.* Where is the man to be found whose mind is enlightened by the doctrines and discoveries of modern science, and who yet remains the slave of superstitious notions and vain fears? Of all the philosophers of America and Europe, is there one who is alarmed at an eclipse, at a comet, at an *ignis fatuus,* or at the notes of a death-watch? or who postpones his experiments on account of what is called an unlucky day? Who ever heard of a specter appearing to such a person, dragging him from bed at the dead hour of midnight, to wander through the forest, trembling with fear? Such beings appear only to the ignorant and illiterate, at least to those who are unacquainted with natural science, and we never hear of their appearing to any who did not previously believe in their existence. But should philosophers be freed from such terrific visions, if substantial knowledge has not the power of banishing them from the mind? Why should supernatural beings feel so shy in conversing with men of science? These would, indeed, be the fittest persons to whom they might impart their secrets, and communicate information respecting the invisible world; but it never falls to their lot to be favored with such visits. It may therefore be concluded that the diffusion of useful knowledge among mankind would infallibly dissipate those groundless fears which have banished much of happiness from the human family, and particularly among the lower orders of society.[34]

I might, perhaps, safely dismiss this subject, and proceed to the consideration of other topics; but, before doing so, it may be well to state that many of the views here presented, and all that come within the range of the subjects discussed by him, are fully sustained by Dr. Lardner, whose popular lectures on science and art have been so well received both in Europe and America. His publishers justly remark, that "probably no public lecturer ever continued, for the same length of time, to collect around him so numerous audiences." The author himself states, in the preface to his Lectures,[35] that from November, 1841, when he commenced his public lectures in the lecture-room of Clinton Hall, in New York, to the close of the year 1844, when he concluded his public labors in this country, he "visited every considerable city and town of the Union, from Boston to New Orleans, and from New York to St. Louis. Most of the principal cities were twice visited, and several courses were given in Boston, New York, and Philadelphia. Nor did the appetite for this species of intellectual entertainment appear to flag by repetition."

I can not forbear making a few quotations from the preface to the work under consideration, which are creditable to the comparative intelligence of the American people, and show the avidity with which they seek instruction and useful knowledge. Dr. Lardner observes, that "it was usual on each evening to deliver from two to four of the essays which compose the contents of the present volumes, and the duration of the entertainment was from two to three hours. On every occasion the most profound interest was evinced on the part of the audience, and the most unremitting and silent attention was given. These assemblies consisted of persons of both sexes, of every age, from the elder classes of pupils in the schools to their grandfathers and grandmothers. Frequently the audiences amounted to twelve hundred, and sometimes, as at the Philadelphia Museum, they exceeded two thousand. Nor was the manifestation of this interest confined, as might be imagined, to the northern Atlantic cities, where education is known to be attended to, and where, as in New England, the diffusion of useful knowledge is regarded as a paramount duty of the state. The same crowded assemblies were collected, for a long succession of nights, in the largest theaters of each of the southern and western cities; in the Charleston Theater; the Mobile Theater; the St. Charles Theater, New Orleans; the Vicksburg and Jackson Theaters, Mississippi; the St. Louis Theater, Missouri; and in the theaters of Cincinnati, Pittsburg, and other western and central cities.

"It can not be denied that such facts are symptomatic of a very remarkable condition of the public mind, more especially among a people who are admitted to be, more than any other nation, engrossed by money-getting and by the more material pursuits of life. The less pretension to eloquence and the attractive graces of oratory the lecturer can offer, the more surprising is the result, and the more creditable to the intelligence of the American people. It is certain that a similar intellectual entertainment, clogged, as it necessarily was, with a pecuniary condition of admission, would fail to attract an audience even in the most polished and enlightened cities of Europe."

While these statements are highly creditable to the American people, the lectures themselves contain paragraphs which show that the popular mind even in our own country is not sufficiently enlightened to eradicate the superstitions just considered.

THE MOON AND THE WEATHER.—Dr. Lardner, in a lecture on the moon, in answer to the question, Does the moon influence the weather? says,[36] It is asserted, first, that at the epochs of new and full moon, and at the quarters, there is generally a change of weather; and, secondly, that the phases of the moon, or, in other words, the relative position of the moon and sun in regard to the earth, is the cause of these changes. Now these and kindred opinions are very extensively held in this country. But the doctor refers to meteorological tables, constructed in various countries after the most extensive and careful observation, and the result is that no correspondence exists between the condition of the weather and the phases of the moon. He hence, after a full examination, comes to the conclusion that "*the condition of the weather as to change, or in any other respect, has, as a matter of fact, no correspondence whatever with the lunar phases.*"

In another lecture on the moon and the weather, the following decisive opinion is expressed: "From all that has been stated, it follows then, conclusively, that the popular notions concerning the influence of the lunar phases on the weather have no foundation in the theory, and no correspondence with observed facts."[37]

TIME FOR FELLING TIMBER.—In another lecture on lunar influences, Dr. Lardner observes that "there is an opinion generally entertained that timber should be felled only during the decline of the moon; for if it be cut down during its increase, it will not be of a good or durable quality. This impression prevails in various countries. It is acted upon in England, and is made the ground of legislation in France. *The forest laws of the latter country interdict the cutting of timber during the increase of the moon.* In the extensive forests of Germany, the same opinion is entertained and acted upon, with the most undoubting confidence in its truth. Sauer, a superintendent of some of these districts, assigns what he believes to be its physical cause. According to him, the increase of the moon causes the sap to ascend in the timber, and, on the other hand, the decrease of the moon causes it to descend. If the timber, therefore, be cut during the decrease of the moon, it will be cut in a dry state, the sap having retired, and the wood, therefore, will be compact, solid, and durable. But if it be cut during the increase of the moon, it will be felled with the sap in it, and will therefore be more spongy, more easily attacked by worms, more difficult to season, and more readily split and warped by changes of temperature.

"Admitting for a moment the reality of this supposition concerning the motion of the sap, it would follow that the proper time for felling the timber would be *the new moon*, that being the epoch at which the descent of the sap would have been made, and the ascent not yet commenced. But can there be imagined, in the whole range of natural science, a physical relation more extraordinary and unaccountable than this supposed correspondence between the movement of the sap and the phases of the moon? Assuredly theory affords not the slightest countenance to such a supposition; but let us inquire as to the fact whether it be really the case that the quality of timber depends upon the state of the moon at the time it is felled.

"M. Duhamel Monceau, a celebrated French agriculturist, has made direct and positive experiments for the purpose of testing this question, and has clearly and conclusively shown that the qualities of timber felled in different parts of the lunar month are the same. M. Duhamel felled a great many trees of the same age, growing from the same soil, and exposed to the same aspect, and never found any difference in the quality of the timber, when he compared those which were felled in the decline of the moon with those which were felled during its increase: in general, they have afforded timber of the same quality. He adds, however, that by a circumstance which was doubtless fortuitous, a slight difference was manifested in favor of timber which had been felled between the new and full moon, *contrary to popular opinion*."

SUPPOSED LUNAR INFLUENCES.—It is an aphorism received by all gardeners and agriculturists in Europe, remarks the same author, that vegetables, plants, and trees, which are expected to flourish and grow with vigor, should be planted, grafted, and pruned during the increase of the moon. This opinion, however, he thinks is altogether erroneous; for the experiments and observations of several French agriculturists have clearly established the fact that the increase or decrease of the moon has no appreciable influence on the phenomena of vegetation.

This erroneous prejudice prevails also on the American continent. A French author states that, in Brazil, cultivators plant during the *decline* of the moon all vegetables whose *roots* are used as food, and that, on the contrary, they plant during the *increasing* moon the sugar-cane, maize, rice, beans, etc., and those which bear the food upon their *stocks* and *branches*. Experiments, however, were made and reported by M. de Chauvalon, at Martinique, on vegetables of both kinds, planted at different times in the lunar month, and no appreciable difference in their qualities was discovered.

There are some traces of a principle adopted by the South American agronomes (farmers), according to which they treat the two classes of plants distinguished by the production of fruit on their roots or on their branches differently; but there are none in the European aphorisms. The directions of Pliny are still more specific: he prescribes the time of the full moon for sowing beans, and that of the new moon for lentils. "Truly," says M. Arago, "we have need of a robust faith to admit, without proof, that the moon, at the distance of two hundred and forty thousand miles, shall, in one position, act advantageously upon the vegetation of *beans*, and that in the opposite position, and at the same distance, she shall be propitious to *lentils*."

Dr. Lardner gives numerous and extended illustrations of the supposed influence of the moon on the growth of grain, on wine-making,[38] on the color of the complexion, on putrefaction, on the size of shell-fish, on the quantity of marrow in the bones of animals, on the number of births, on mental derangement, and other human maladies, etc., etc.

The influence on the phenomena of human maladies imputed to the moon is very ancient. Hippocrates had so strong a faith in the influence of celestial objects upon animated beings, that he expressly recommends no physician to be trusted who is ignorant of astronomy. Galen, following Hippocrates, maintained the same opinion, especially of the influence of the moon. The critical days, or *crises*, were the seventh, fourteenth, and twenty-first of the disease, corresponding to the intervals between the moon's principal phases. While the doctrine of alchemists prevailed, the human body was considered as a microcosm, or an epitome of the universe, the heart representing the sun, and the brain the moon. The planets had each his proper influence: Jupiter presided over the lungs, Saturn over the spleen, Venus over the kidneys, and Mercury over the organs of generation. The term *lunacy*, which still designates unsoundness of mind, is a relic of these grotesque notions, and is defined by Dr. Webster as "a species of insanity or madness, formerly supposed to be influenced by the moon, or periodical in the month." But even this term may now be said, in some degree, to be banished from the nomenclature of medicine; it has, however, taken refuge in that receptacle of all antiquated absurdities of phraseology—the law—lunatic being still the term for the subject who is incapable of managing his own affairs.

Sanctorius, whose name is celebrated in physics for the invention of the thermometer, held it as a principle that a healthy man gained two pounds' weight at the beginning of every lunar month, which he lost toward its completion. This opinion appears to have been founded on experiments made upon himself, and affords another instance of a fortuitous coincidence hastily generalized.

For all the progress that has been made in this country toward the removal from the popular mind of the numerous corrupting and debasing absurdities which have hitherto enslaved it, we are indebted to our enlightened and chastened systems of popular education; and to these, and to these only, may we confidently look for entire freedom from the thraldom.

EDUCATION INCREASES THE PRODUCTIVENESS OF LABOR.

Education has a power of ministering to our personal and material wants beyond all other agencies, whether excellence of climate, spontaneity of production, mineral resources, or mines of silver and gold. Every wise parent, every wise community, desiring the prosperity of its children even in the most worldly sense, will spare no pains in giving them a generous education.—HORACE MANN.

The best educated are always the best paid.—*Foreign Report.*

The desirableness of education is manifest, view it in what light we may, and whether as affecting individuals or communities. We have already seen that education, and that alone, will dissipate the evils of ignorance. We now propose to discuss the equally tenable proposition that education increases the productiveness of labor.

That knowledge is power has become a proverb. If it be asked why the labor of a man is more valuable than the same amount of physical effort put forth by a brute, the ready answer is, It is because man combines *intelligence* with his labor. A single yoke of oxen will do more in one day at plowing than forty men; yet the oxen may be had for fifty cents a day, while each of the men can earn a dollar. Physical exertion in this case, combined with ordinary skill, is eighty times more valuable than the same amount of brute force. The strength of the ox is of no account without some one to guide and apply it, while the power of man is guided by intelligence within.

In proportion as man's intelligence increases is his labor more valuable. A small compensation is the reward of mere physical power, while skill, combined with a moderate amount of strength, commands high wages. The labor of an ignorant man is scarcely more valuable than the same amount of brute force; but the services of an intelligent, skillful person are a hundred fold more productive. I will pause and illustrate, for I wish to have every person who arises from the perusal of these pages do so with the fullest conviction that mental culture is of the highest importance even in the ordinary departments of human industry. It is, indeed, hardly less important for the man of business, the farmer, or the mechanic, than for statesmen, legislators, and members of the so-called learned professions.

An intelligent farmer of my acquaintance having a piece of greensward to break up, and having three work-horses, determined to employ them all. He hence, possessing some mechanical skill, himself constructed a three-horse whipple-tree, by means of which he advantageously combined the strength of his horses. A less intelligent neighbor, pleased with the novel appearance of three horses working abreast, resolved to try the experiment himself. But not possessing the skill requisite to construct such a whipple-tree, he waited till his better-informed and more expert neighbor had got through with his, and then, borrowing it, tried the experiment with his own team. Early one morning, and full of expectation, aided by his two sons and a hired man, he harnessed his three horses to the plow. But one of them, for the first time, refused to draw. After several fruitless attempts to make the team work as first harnessed, the relative position of the horses was changed, when, lo! although *this* horse would draw as formerly, one of the others would not. By and by another change was made, and the third horse, in turn, refused to draw. The farmer could not understand it, nor his sons, nor his hired man. His three horses, for the first time, were each fickle in turn. And, what was most surprising, they would all work in either of two positions, but in the third none of them would draw. The honest farmer thought the age of witchcraft had not yet passed. At the conclusion of the forenoon he gave up the undertaking in disgust, and, carrying the whipple-tree home, told the story of his unsuccessful and vexatious experiment.

"And how did you harness the horses to the whipple-tree?" inquired the more intelligent farmer. "Why, one at the short end, and two at the long end, where there is the most room for them, to be sure!" was the frank reply.

The power at the short end, I need not say, should be twice that at the long end; whereas he had it reversed. One horse drew against two with a double purchase. He then would have to draw twice as much as both of them, or four times as much as one of them. The fickleness of the horses, then, instead of being the result of *witchcraft,* as he was inclined to believe, was chargeable solely to the *ignorance* of their hardly more intelligent master. A knowledge of the first principles of mechanics, or, in the absence of this, an ordinary degree of active, available common sense, would teach the proper use of such a whipple-tree. For want of this knowledge, the farmer suffered much chagrin, lost the time of four men, and did great injury to his team.

After mentioning this circumstance on a certain occasion, a gentleman present gave a parallel case, that occurred under his immediate observation. His neighbor had a yoke of oxen, one of which was large, strong, and beautiful. One day, as the neighbor was passing the residence of the gentleman, the latter remarked to him, "You have one very fine-looking ox." "Yes," replied the neighbor, with apparent satisfaction, "and a bonny fellow he is too. He can carry the *long end of the yoke, and grow fat under it*." Here, again, the weaker ox had to tax his strength doubly on account of the advantage which the ignorance of his kind master had unintentionally given to his superior yoke-fellow.

A farmer, or laborer of any kind, who possesses a knowledge of the merest elements of science, and is accustomed to think and investigate, can not only work more advantageously with his team, but he can do more work himself, and do it easier too, than his neighbor of superior physical strength, though of inferior mental capacity. The correctness of this statement may be satisfactorily proved and amply illustrated in loading timber, in moving buildings, in plowing, and in almost every kind of work done on a farm or among men, either on land or at sea. The ignorant man will spend more time in running after help to do a supposed difficult job, than it will require for a skillful one to do it alone. This is true in carpentry, and in all of the mechanic arts. Increase the practical and available education of the laborer, and you enable him to do more work, and better work too, than his less informed associate. The following is a striking illustration.

A practical teacher employed some mechanics to build him a barn. The day after the frame was raised, the teacher discovered that it needed to be turned a few inches upon its foundation, to range properly with other buildings. While the mechanics went in several directions to procure what they regarded as necessary help, the teacher, who was familiar with the various combinations of the lever, effected the work alone, and before their return! Other equally striking illustrations might be cited.

But education increases the productiveness of labor in a wider and more extended sense. By its omnipotent influence, man is enabled to lay the elements under tribute. The water and the wind, by its mysterious power, are made to propel his machinery for various purposes. The utmost skill of the untutored savage enables him to construct a rude canoe which two can carry upon their shoulders by land, which is barely capable of plying upon our rivers and coasting our inland seas, and which can be propelled only by human muscles, but the *educated man* erects a magnificent vessel, a floating palace, and, spreading his canvas to the breeze, aided by the mariner's compass, can traverse unknown seas in safety. To such perfection has he attained in the science and art of navigation, that he contends successfully with wind and tide, and makes headway against both, even when he depends upon the former for his motive power. Yes, education enables man even to tax the gentle breeze to urge a proud ship, heavily laden, up an inclined plane, thousands of miles, against the current of a mighty river.

I can not, perhaps, so satisfactorily establish the proposition which I am now endeavoring to elucidate, nor so well maintain the universality of its application, as by referring to the writings of the most indefatigable and successful laborer in the department of popular education of which our country can boast. I refer to the Hon. Horace Mann,[39] who, a few years ago, in his official capacity, opened a correspondence, and availed himself of all opportunities to hold personal interviews with many of the most practical, sagacious, and intelligent business men in our country, who for many years had had large numbers of persons in their employment. His object was to ascertain the difference in the productive ability, where natural capacities were equal, between the educated and the uneducated; between a man or a woman whose mind has been awakened to thought, and supplied with the rudiments of knowledge by a good common school education, and one whose faculties have never been developed, or aided in emerging from their original darkness and torpor by such a privilege. For this purpose he conferred and corresponded with manufacturers of all kinds —with machinists, engineers, rail-road contractors, officers in the army, etc.; classes which have means of determining the effects of education on individuals equal in their natural abilities that other classes do not possess.

A farmer hiring a laborer for one season who has received a good common school education, and the ensuing season hiring another who has not enjoyed this advantage, although he may be personally convinced of the relative value or profitableness of their services, yet he will rarely have any exact data or tests to refer to by which he can measure the superiority of the former over the latter. They do not work side by side, so that he can institute a comparison between the amounts of labor they perform. They may cultivate different fields, where the ease of tillage or the fertility of the soils may be different. They may rear crops under the influence of different seasons, so that he can not discriminate between what is referable to the bounty of nature and what to superiority in judgment or skill.

Similar difficulties exist in estimating the amount and value of female labor in the household. And as to the mechanic also—the carpenter, the mason, the blacksmith, the tool-maker of any kind—there are a thousand circumstances, which we call accidental, that mingle their influence in giving quality and durability to their work, and prevent us from making a precise estimate of the relative value of any two men's handicraft. Individual differences, too, in regard to a single article or a single days' work, may be too minute to be noticed or appreciated, while the aggregate of these differences at the end of a few years may make all the difference between a poor man and a rich one. No observing man can have failed to notice the difference between two workmen, one of whom, to use a proverbial expression, always "hits the nail on the head," while the other loses half his strength and destroys half his nails by the awkwardness of his blows; but perhaps few men have thought of the difference in the results of two such men's labor at the end of twenty years.

But when hundreds of men or women work side by side in the same factory, at the same machinery, in making the same fabrics, and, by a fixed rule of the establishment, labor the same number of hours each day; and when, also, the products of each operative can be counted in number, weighed by the pound, or measured by the yard or cubic foot, then it is perfectly practicable to determine, with arithmetical exactness, the productions of one individual and class as compared with those of another individual and class.

So, where there are different kinds of labor, some simple, others complicated, and of course requiring different degrees of intelligence and skill, it is easy to observe what class of persons rise from a lower to a higher grade of employment.

This, too, is not to be forgotten, that in a manufacturing or mechanical establishment, or among a set of hands engaged in filling up a valley or cutting down a hill, where scores of people are working together, the absurd and adventitious distinctions of society do not intrude. The capitalist and his agents are looking for the greatest amount of labor or the largest income in money from their investments, and they do not promote a dunce to a station where he will destroy raw material or slacken industry because of his name, or birth, or family connections. The obscurest and humblest person has a fair field for competition. That he proves himself capable of earning more money for his employers is a testimonial better than a diploma from all the colleges.

Now many of the most intelligent and valuable men in the community, in compliance with Mr. Mann's request, examined their books for a series of years, and ascertained both the quality and the amount of work performed by persons in their employment, and the result of the investigation is a most astonishing superiority in productive power on the part of the educated over the uneducated laborer. The hand is found to be another hand when guided by an intelligent mind. Processes are performed not only more rapidly, but better, when faculties which have been exercised in early life furnish their assistance. Individuals who, without the aid of knowledge, would have been condemned to perpetual inferiority of condition, and subjected to all the evils of want and poverty, rise to competence and independence by the uplifting power of education. In great establishments, and among large bodies of laboring men, where all services are rated according to their pecuniary value; where there are no extrinsic circumstances to bind a man down to a fixed position after he has shown a capacity to rise above it; where, indeed, men pass by each other, ascending or descending in their grades of labor just as easily and certainly as particles of water of different degrees of temperature glide by each other—under such circumstances it is found, as an almost invariable fact, other things being equal, that those who have been blessed with a good common school education rise to a higher and a higher point in the kinds of labor performed, and also in the rate of wages received, while the ignorant sink like dregs, and are always found at the bottom.

James K. Mills, Esq., of Boston, who has been connected with a house that has had for the last ten years the principal direction of cotton-mills, machine shops, and calico-printing works, in which are constantly employed about three thousand persons, and whose opinions of the effects of a common school education upon a manufacturing population are the result of personal observation and inquiries, and are confined to the testimony of the overseers and agents who are brought into immediate contact with the operatives, expresses the conviction that the rudiments of a common school education are essential to the attainment of skill and expertness as laborers, or to consideration and respect in the civil and social relations of life; that very few who have not enjoyed the advantages of a common school education ever rise above the lowest class of operatives, and that the labor of this class, when it is employed in manufacturing operations which require even a very moderate degree of manual or mental dexterity, is unproductive; that a large majority of the overseers and others employed in situations which require a high degree of skill in particular branches—which oftentimes require a good general knowledge of business, and *always* an unexceptionable moral character—have made their way up from the condition of common laborers, with no other advantage over a large proportion of those they have left behind than that derived from a better education.

A statement made from the books of one of the manufacturing companies will show the relative number of the two classes, and the earnings of each; and this mill, we are assured, may be taken as a fair index of all the others. The average number of operatives employed for the last three years is twelve hundred. Of this number there are forty-five unable to write their names, or about three and three fourths per cent. The average of women's wages, in the departments requiring the most skill, is two dollars and fifty cents per week, exclusive of board. The average wages of the lowest departments is one dollar and twenty-five cents per week.

Of the forty-five who are unable to write, twenty-nine, or about two thirds, are employed in the lowest department. The difference between the wages earned by the forty-five and the average wages of an equal number of the better-educated class is about twenty-seven per cent. in favor of the latter. The difference between the wages earned by twenty-nine of the lowest class and the same number in the higher is sixty-six per cent. Of seventeen persons filling the most responsible stations in the mills, ten have grown up in the establishment from common laborers or apprentices.

This statement does not include an importation of sixty-three persons from Manchester, in England, in 1839. Among these persons there was scarcely one who could read or write; and although a part of them had been accustomed to work in cotton-mills, yet, either from incapacity or idleness, they were unable to earn sufficient to pay for their subsistence, and at the expiration of a few weeks not more than half a dozen remained in the employment of the company.

In some of the print-works a large proportion of the operatives are foreigners. Those who are employed in the branches which require a considerable degree of skill are as well educated as our people in similar situations. But the common laborers, as a class, are without any education, and their average earnings are about two thirds only of those of *our* lowest classes, although the prices paid to each are the same for the same amount of work.

Among the men and boys employed in the machine shops, the want of education is quite rare. Mr. Mills does not know an instance of a person so employed who is unable to read and write; and many have a good common school education. To this, he thinks, may be attributed the fact that a large proportion of persons who fill the higher and more responsible situations come from this class of workmen. From these statements the reader will be able to form some estimate, in dollars and cents, at least, of the advantages of even a little education to the operative; and *there is not the least doubt*, says the same authority, that the *employer is equally benefited*. He has the security for his property that intelligence, good morals, and a just appreciation of the regulations of his establishment always afford. His machinery and mills, which constitute a large part of his capital, are in the hands of persons who, by their skill, are enabled to use them to their utmost capacity, and to prevent any unnecessary depreciation.

Each operative in a cotton-mill, according to the estimate of Mr. Mills, may be supposed to represent from one thousand to twelve hundred dollars of the capital invested in the mill and its machinery. It is only from the most diligent and economical use of this capital that the proprietor can expect a profit. A fraction less than one half of the cost of manufacturing common cotton goods when a mill is in full operation, is made up of charges which are permanent. If the product is reduced in the ratio of the capacity of the two classes of operatives mentioned in this statement, it will be seen that the cost will be increased in a compound ratio. Mr. Mills expresses the opinion "that the best cotton-mill in New England, with such operatives only as the forty-five mentioned above, who are unable to write their names, would never yield the proprietor a profit; that the machinery would be soon worn out, and he would be left, in a short time, with a population no better than that which is represented by the importation from England. I can not imagine any situation in life," he continues, "where the want of a common school education would be more severely felt, or be attended with worse consequences, than in manufacturing villages; nor, on the other hand, is there any where such advantages can be improved with greater benefit to all parties. There is more excitement and activity in the minds of people living in masses, and if this expends itself in any of the thousand vicious indulgences with which they are sure to be tempted, the road to destruction is traveled over with a speed exactly corresponding to the power employed."

H. Bartlett, Esq., of Lowell, who has been engaged ten years in manufacturing, and has had the constant charge of from four hundred to nine hundred persons during that time, has come in contact with a very great variety of character and disposition, and has seen mind applied to production in the mechanic and manufacturing arts possessing different degrees of intelligence, from gross ignorance to a high degree of cultivation, and he has no hesitation in affirming that he finds the best educated to be the most profitable help. *Even those females who merely tend machinery give a result somewhat in proportion to the advantages enjoyed in early life for education*, those who have a good common school education giving, as a class, invariably a better production than those brought up in ignorance.

In regard to the domestic and social habits of persons in his employ, the same gentleman adds, "I have never considered mere knowledge, valuable as it is to the laborer, as the only advantage derived from a good common school education. I have uniformly found the better educated, as a class, possessing a higher and better state of morals, more orderly and respectful in their deportment, and more ready to comply with the wholesome and necessary regulations of an establishment. And in times of agitation, on account of some change in regulations or wages, I have always looked to the most intelligent, best educated, and the most moral for support, and have seldom been disappointed; for, while they are the last to submit to imposition, they *reason*, and if your requirements are reasonable, they will generally acquiesce, and exert a salutary influence upon their associates. But the ignorant and uneducated I have generally found the most turbulent and troublesome, acting under the influence of excited passion and jealousy.

"The former appear to have an interest in sustaining good order, while the latter seem more reckless of consequences. And, to my mind, all this is perfectly natural. The better educated have more and stronger attachments binding them to the place where they are. They are generally neater in their persons, dress, and houses; surrounded with more comforts, with fewer of 'the ills flesh is heir to.' In short, I have found the educated, as a class, more cheerful and contented, devoting a portion of their leisure time to reading and intellectual pursuits, more with their families, and less in scenes of dissipation. The good effect of all this is seen in the more orderly and comfortable appearance of the whole household, but nowhere more strikingly than in the children. A mother who has a good common school education will rarely suffer her children to grow up in ignorance. As I have said, this class of persons are more quiet, more orderly, and, I may add, more regular in their attendance upon public worship, and more punctual in the performance of all their duties."

Mr. Bartlett thinks it would be very difficult, if not impossible, for a young man, who has not an education equal to a good common school education, to rise from grade to grade until he should obtain the berth of an overseer, and that, in making promotions, as a general thing, it would be unnecessary to make inquiry as to the education of the young men from whom you would select. Very seldom indeed, he says, would an uneducated young man rise to "*a better place and better pay*. Young men who expect to resort to manufacturing establishments for employment, can not prize too highly a good education. *It will give them standing among their associates, and be the means of promotion among their employers.*"

The final remark of this gentleman, in a lengthy letter, showing the advantages of education in a pecuniary, social, and moral point of view, is, that "*those who possess the greatest share in the stock of worldly goods are deeply interested in this subject, as one of mere insurance*; that the most effectual way of making insurance on their property would be *to contribute from it enough to sustain an efficient system of common school education, thereby educating the whole mass of mind, and constituting it a police more effectual than peace officers and prisons.*" By so doing he thinks they would bestow a benefaction upon those who, from the accident of birth or parentage, are subjected to the privations and temptations of poverty, and would do much to remove the prejudice and to strengthen the bands of union between the different and extreme portions of society. He very justly regards it a wise provision of Providence which connects so intimately, and, as he thinks, so indissolubly, the greatest good of the many with the highest interest of the few; or, in other words, which unites into one brotherhood all the members of the community, and in the existing partnership connects inseparably the interests of Labor and Capital.[40]

John Clark, Esq., of Lowell, who has had under his superintendence for eight years about fifteen hundred persons of both sexes, gives concurrent testimony. He has found, with very few exceptions, the best educated among his hands to be the most capable, intelligent, energetic, industrious, economical, and moral, and that they produce the best work, and the most of it, with the least injury to the machinery. They are, in short, in all respects the most useful, profitable, and the safest operatives; and as a class, they are more thrifty, and more apt to accumulate property for themselves. "I am very sure," he remarks, "that neither men of property nor society at large have any thing to fear from a more general diffusion of knowledge, nor from the extension and improvement of our system of common schools. On our pay-roll for the last month are borne the names of twelve hundred and twenty-nine female operatives, forty of whom receipted for their pay by 'making their mark.' Twenty-six of these have been employed in job work; that is, they are paid according to the quantity of work turned off from their machines. The average pay of these twenty-six falls eighteen and one half per cent. below the general average of those engaged in the same departments.

"Again: we have in our mills about one hundred and fifty females who have at some time been engaged in *teaching schools.* Many of them teach during the summer months, and work in the mills in winter. The average wages of these ex-teachers I find to be seventeen and three fourths per cent. *above the general average of our mills, and about forty per cent. above the twenty-six who can not write their names.* It may be said they are generally employed in the higher departments, where the pay is better. This is true; but this again may be, in most cases, fairly attributed to their better education, which brings us to the same result. If I had included in my calculations the remaining fourteen of the forty, who were mostly sweepers and scrubbers, and who are paid by the day, the contrast would have been still more striking; but, having no well-educated females in this department with whom to compare them, I have omitted them altogether. In arriving at the above results, I have considered the *net wages* merely, the price of board being in all cases the same. I do not consider these results as either extraordinary or surprising, but as a part only of the legitimate and proper fruits of a better cultivation, and fuller development of the intellectual and moral powers."

Mr. Mann gives the entire letters from which I have so freely drawn, and also introduces into his report extracts from a letter of Jonathan Crane, Esq., who has been for many years a large rail-road contractor, and has had several thousand men in his employment. The testimony of this gentleman is corroborative of that already presented. Testimony similar to the preceding might be introduced from the proprietors and superintendents of the principal manufacturing establishments in America not only, but from every part of the civilized world. Before concluding this chapter, I shall, for another purpose, refer to statements made by extensive manufacturers in England and Switzerland.

These are no more than a fair specimen of a mass of facts which Mr. Mann obtained from the most authentic sources. They seem to prove incontestably that education is not only a moral renovator, and a multiplier of intellectual power, but that it is also the most prolific parent of material riches. It has a right, therefore, not only to be included in the grand inventory of a nation's resources, but to be placed at the very head of that inventory. It is not only the most honest and honorable, but the surest means of amassing property. Considering education, then, as a producer of wealth, it follows that the more educated a people are, the more will they abound in all those conveniences, comforts, and satisfactions which money will buy; and, other things being equal, *the increase of competency and the decline of pauperism will be measurable on this scale.*

EDUCATION AND AGRICULTURE.—The healthful and praiseworthy employment of agriculture requires knowledge for its successful prosecution. In this department of industry we are in perpetual contact with the forces of nature. We are constantly dependent upon them for the pecuniary returns and profits of our investments, and hence the necessity of knowing what those forces are, and under what circumstances they will operate most efficiently, and will most bountifully reward our original outlay of money and time.

Our country yields a great variety of agricultural productions, and this brings into requisition all that chemical and experimental knowledge which pertains to the rotation of crops and the enrichment of soils. If rotation be disregarded, the repeated demands upon the same soil to produce the same crop will exhaust it of the elements on which that particular crop will best thrive. If the chemical ingredients and affinities of the soil are not understood, an attempt may be made to reenforce it by substances with which it is already surcharged, instead of renovating it with those of which it has been exhausted by previous growths. But for these arrangements and adaptations knowledge is the grand desideratum, and the addition of a new fact to a farmer's mind will often increase the amount of his harvests more than the addition of acres to his estate.

Why is it that, if we except Egypt, all the remaining territory of Africa, containing nearly ten millions of square miles, with a soil most of which is incomparably more fertile by nature, produces less for the sustenance of man and beast than England, whose territory is only fifty thousand square miles? In the latter country, knowledge has been a substitute for a genial climate and an exuberant soil; while in the former, it is hardly a figurative expression to say that all the maternal kindness of nature, powerful and benignant as she is, has been repulsed by the ignorance of her children. Doubtless industry as well as knowledge is indispensable to productiveness; but knowledge must precede industry, or the latter will work to so little effect as to become discouraged, and to relapse into the slothfulness of savage life. This is illustrated by the condition of the inhabitants of Lower California, as described by an intelligent friend of the author, who left this country a year ago. He says this is a "most beautiful country, with the finest climate in the world. But its inhabitants, who are principally Spaniards and Indians, are in a state of semi-barbarism, and consequently its resources are, to a certain extent, undeveloped. The land, which is generally level and of the richest quality, is divided into ranchos or plantations, the largest of which are twenty miles square, and feed twenty or thirty thousand head of wild cattle, with horses and mules in proportion. But these are all. The arts are in the lowest state imaginable. Their houses are mere pens, without pen floors; their plows are pointed logs; their yokes are straight sticks, which they tie to the horns of their oxen; and every implement of industry shows an equal want of ingenuity and enterprise. They are too indolent to raise much grain, though the soil will yield, I am told, eighty bushels of wheat to an acre; consequently, wheat is sold to the immigrants at three dollars per bushel, while the finest beef cattle in the world bring from eight to ten dollars per head. Butter, cheese, and even milk, you can not obtain at all, for they are too lazy to tame their cows. A few Americans, who own large ranchos, have American plows, and are doing better than the rest. Many ranchos have been abandoned, and their owners have gone to the mines. This state of things the energetic Anglo-Saxon will soon change. The immigration for the next few years will be immense, and the whole community will yield to American customs. The large ranchos will be cut up into farms, and their products will supply the wants of a dense population. Property will rapidly change hands, and it will be easy for the shrewd Yankee to reap the benefit of the change."

But, without further exposition, it may be remarked generally, that the spread of intelligence, through the instrumentality of good books, and the cultivation in our children of the faculties of observing, comparing, and reasoning, through the medium of good schools, would add millions to the agricultural products of nearly every state of the Union, without imposing upon the husbandman an additional hour of labor.

EDUCATION AND THE USEFUL ARTS.—For the successful prosecution among us of the manufacturing and mechanic arts, if not for their very existence, there must be not only the exactness of science, but also exactness or skill in the application of scientific principles throughout the whole processes, either of constructing machinery, or of transforming raw materials into finished fabrics. This ability to make exact and skillful applications of science to an unlimited variety of materials, and especially to the subtile but most energetic agencies of nature, is one of the latest attainments of the human mind. It is remarkable that astronomy, sculpture, painting, poetry, oratory, and even ethical philosophy, had made great progress thousands of years before the era of the manufacturing and mechanic arts. This era, indeed, has but just commenced; and already the abundance, and, what is of far greater importance, the *universality* of the personal, domestic, and social comforts it has created, constitute one of the most important epochs in the history of civilization.

The cultivation of these arts is conferring a thousand daily accommodations and pleasures upon the laborer in his cottage, which, only two or three centuries ago, were luxuries in the palace of the monarch. Through circumstances incident to the introduction of all economical improvements, there has hitherto been great inequality in the distribution of their advantages; but their general tendency is greatly to ameliorate the condition of the mass of mankind. It has been estimated that the products of machinery in Great Britain, with a population of eighteen millions, is equal to the labor of hundreds of millions of human hands. This vast gain is effected without the conquest or partitioning of the territory of any neighboring nation, and without rapine or the confiscation of property already accumulated by others. It is an absolute creation of wealth—that is, of those articles, commodities, and improvements which we appraise and set down as of a certain moneyed value alike in the inventory of a deceased man's estate and in the grand valuation of a nation's capital. These contributions to human welfare have been derived from knowledge; from knowing how to employ those natural agencies which from the beginning of the race had existed, but had lain dormant or run uselessly away. For mechanical purposes, what is wind, or water, or the force of steam worth, until the ingenuity of man comes in, and places the wind-wheel, the water-wheel, or the piston *between* these mighty agents and the work he wishes them to perform? But after the intervention of machinery, how powerful they become for all purposes of utility! In a word, these great improvements, which distinguish our age from all preceding ages, have been obtained from Nature by addressing her in the language of Science and Art, the only language she understands, yet one of such all-pervading efficacy that she never refuses to comply to the letter with all petitions for wealth or physical power, if they are preferred to her in that dialect.

Now it is easy to show, from reasoning, from history, and from experience, that an early awakening of the mind is a prerequisite to success in the useful arts. But it must be an awakening to thought, not to feeling merely. In the first place, a clearness of perception must be acquired, or the power of taking a correct mental transcript, copy, or image of whatever is seen This, however, though indispensable, is by no means sufficient.

The talent of improving upon the labors of others requires not only the capability of receiving an exact mental copy or imprint of all the objects of sense or reasoning; it also requires the power of reviving or reproducing at will all the impressions or ideas before obtained, and the power of changing their collocations, of re-arranging them into new forms, and of adding something to or removing something from the original perceptions, in order to make a more perfect plan or model. If a ship-wright, for instance, would improve upon all existing specimens of naval architecture, he would first examine as great a number of ships as possible; this done, he would revive the image which each had imprinted upon his mind, and, with all the fleets which he had inspected present to his imagination, he would compare each individual vessel with all others, make a selection of one part from one, and of another part from another, apply his own knowledge of the laws of moving and of resisting forces to all, and thus create, in his own mind, the complex idea or model of a ship more perfect than any of those he had seen.

Now every recitation in a school, if rightly conducted, is a step toward the attainment of this wonderful power. With a course of studies judiciously arranged and diligently pursued through the years of minority, all the great phenomena of external nature, and the most important productions in all the useful arts, together with the principles on which they are evolved or fashioned, would be successively brought before the understanding of the pupil. He would thus become familiar with the substances of the material world, and with their manifold properties and uses; and he would learn the laws, comparatively few, by which results infinitely diversified are produced. When such a student goes out into life, he carries, as it were, a plan or model of the world in his own mind. He can not, therefore, pass, either blindly or with the stupid gaze of the brute creation, by the great objects and processes of nature; but he has an intelligent discernment of their several existences and relations, and their adaptation to the uses of mankind. Neither can he fasten his eye upon any workmanship or contrivance of man without asking two questions: first, How is it? and, secondly, How can it be improved?

Hence it is that all the processes of nature and the contrivances of art are so many lessons or communications to an instructed man; but an uninstructed one walks in the midst of them like a blind man among colors, or a deaf man among sounds. The Romans carried their aqueducts from hill-top to hill-top, on lofty arches erected at immense expenditure of time and money. One idea—that is, a knowledge of the law of the equilibrium of fluids; a knowledge of the fact that water in a tube will rise to the level of the fountain—would have enabled a *single individual* to do with ease what, *without that knowledge,* it required the *wealth of an empire to accomplish.*

It is in ways similar to this—that is, by accomplishing greater results with less means; by creating products at once cheaper, better, and by more expeditious methods; and by doing a vast variety of things otherwise impossible—that the cultivation of mind may be truly said to yield the highest pecuniary requital.

Intelligence is the great money-maker, not by extortion, but by PRODUCTION. There are ten thousand things in every department of life which, if done in season, can be done in a minute, but which, if not seasonably done, will require hours, perhaps days or weeks for their performance. An awakened mind will see and seize the critical juncture; the perceptions of the sluggish one will come too late, if they come at all.

A general culture of the faculties, also, gives versatility of talent, so that, if the customary business of the laborer is superseded by improvements, he can readily betake himself to another kind of employment. But an uncultivated mind is like an automaton, which can do only the thing for which its wheels or springs were made. Brute force expends itself unproductively. It is ignorant of the manner in which Nature works, and hence it can not avail itself of her mighty agencies. Often, indeed, it attempts to oppose Nature. It throws itself across the track where her resistless car is moving. But knowledge enables its possessor to employ her agencies in his own service, and he thereby obtains an amount of power, without fee or reward, which thousands of slaves could not give.

Every man who consumes a single article in whose production or transportation the power of steam is used, has it delivered to him cheaper than he could otherwise have obtained it. Every man who can avail himself of this power in traveling, can perform the business of three days in one, and so far add two hundred per cent. to the length of his life as a business man. What innumerable millions has the invention of the cotton-gin, by Whitney, added, and will continue to add, to the wealth of the world! a part of which is already realized, but vastly the greater part of which is yet to be received, as each successive day draws for an installment which would exhaust the treasury of a nation. The instructed and talented man enters the rich domains of Nature not as an *intruder*, but, as it were, a PROPRIETOR, and makes her riches his own.

Why is it that, so far as the United States are concerned, four fifths of all the improvements, inventions, and discoveries in regard to machinery, to agricultural implements, to superior models in ship-building, and to the manufacture of those refined instruments on which accuracy in scientific observations depends, have originated in New England? I believe no adequate reason can be assigned but the early awakening and training of the power of thought in her children. Improvements, inventions, and discoveries have been made in other states of the Union to an extent commensurate with the progress they have made in perfecting their systems of public instruction, and these improvements will ever keep pace with the attentions which a people bestow upon their common schools.

Mr. Mann remarks that, in conversing with a gentleman who had possessed most extensive opportunities for acquaintance with men of different countries and of all degrees of intellectual development, he observed that he could employ a common immigrant or a slave, and, if he chose, could direct him to shovel a heap of sand from one spot to another, and then back into its former place, and so to and fro through the day; but, added he, neither love nor money would prevail on a New Englander to prosecute a piece of work of which he did not see the utility.

There is scarcely any kind of labor, however simple, pertaining to the farm, to the work-shop, or to domestic employments, and whether performed by male or female, which can be so well done without knowledge in the workman or domestic as with it. It is impossible for an overseer or employer at all times to supply mind to the laborer. In giving directions for the shortest series or train of operations, something will be omitted or misunderstood; and without intelligence in the workman, the omission or mistake will be repeated in the execution.

It is a fact of universal notoriety, that the manufacturing population of England, as a class, work for half, or less than half the wages of our own. The cost of machinery there, also, is about half as much as the cost of the same articles with us; while our capital, when loaned, produces nearly double the rate of English interest; yet against these grand adverse circumstances our manufacturers, with a small per centage of tariff, successfully compete with English capitalists in many branches of manufacturing business. No explanation can be given of this extraordinary fact which does not take into the account the difference of education between the operatives in the two countries.

One of our most careful and successful manufacturers remarks that, on substituting in one of his cotton-mills a better for a poorer educated class of operatives, he was enabled to add twelve or fifteen per cent. to the speed of his machinery, without any increase of damage or danger from the acceleration. How direct and demonstrative the bearing which facts like this have upon the wisdom of our laws respecting the education of children in manufacturing establishments.[41]

The number of females in the State of Massachusetts engaged in the various manufactures of cotton, straw-platting, etc., has been estimated at forty thousand, and the annual value of their labor at one hundred dollars each on an average, or four millions of dollars for the whole. From the facts stated in the letters of Messrs. Mills and Clark above cited, it appears there is a difference of not less than fifty per cent. between the earnings of the least educated and of the best educated operatives—between those who make their marks instead of writing their names, and those who have been acceptably employed in school-keeping. Now suppose the whole forty thousand females engaged in the various kinds of manufactures in that commonwealth to be degraded to the level of the lowest class, it would follow that their aggregate earnings would fall at once to two millions of dollars. But, on the other hand, suppose them all to be elevated by mental cultivation to the rank of the highest, and their earnings would rise to the sum of six millions of dollars annually.

There can be no doubt but that education, or the want of it, affects the pecuniary value of female labor in the ordinary domestic employments of the sex not less than in manufactures. If, then, the females of the thirty states of the Union be estimated at eight millions—and the number sustaining the relations of daughters, wives, and mothers must exceed the supposition—the effect of giving them all an education equal to the best would at once raise their earnings, annually, two hundred millions of dollars! But this is the lowest sense in which we can estimate the value of education, even in the sterner sex. This sum, vast as it may seem, is as dross to gold when compared with the refining and elevating influence which eight millions of educated females would exert upon the domestic and social institutions of our country, in uplifting our national character and improving the condition of the race.

Not more than thirty years ago it was uncommon for a glazier's apprentice, even after having served an apprenticeship of seven years, to be able to cut glass with a diamond without spending much time and destroying much of the glass upon which he worked. But the invention of a simple tool has put it into the power of the merest tyro in the trade to cut glass with facility, and without loss. A man who had a *mind*, as well as *fingers*, observed that there was one direction in which the diamond was almost incapable of abrasion or wearing by use. The tool not only steadies the diamond, but fastens it in that direction.

The operation of tanning leather consists in exposing a hide to the action of a chemical ingredient, called tannin, for a length of time sufficient to allow every particle of the hide to become saturated with the solution. In making the best leather, the hides used to lay in the pit for six, twelve, or eighteen months, and sometimes for two years, the tanner being obliged to wait all this time for a return of his capital. By the modern process, the hides are placed in a close pit, with a solution of the tannin matter, and the air being exhausted, the liquid penetrates through every pore and fiber of the skin, and the whole process is completed in a few days.

The bleaching of cloth, which used to be effected in the open air, and in exposed situations where temptation to theft was offered, and in England hundreds and probably thousands of men have yielded and forfeited their lives, is now performed in an unexposed situation, and in a manner so expeditious, that cloth is bleached as much more rapidly than it formerly was as hides are tanned.

It is stated by Lord Brougham, in his beautiful Discourse on the Advantages of Science, that the inventor of the new mode of refining sugar made more money in a shorter time, and with less risk and trouble, than perhaps was ever realized from any previous invention.

Intelligence also *prevents loss* as well as *makes profits*. How much time and money have been squandered in repeated attempts to invent machinery, after a principle had been once tested and had failed through some defect inherent and natural, and therefore insuperable! Within thirty years not less than five patents have been taken out, in England and the United States, for a certain construction of paddle-wheels for a steamboat, which construction was tested and condemned as early as 1810.[42] A case once came within my own knowledge, says Mr. Mann, of a person who spent a fortune in mining for coal, when a work on geology, which would have cost but a dollar, and might have been read in a week, would have informed him that the stratum where he began to excavate belonged to a formation lower down in the natural series than coal ever is, or, according to the constitution of things, ever can be found. He therefore worked into a stratum which must have been formed before a particle of coal, or even a tree, or a vegetable existed on the planet. Numerous similar and equally striking illustrations might be cited, but this is not necessary.

These are a few specimens, on familiar subjects, taken almost at random, for the purpose of showing the inherent superiority of any association or community, whether small or great, where *mind* is a member of the partnership. What is true of the above-mentioned cases is true of the whole circle of those arts by which human life is sustained and human existence comforted, elevated, and embellished. Mind has been the improver, for matter can not improve itself, and improvement has advanced in proportion to the number and culture of the minds excited to activity and applied to the work.

Similar advancements have been effected throughout the whole compass of human labor and research; in the arts of Transportation and Locomotion, from the employment of the sheep and the goat as beasts of burden, to the steam-engine and the rail-road car; in the art of Navigation, from the canoe clinging timidly to the shore, to steam-ships which boldly traverse the ocean; in Hydraulics, from carrying water by hand in a vessel or in horizontal aqueducts, to those vast conduits which supply the demands of a city, and to steam fire-engines which throw a column of water to the top of the loftiest buildings; in the arts of Spinning and Rope-making, from the hand distaff to the spinning-frame, and to the machine which makes cordage or cables of any length, in a space ten feet square; in Horology or Time-keeping, from the sun-dial and the water-clock to the watch, and to the chronometer, by which the mariner is assisted in measuring his longitude, and in saving property and life; in the extraction, forging, and tempering of Iron and other ores having malleability to be wrought into all forms and used for all purposes, and supplying, instead of the stone hatchet or the fish-shell of the savage, an almost infinite variety of instruments, which have sharpness for cutting or solidity for striking; in the art of Vitrification or Glass-making, giving not only a multitude of commodious and ornamental utensils for the household, but substituting the window for the unsightly orifice or open casement, and winnowing light and warmth from the outward and the cold atmosphere; in the arts of Induration by Heat, from bricks dried in the sun to those which withstand the corrosion of our climate for centuries or resist the intensity of the furnace; in the arts of Illumination, from the torch cut from the fir or pine tree to the brilliant gas-light which gives almost a solar splendor to the nocturnal darkness of our cities; in the arts of Heating and Ventilation, which at once supply warmth for comfort and pure air for health; in the art of Building, from the hollowed trunk of a tree or the roof-shaped cabin, to those commodious and lightsome dwellings which betoken the taste and competence of our villages and cities; in the art of Copying or Printing, from the toilsome process of hand-copying, where the transcription of a single book was the labor of months or years, and sometimes almost of a life, to the power printing-press, which throws off sixty printed sheets in a minute; in the art of Paper-making, from the preparation of the inner bark of a tree, cleft off and dried at immense labor, to machinery from which there jets out an unbroken stream of paper with the velocity and continuousness of a current of water; in the art of Painting, from the use of the crayon, and artificial colors imperfectly blended, requiring whole days to present an incomplete picture, to the production, as by enchantment, of perfect likenesses in nature's own penciling, executed in a few seconds; in the art of Telegraphing, from communicating information by signs which may be seen from one station to another, to conveying intelligence to any given distance with the velocity of lightning; and, in addition to all these, in the arts of Moulding and Casting, of Designing and Engraving, of Preserving materials and of Changing their color, of Dividing and Uniting them, etc., etc., an ample catalogue, whose very names and processes would fill volumes.

Now, for the perfecting of all these operations, from the tedious and bungling process to the rapid and elegant; for the change of an almost infinite variety of crude and worthless materials into useful and beautiful fabrics, *mind* has been the agent. Succeeding generations have outstripped their predecessors just in proportion to the superiority of their mental cultivation. When we compare different people or different generations with each other, the diversity is so great that all must behold it. But there is the same kind of difference between contemporaries, fellow-townsmen, and fellow-laborers. Though the uninstructed man works side by side with the intelligent, yet the mental difference between them places them in the same relation to each other that a *past age* bears to the *present.* If the ignorant man knows no more respecting any particular art or branch of business than was generally known during the last century, *he belongs to the last century*, and he must consent to be outstripped by those who have the light and knowledge of the present. Though they are engaged in the same kind of work, though they are supplied with the same tools or implements for carrying it on, yet, so long as one has only an *arm*, but the other has an arm and a MIND, their products will come out stamped and labeled all over with marks of contrast; inferiority and superiority, both as to quantity and quality, will be legibly written on their respective labors.

It is related by travelers among savage tribes that when, by the aid of an ingeniously devised instrument or apparatus, they have performed some skillful manual operation, the savages have purloined from them the instrument they had used, supposing there was some magic in the apparatus itself, by which the seeming miracle had been performed; but, as they could not steal *the art of the operator* with the instrument which he employed, the theft was fruitless. Any person who expects to effect with less education what another is enabled to do with more, ought not to smile at the delusion of the savage or the simplicity of his reasoning.

On a cursory inspection of the great works of art—the steam-engine, the printing-press, the power-loom, the mill, the iron foundery, the ship, the telescope, etc., etc.—we are apt to look upon them as having sprung into sudden existence, and reached their present state of perfection by one, or, at most, by a few mighty efforts of creative genius. We do not reflect that they have required the lapse of centuries and the successive application of thousands of minds for the attainment of their present excellence; that they have advanced from a less to a more perfect form by steps and gradations almost as imperceptible as the growth by which an infant expands to the stature of a man; and that, as later discoverers and inventors had first to go over the ground of their predecessors, so must future discoverers and inventors first master the attainments of the present age before they will be prepared to make those new achievements which are to carry still further onward the stupendous work of improvement.

www.ingramcontent.com/pod-product-compliance
Lightning Source LLC
Chambersburg PA
CBHW081616100526
44590CB00021B/3467